W

Cyber Threat

Cyber Threat

The Rise of Information Geopolitics in U.S. National Security

CHRIS BRONK

Praeger Security International

 PRAEGER™

An Imprint of ABC-CLIO, LLC
Santa Barbara, California • Denver, Colorado

Library of Congress Cataloging-in-Publication Data

Names: Bronk, Chris, author.
Title: Cyber threat : the rise of information geopolitics in U.S. national
  security / Chris Bronk.
Description: Santa Barbara, California : Praeger, [2016] | Includes bibliographical
  references and index.
Identifiers: LCCN 2015034347 | ISBN 9781440834981 (hardcopy : alk. paper) | ISBN
  9781440834998 (ebook)
Subjects: LCSH: Internet governance—United States. | Cyberspace—Political aspects—
  United States. | Computer security—Political aspects—United States. | Internet in
  espionage—United States. | Cyberterrorism—United States. | National security—
  United States. | Geopolitics.
Classification: LCC TK5105.8854 .B76 2016 | DDC 355/.03302854678—dc23 LC record
available at http://lccn.loc.gov/2015034347

ISBN: 978–1–4408–3498–1
EISBN: 978–1–4408–3499–8

20 19 18 17 16   1 2 3 4 5

This book is also available on the World Wide Web as an eBook.
Visit www.abc-clio.com for details.

Praeger
An Imprint of ABC-CLIO, LLC

ABC-CLIO, LLC
130 Cremona Drive, P.O. Box 1911
Santa Barbara, California 93116-1911

This book is printed on acid-free paper ∞

Manufactured in the United States of America

Contents

Acknowledgments   vii

Timeline of Major Cyber Security Events, 2005–2015   xi

  1. A New Great Game   1

  2. Checking Facebook on an iPhone   10

  3. Tunis, Room 641A, and the Politics of the Information Society   26

  4. The Great Cyberwar of 2007   41

  5. Securing Cyberspace in the Homeland   54

  6. A Commission, a Review, but Little Policy   68

  7. Hard Cyber Power, from Stuxnet to Shamoon   80

  8. Diplomacy, Social Software, and the Arab Spring   93

  9. Espionage, Radical Transparency, and National Security   105

10. Snowden   124

11. Cybercrime and Punishment   138

12. Virtual Policy in the Real World   149

Notes   159

Bibliography   203

Index   227

Acknowledgments

Sometimes it really is about being in the right place at the right time. For me, that moment was at the annual convention of the International Studies Association in 2010. In a cramped New Orleans hospitality suite, in which heaven knows how many possibly shady deals were concluded, I chaired a panel of international relations grad students who all were basically asking, "Is it ok for us to study this cyberspace thing?" In the ridiculously crowded room was Lene Hansen, who asked me later to attend a workshop, postponed once by Eyjafjallajökull's eruption, held at Central European University in Budapest. At that gathering, I realized the answer to my panelists' question was an emphatic yes. Also in the room was Aaron Brantly, then a grad student, now a brilliant researcher at the Army Cyber Institute, who followed his intuition to finish his cybersecurity policy doctorate.

This book is the account of a spectator who observed the arrival of geopolitics to cyberspace. It spans three careers, at the State Department, Rice University's Baker Institute, and the University of Houston's College of Technology, where I currently spend much time preparing new entrants into the cybersecurity workforce. At this point, educating as many high-quality professionals in the field may be our best bet for securing cyberspace.

In January 2000, I began writing a doctoral thesis on the international politics of cybersecurity. Although one of my professors said I was probably nuts to take on the topic, my advisor, Stuart Thorson, felt that such foolhardy endeavors were worth pursuing. I can thank Stu as well for nominating my thesis for the award it received and then-dean Mitchel

Wallerstein for conferring it. At Syracuse, my professors, David Berteau, Matt Bonham, Shiu-Kai Chin, Vernon Dale Jones, Harry Lambright, Susan Wadley, Melvyn Levitsky, and Milton Mueller, enriched me enormously on the topics of bureaucracy, diplomacy, computer security, Internet engineering, and of course, international politics. I wish I could have stuck around longer.

When the Foreign Service called in 2001, I went, and got the chance to continue my research while learning the business of security through on-the-job training. I had some great colleagues and bosses shape my thinking, including Alfred Anzaldua, Michael Bishton, Richard Boly, Bruce Burton, Greg Garland, John Janek, Eric Johnson, Dan Sheerin, Buck Shinkman, Tiffany Smith, Wilson Dizard, and David Stewart. Gerry Gallucci talked me into joining the staff of the Office of eDiplomacy by suggesting that I eschew taking a job in which I would learn how paper moved through the building for one that would show me "how the bits flowed through it." Tom Niblock did me the great service of going to bat for me so that I could speak at Wikipedia's convention at Harvard in 2006, when the State bureaucracy thought it unnecessary. Incredibly supportive as well has been Alec Ross, who always finds time to lend an ear despite his ridiculous schedule.

In my job interview for the fellow in information technology, society, and policy at Rice University, I was thoroughly grilled by Moshe Vardi. Over the decade since, Moshe has never allowed me to take the easy way out or engage in insufficiently critical thinking. My Baker Institute "boss," Ambassador Edward Djerejian, gave me the platform to think and write about cyberspace, I think because he was genuinely fascinated by the global transformation produced by the Internet and computing or possibly to keep tabs on Mrs. Djerejian's interest in online commerce. Also at Rice came the day Secretary James A. Baker III asked me to come in and talk about hacking was another strong indicator that this cyber business mattered.

Many others at Rice pushed me to think bigger and do more. Jan Odegard always was able to make ideas happen and Christine Kimmel could figure out how to fund them. Among the faculty and staff I can thank for their time and dedication are: Joe Barnes, Tony Elam, Ric Stoll, Devika Subramanian, Ken Medlock, Steven Lewis, Neal Lane, Allen Matusow, Bill Arnold, Matthew Wettergreen, Liane Hart, Amy Kavalewitz (the other red Swingline person), Sidney Burrus, and Bob Brito. I had some amazing student interns and Ph.D. students as well, including Andi Bandyopadhyay, Anhei Shui, Judson Dressler, Theodore Book, Adam Pridgen, Sofia Haase, Max Ingraham-Rakatansky, Rima Tanash, Sean Graham, and Holt Weeks.

The cybersecurity academic cohort in Houston is rather small, but I am lucky to work with both Wm. Arthur Conklin and Dan Wallach. They are wonderful collaborators. My conversations with Art were critical in establishing the bounds of this book, and included lengthy deliberations on the ethics of security. Dan's ideas for getting to the bits on things like Chinese Internet censorship (or Turkish censorship) continue to amaze me.

At the University of Houston, I interact with wonderful colleagues including Deniz Gurkan, Stephen Huang, Jaspal Subhlok, Greg Vetter, Hesam Panahi, Paula deWitte, and Emily Berman. I owe enormous gratitude to my department chair, Ray Cline, and to my incredibly supportive dean, William Fitzgibbon. Thanks also go to those who have supported my research, including Victor Piotrowski, Hriar Cabayan, Adnan Amjad, Alice Aanstoos, and Llayron Clarkson as well as Amy Jones, the über-administrator who holds the UH Center for Information Security Research and Education together on a day-to-day basis. My UH graduate assistants, Vishal Gulati and Anthony Moyegun, were both enormously helpful in this project.

I am also fortunate to be part of a fascinating group of researchers and practitioners spread around the globe who think about not just cybersecurity, but how it fits into global politics. It was pure joy writing the *Shamoon* case study with Eneken Tikk-Ringas and teaching with Chris Spirito at West Point. The same goes for work I've been lucky enough to do with Cody Monk and John Villaseñor. Jim Lewis provided me tremendous advice after an interesting meeting with Huawei. Blake Clayton and Adam Segal at the Council on Foreign Relations gave me an experience that the 17-year-old me couldn't believe, to speak at 58 East 68th Street. Gene Spafford has gently nudged me into not giving up on providing advice to government and encourages my curmudgeonly behavior. Herbert Lin continues to inspire me with his "What if?" questions. John Sheldon has the distinction of providing me the most "out there" ideas on cyberspace. Last off, I still pine for a summer at CEU working in Kate Coyer's shop and I can thank her for plugging me into the European cyber community.

While there are now many cyber conferences, including the one that fills San Francisco's Moscone Center with thousands every spring, two have been amazing standouts for me, the University of Toronto's Cyber Dialogue events and the Cyber Norms meetings held at MIT. I think I have Rex Hughes to thank for getting me my first invite to the Cyber Dialogue and introducing me to Ron Deibert. Ron's Citizen Lab is an amazing place, and every day they are fighting in cyberspace to protect the weak from the despotic in the global struggle for freedom of expression and honest governance. The lab's staff and those who have passed through it are an inspiration. Masashi Crete-Nishihata, Jakub Dalek, Irene Poetranto, Chris Parsons, Camino Kavanaugh, Nart Villeneuve, and Morgan Marquis-Boire, take a bow. I will never forget the impromptu debate between former NSA senior counsel Joel Brenner and NSA whistleblower (and former senior executive) Thomas Drake at the last Dialogue.

Participating in the Cyber Norms conferences co-chaired by Ron, Roger Hurwitz, and Joseph Nye also gave me much. It brought an awfully interesting group of people together to ask, "Was Stuxnet worth it?" a few years back. Conversations late into the evening on the north bank of the Charles with Andrew Cushman, Chris Demchak, Martha Finnemore, Sandro Gaycken, Nigel Inkster, Alexander Klimburg, Catherine Lotrionte, Tim Maurer, Greg Rattray, Harvey Rishikoff, Eric Sears, and Pano Yanna-kogeorgos gave me much to think about. We lost Roger, the driving force of the Cyber Norms conference, in April 2015. I miss our conversations and wish he could have provided his comments on this book. Anything he touched was made better. At least we got to Café du Monde one last time together before he passed.

Great comments I did receive from my friend Michael Ard, a member of my "guys who worked in Washington club" here in Houston. Also in this group is Steve Young, who has taught me everything I could want to know about the craft of intelligence. And for several years now, my dear friend Cody Monk and I have dedicated significant time to cyber deep dive discussions on the motivations of Anonymous, national cyber capabilities, "hackability" of critical infrastructure, and the managerial failings of the Houston Astros. The ideas in this book are as much his as mine.

Finally, I'm lucky to have a wonderful family as well as that family we choose and call our friends. John Cassaro, David Cyprus, and Tory Gattis let me be one of the guys. And then there is my family. My parents gave me a great start in life. From my father I got a love of history, commitment to public service, and passion for baseball. My mom, a newspaperwoman and editor, taught me how to write and always read my best and worst work going back to when crayon was my medium. I am lucky to have them, as well as my sister, Juli, in my life still. My work has too often taken me away from Annaka-Joy and Gabriela Lynn, my amazing daughters. They are incredible young women who will grow to stand just as capably in any role as a man could. How much they teach me about cyberspace every day, they have no idea.

Houston, Texas
July 6, 2015

Timeline of Major Cyber Security Events, 2005–2015

January 2006	Mark Klein reveals NSA data collection effort
March 2007	Thomas Drake's home raided by FBI
April 2007	Russia DDoS attack on Estonia
March 2008	WikiLeaks releases videos of unrest in Tibet
July–August 2008	Russia DDoS attacks on Georgian government websites
August 2008	Obama campaign HQ hacked
February 2009	WikiLeaks publishes CRS reports
March 2009	Dalai Lama's compromise discovered (GhostNet)
April 2009	Conficker worm infiltrates millions of computers
January 2010	China hacks Google and Gmail accounts (Aurora)
April 2010	Chelsea Manning documents published to WikiLeaks
June 2010	Stuxnet discovered
January 2011	WikiLeaks posts customer information of a Swiss bank
January 2011	Facebook hacked by Tunisian government (Arab Spring)
March 2011	RSA Security compromised
August 2011	Shady RAT discovered
September 2011	Duqu discovered

May 2012   Flame discovered

August 2012   Saudi Aramco cyber attacked by Shamoon worm

September 2012   Iran DDoS attack against major U.S. banks begins

April 2013   AP Twitter account hacked by Syrian Electronic
                      Army

May–June 2013   Edward Snowden leaks NSA documents

August 2013   The *New York Times* hacked by Syrian Electronic
                      Army

October 2014   White House computer network compromised

November–   Sony hacked by North Korean Government
December 2014

June 2015   Office of Personnel Management breached

CHAPTER 1

A New Great Game

A few days before the 2014 Thanksgiving holiday, North Koreans hacked Sony Entertainment to block the theatrical release of *The Interview,* a Seth Rogen and James Franco comedy about a plot to assassinate Kim Jong Un. Unlike the movie's plot, the hack was not fiction. According to the FBI, a North Korean or a proxy of the country breached computer systems at Sony. Full versions of several unreleased forthcoming motion pictures as well as embarrassing emails were leaked from Sony's control. The company suffered immediate financial losses involved with incident response, faced diminished returns on the box office take for leaked films, and for some time experienced fallout from the damage produced by the loss of confidentiality of its internal emails.[1] Women at the company were shown that they were likely unfairly compensated, and the movie division's co-chair Amy Pascal left to form her own firm, underwritten by Sony for its first four years.[2]

North Korea, a sovereign state, hacked Sony, a multinational corporation, causing it significant damage. After warning that the act would have consequences, President Obama signed into effect an executive order creating new punishments for the perpetrators of such acts, in the form of international sanctions.[3] Welcome to the geopolitics of cyberspace.

Hacking computers is now a vehicle for spying, theft, expressing disobedience, exerting influence, and even perpetrating covert action. The days when computing or Internet could be downplayed as a niche issue in international security have passed. This book is written to explain how cyber threats have gone from a relatively trivial matter to a major national security issue for the United States in the last decade. The U.S. Department of Defense has named cyberspace a domain for military operations, standing alongside land, sea, air, and space. Cybercrime costs inestimable billions of dollars to individuals and institutions in the United States alone. Operators of critical infrastructure worry of attacks via computer against the machines that deliver water, energy, and data. Cyberspace, once a marvel, is now very much a mess.

GEOPOLITICS AND INFORMATION TECHNOLOGIES

This book illustrates the international security issues arising for the United States as cyberspace becomes a prominent venue for international competition, cooperation, and conflict. The politics of cyberspace is new. Over the last decade, federal government offices have sprung up or grown all over—at the Departments of Defense, State, Homeland Security, and Treasury; the FBI; and the White House—to manage the policy and security issues that cyberspace produces.

Cybersecurity issues are a manifestation of the employment of power in cyberspace. Power has traditionally been the province of states and their rulers. In the last days before World War II, E. H. Carr described three forms of power existing in the international system—military, economic, and information.[4] Power can still be described as falling into these three areas, but each is considerably altered by cyberspace. Cyber weapons can be employed to attack a nuclear facility via software that manipulates and breaks centrifuges.[5] Stock exchanges may lose billions in value from a single false input of data delivered by a hacking operation.[6] Data breaches can undermine corporate or state secrecy, causing great military or economic harm or both.[7] So many of the ways in which cyber capabilities may be applied remain in the realm of the imagination, but new functionality opens up new vulnerabilities at a rapid pace. For instance, Wi-Fi Internet is now available on commercial aircraft. What can go wrong there?[8]

For the U.S. government, cyber issues are plentiful. In military and homeland defense areas, there is the matter of how to protect information resources while disrupting those of the enemy in times of both war and peace. Then there is the matter of cyber equities, the thorny problem of deciding whether to fix vulnerabilities in computer software or secretly stockpile them for use in intelligence operations or cyber conflicts.[9] Crime is rife in cyberspace. While computer-enabled thieves steal an immeasurable but massive sum, the FBI struggles to identify, locate, and, most importantly, extradite those stealing data from half a world away. Agencies also work to protect critical infrastructure, which is increasingly managed by computer each year, opening new vulnerabilities to attack. Finally, there is the diplomacy of cyberspace. The State Department, which coped with one of the most enormous and consequential data breaches in history,[10] must grapple with international agreements on cybersecurity, the right of open expression on the Internet, and how the governance of the Internet shall be conducted. Where computer security and international relations merge is the venue for *cyber geopolitics*.

WHAT IS CYBERSPACE?

The concept of cyber—a tie between humans and computers—had its beginnings with Norbert Weiner's thinking on cybernetics.[11] Weiner considered thinking machines in the period immediately following World War II in a book described as "a hodge podge of notions and analysis."[12] Weiner's concepts of cybernetics produced a platform for discussion on the intersection of math and logic with social science and human behavior. Decades later Novelist William Gibson considered the connection of computers and people in his science fiction/cyberpunk novels, most notably in *Neuromancer* (1984). He described a virtual space of interconnected human beings and computers around the globe that served as a backdrop for his novels of intrigue in the urban sprawl of a not-too-distant future.[13]

Cyberspace is a newer concept than cybernetics. The term was coined by Gibson in "Burning Chrome," a short story published in a 1982 issue of *Omni* magazine.[14] He used the word to describe a "mass consensual hallucination," where characters interacted heavily in computer-mediated environment. Cyberspace in Gibson's story of a dystopian near future was science fiction when he wrote of it. Now it seems much more a real thing than a fictional concept, much in the way Jules Verne's *Nautilus* was imagined, built, and institutionalized in the form of Rickover's nuclear navy. Ray Bradbury's belief certainly appears valid. *"Anything you dream is fiction, and anything you accomplish is science, the whole history of mankind is nothing but science fiction"* (author's italics).[15]

The cybernetics Weiner practiced and the cyberspace Gibson envisioned are pieces of a revolutionary change under way in the processing and transmission of information. We may well be living through the most profound change in the creation and dissemination of information since Gutenberg's movable type made publishing to mass audiences possible in the 15th century.[16] How much the printing press changed the Western civilization may be debated, but certainly it played a hand in the Protestant Reformation, the growth of universities, and even the creation of the Westphalian system of states and the birth of democracies. Suspending disbelief, let us suppose what interconnected thinking machines may produce. If the printing press represented the key technology of Western society's first information revolution, the period of Europe's enlightenment and the Renaissance, what then may we expect from digital computers communicating via Internet Protocol (IP)? (See Table 1.1.)

While Charles Babbage and Ada Lovelace toiled to build and program mechanical computers in the 19th century, another Briton, Alan Turing, produced the first digital computer during World War II. It remained a secret for decades, as did the Allied project to decrypt Axis messages. But when computing came, it came quickly. In a period of just 40 years, the main pieces of our contemporary information infrastructure were

Table 1.1

Key Technologies of the Information Revolution

Technology	Year of Development
Digital Computer (ENIAC)	1946
Integrated Circuit (Texas Instruments)	1958
Packetized Network (ARPANET)	1969
Personal Computer (Altair 8800)	1975
Graphical User Interface (Xerox Star)	1981
Cellular Phone (Motorola DynaTAC)	1983

dreamed up and built, largely in the United States. This chain of innovation represents an important plank of U.S. national power. American firms largely built computing as we know it and forged the interconnection between computers. Cyberspace was created in the United States but has leapt across the world.

The boundaries of cyberspace are fuzzy. As Joseph Nye offers, "Cyber is a prefix standing for computer and electromagnetic spectrum–related activities."[17] Martin Libicki argued that cyberspace is composed of three layers: physical, syntactic, and semantic.[18] It is the cables, antennae, and machines; the software code and protocols; and the images, text, and ideas transmitted and processed. Cyberspace is the interconnection of computing and communications that began with the introduction of the Defense Advanced Research Projects Agency's (DARPA) network, ARPA-NET. The protocols, standards, and technology that emerged from the late 1960s ARPANET have grown to become the global cyber infrastructure. A set of technologies developed in a few decades have been stitched together into an infrastructure that is now vitally important, but very brittle. IP now interconnects more computers than there are humans, and they are not just desktops, laptops, or mobile phones, but computers that reside inside cars, home appliances, medical devices, pipelines, and all manner of industrial plants. Unfortunately, they are often very easy to access, manipulate, or destroy.

CYBER (IN)SECURITY

The big problem with cyberspace is that it is built on a set of technologies that were designed without consideration for their contestation or abuse. Leonard Kleinrock, whose lab was one of the first two nodes connected via the Defense Department's ARPANET, noted that the first major outage of the Internet, caused by the Morris Worm in 1988, should have been a wakeup call.[19] Had the Internet pioneers re-engineered their creation to be more secure rather than more interoperable, perhaps there wouldn't be the copious problems with it today. But because cyberspace is so insecure, the prefix "cyber" alone has become synonymous with security concerns. In policy circles, one need not say more than cyber to mean cybersecurity.

Unfortunately, information assurance and security has largely been an afterthought in systems design, taking a backseat to performance, innovation, and marketable features. The canon of security revolves around three maxims, *confidentiality, integrity,* and *availability*: a holy trinity of information assurance. While these principles are desirable for any computer system, the ever-growing record of data breaches, cyber attacks, and other technological calamities indicates just how little thought typically goes into security. Computer scientists considered the issues of information security as far back as the 1960s.[20] But work on secure operating system and application design was largely ignored.[21] Only recently has Silicon Valley begun to seriously consider how incentives, often in the form of bounties for finding software bugs, can locate security problems in the code that makes cyberspace run.[22]

So cyberspace is a rickety ship, yet at the same time it is resilient. The Internet architecture was designed to get packets of data from sender to receiver through whatever path would work and that led to great reliability in the delivery of messages, but we have learned that monitoring or tampering with those packets is often very easy. Today, computing continues to advance in capability and application, as Big Data initiatives attempt to explain complex relationships while an Internet of Things (IoT) interconnects the computers embedded in everything from refrigerators to house pets. The recurring problem is the failure to consider security while Internet-enabled technologies continue to evolve at a rapid pace. New platforms and applications appear holding ample indication that their developers likely don't know much about security or don't have the time or resources to deal with security problems. Once an application or infrastructure is deployed, applying security becomes somewhat akin to conducting preventative automotive maintenance on a car speeding down the interstate highway.

What this all means is that despite the tremendous emphasis emplaced on the application of networked computing to almost all facets of human endeavor, significant flaws with enormous ramifications for military and economic security as well as individual liberty and privacy persist. IP is probably the most successful technological standard ever conceived in terms of global adoption. Unfortunately, there is also the problem that any computer connected to the Internet via IP can be compromised given enough time and effort. Cyberspace is a huge success, but cyberspace is also broken.

WHAT FOLLOWS

David Byrne reflected in his song "Once in a Lifetime," "Well, how did I get here?" We got cyberspace without thinking a lot about it. There were architects, but there was no monolithic plan. The system that is cyberspace evolved from the efforts of many hands with little coordination. Understanding cybersecurity necessitates the knowledge of computing, its origins, what computers can do, and the evolving business models of IT. Only then may we consider the policy issues of securing cyberspace. It is important to understand why the Tunisian government had Facebook hacked as protesters used it to organize against the Ben Ali government in 2011, but it is also necessary to know how the economic engine supplies Silicon Valley firms like Facebook with the wherewithal to produce disruptive innovation and fund start-up firms. Knowing how Internet companies like Facebook and Google produce revenue explains a great deal about the value of data for those who can aggregate a lot of it. This technological innovation-investment nexus is covered in Chapter 2.

In Chapter 3, we approach two distinct issues that have become deeply interrelated in geopolitics that will determine who has a seat at the table in determining the future of cyberspace as a global issue. Here, we investigate the multi-stakeholder process of Internet governance, a process managed by dotted line and contract by the U.S. Commerce Department largely through the Internet Corporation for Assigned Names and Numbers (ICANN). U.S. stewardship in Internet governance has increasingly been called into question by many other countries after the level of surveillance, for intelligence purposes, of cyberspace by the U.S. Intelligence Community became public knowledge. When an AT&T retiree provided evidence of massive tapping of the Web in 2006, critics immediately called into question the unique U.S. role in Internet governance.

Beyond the diplomacy of Internet governance and the intelligence effort directed and undertaken via the Internet is the matter of the militarization of cyberspace, the topic of Chapter 4. When Estonia displeased Russia in 2007, Moscow pushed back by blasting the Baltic republic's information infrastructure with massive distributed denial of service (DDoS) cyber attacks. While strategic thinkers have pondered the concept of cyber conflict at least since the networked and computer-enabled U.S. military delivered a withering barrage of precision ordnance on Iraq in 1991, cyber attacks have become a facet of contemporary conflict. From the Estonia affair to the most recent efforts of the Islamic State to develop its cyber capability, the application of cyber weapons in conflict has gone from strategic thinking to an integral component of military operations.

With cyberspace militarized, we next consider the civil defense of cyberspace undertaken by the U.S. government. Chapter 5 lays out the evolution of the civilian cybersecurity mission and edifice at the

Department of Homeland Security (DHS). DHS's effort to develop a civilian defensive cyber capability for the U.S. government and the nation is a torturous history of bureaucratic infighting, fuzzy focus, and an incomplete mandate or set of powers. At the midpoint of DHS's short history, a study of national cybersecurity policy was undertaken at the behest of Congress and then considered in great detail by the Obama administration in its early days. Despite this work, comprehensive legislation on cybersecurity remains a work in progress. Chapter 6 studies these proposals for a more secure cyberspace and offers evidence of why suggestions failed to become policy.

While commissions and reviews were conducted in Washington, cyber attacks grew far more efficacious. At the center of Chapter 7 is the story of Stuxnet, the malicious software designed to delay and disrupt Iran's nuclear enrichment program. Beyond Stuxnet, we consider the impact of cyber espionage directed against U.S. firms as well as the cyber attack undertaken against Saudi Aramco, the world's largest oil producer, in 2012. Also discussed here is the other leg of cyber defense, the odd collection of firms, freelancers, and academics who compete and collaborate to identify malicious software and increasingly engage in private intelligence operations to identify attackers and provide attribution for attacks.

Chapter 8 visits another aspect of cyber diplomacy, the role of information technologies, social media, and computer hacking in undermining repressive regimes as well as the responses of those governments. The relationship between cyberspace and the Arab Spring, along with the agenda of Internet Freedom, an extension of speech freedoms found in the United States extended to the world via the Internet, appears here. Turning to another thorny problem, the problem of keeping closely held digital information that way is the subject of Chapter 9. China's massive effort to vacuum proprietary data from corporations, foreign governments, and other organizations is detailed, as well as the activities of WikiLeaks, the organization that eventually published thousands of classified U.S. diplomatic cables taken by Chelsea Manning, a disgruntled enlisted intelligence analyst.[23]

Reserved for Chapter 10 is perhaps the most explosive event in international cyber geopolitics thus far, the release of a massive trove of classified documents from the National Security Agency (NSA) by Edward Snowden. The revelation of the NSA's extraordinary cyber-enabled signals intelligence capabilities has recast relationships for the United States from Berlin to Brasilia. Here we consider not Snowden himself, but rather the impact of his actions on international partners, Silicon Valley, and the academic community that drives advances in computing and computer security. Perhaps most important among the question raised by the NSA and Government Communications Headquarters (GCHQ) documents reported on in the *Guardian* newspaper in 2013 is the issue of whether the United States belongs at the head of Internet governance.

While intelligence in cyberspace stands as a divisive issue, in Chapter 11 we consider a less-polarizing one, the problem of international cybercrime. While the robbing of banks in the United States has become an almost insignificantly small-change endeavor, cybercrime continues to mushroom. Even the best estimates of cybecrime's domestic and global cost are flawed, but incidents like the data breach at Target in 2013 indicate not only how pervasive the problem has become but also that a breach of such magnitude can cost a CEO his or her job. Cyberspace is costing us.

FIXING CYBERSPACE

Ask anyone who has gone without connectivity to the Internet and you may get an interesting placement for it in his or her personal contemporary interpretation of Maslow's hierarchy. Similarly, with the United States deeply dependent on the computers and networks of cyberspace, the question of just how much disruption in cyberspace can undermine civil society, the economy, and national security requires attention. Generally, there is agreement in Washington, Silicon Valley, and the rest of the world that a more secure cyberspace is desirable. Although that is the case, it's hard to say that either government or industry is making consistent or significant progress.[24]

The list of those who can and will fix cybersecurity issues is long and broad. "We must recognize that cyberspace spans measures that are personal, corporate, federal, and international. It is necessarily a distributed function: one that is not solely a mission of government, the private sector, or individuals, but is a function shared among them."[25] Rare is mention of individual responsibility for securing one's system. So too is discussion regarding liability in software, despite bugs producing significant costs to users.[26] And when the issue of regulated cybersecurity arises, in the United States, industry bristles.[27] This is for good reason, however, as attempts to routinize and enforce security practices in the federal government can hardly be considered a rousing success. So with regard to security, in cyberspace, nobody is really all that responsible for security, yet.

Despite the security problems, we most definitely live in interesting times. A decade ago, voices decried the issue of a digital divide, in which the world's poorest were unfairly disadvantaged in lacking computers and Internet connectivity. While access is hardly universal, the Global South's representation in cyberspace is surging. What this will mean to policymakers in the next decade is hard to know.[28] But because so many around the globe have grown so reliant on information technologies, the need to improve their resiliency and security is imperative. The global communication linkages that connect the telephone handset factory in Shenzhen with the Internet-based reseller in San Francisco, the parcel service in Memphis, and the customer in Peoria are remarkable. The current wave of globalization is a product of information and computing technology, connecting the developed world with the developing. For globalization, cyberspace is indispensable.

While we enjoy the fruits of global connectivity, we should feel concern for the activity of carving up cyberspace into sovereign blocks, something well under way as China erects its Great Firewall and shows repressive regimes how to do the same.[29] These countries fear not only hacking and cyber attacks but also many forms of information itself. For this reason, this book takes the position that cyber threats are not simply the matter of breaches, hacks, disruptions, or other nefarious activity. To separate the syntactic elements of cybersecurity from the semantic ones is foolhardy. When Chinese or Russian officials speak of information security, they may well be considering the protection of state secrets or closely held information, but it is more likely they are offering warning that certain forms of information or expression are unwelcome in their political system. To some, information should be free. To others, it should be feared. Cyberspace has manifold meanings.

And finally, when we consider what cyberspace may need to be resilient, reliable, and trustworthy, we must dispense with the idea that either technological innovation or policy alone will fix the world's cybersecurity problems. What is the key to a secure cyberspace? Perhaps it is ubiquitous encryption in all online activity. Or maybe, a set of regulations that can be enacted by the federal government for IT developers or providers? Education? Law suits? Global frameworks? No one item is a panacea. The issue is too complex. But it's good to accept, as Herbert Lin has suggested, that neither policy nor technology alone will close the gap on our cybersecurity issues.[30] Cyberspace is one of humanity's more complex creations, so the idea of fixing it should be seen as a bit of an absurdity. When we seek to secure cyberspace, we are asking to tame it, and in so doing tame what may be a global consciousness of sorts. To completely secure cyberspace is akin to erasing crime, silencing disagreement, banishing risk, or ending conflict. *That is because cyberspace is a reflection of the human condition.*

Do not despair. There are plenty of little problems in cyberspace that need fixing and can be fixed. Policymakers and technologists alike have a part and can work to preserve the desirable elements of cyberspace and mitigate its problems. But to do so will require much more significant effort within both the policy and tech camps, as well as more interchange between them. Cyberspace can be helped, but cyberspace deserves far more respect than it has been accorded.

CHAPTER 2

Checking Facebook on an iPhone

Cybersecurity is undertaken in an environment of connected computing that has largely evolved since World War II, mostly in the United States. To understand why securing information systems is hard, a brief study of the American IT innovation engine is necessary. This means understanding Silicon Valley and the other innovation hubs and how they create economic value. In addition, to make good decisions on cyber security requires understanding what computers do, what they can't do, and how they have evolved from the massive mainframes of early computing to the far more powerful devices some 2 billion people use and quaintly call "phones."[1] Understanding contemporary computing is requisite to make good decisions on IT risk, to be sure. But it is also a necessity for those who must cope with the cyber components of national security issues, in the military, diplomatic, and homeland defense areas. For these reasons a brief explanation of the technology and economics of cyberspace is necessary.

SELLING THE INTERNET

American professional football's Super Bowl Sunday is the most widely viewed sporting event of the year in the United States and has been so for decades. It is also the biggest day of the year for television advertisers. Typically, snack and beer conglomerates—Budweiser, Coca-Cola, and Frito-Lay—as well as auto manufacturers and motion picture studios dominate the allocation of television's most expensive advertising event. Fox, the game's broadcaster for 2014's Super Bowl XLVIII, charged as much as $4.5 million per 30-second advertisement block.[2]

Beginning in 2000, the Super Bowl drew a rather different breed of advertisers: lots of Silicon Valley dot-coms. Flush with venture capital, 19 websites from Pets.com to a company called LifeMinders bought time.[3]

Technology companies bought Super Bowl spots before, most notably Apple with its 1984 commercial for the Macintosh computer, but these were typically outliers. Start-ups expecting continued venture funding and eventual initial public offerings (IPOs) of their stock saw the ad expense as small potatoes on their march to incredible success.[4] And then the money dried up. On March 10, 2000, the tech-heavy NASDAQ stock exchange reached its dot com bubble peak of 5,048.62. In the following weeks it skidded mightily, and by the end of the year the NASDAQ composite stood at 2,470.52, a 48 percent decline in value. The causes of the bust were argued to be many, from the Department of Justice's monopoly case against Microsoft to a long overdue correction of market behavior in tempering expectations of what Internet technologies could do or were worth.[5]

An interesting footnote on the dot com bubble's burst is the first widely noticed denial-of-service attacks against highly visible websites. Michael Calce aka *MafiaBoy*, then a Montreal high school student, overwhelmed a series of major websites, starting with Yahoo! on February 7, 2000. Calce, who operated under the hacker alias of *MafiaBoy* brought down the Yahoo! website and search engine for an hour. After Yahoo! restored service, Calce shifted his attention to eBay, Amazon, and CNN websites.[6] Although there is no reason to infer any deep causal linkage between the MafiaBoy cyber attacks and the precipitous decline of the dot com sector in 2000, it was yet another factor for investors to consider in making an accurate valuation of IT firms or even corporate investment in IT, a figure reaching roughly half of corporate capital expenditures by 2000. In the 1980s, economist Robert Solow had asked his peers to consider what firms were gaining in productivity through the adoption of the computer.[7] The answers he received left him deeply unimpressed. A decade of IT-facilitated productivity growth in the 1990s rendered Solow's question irrelevant.

After the dot com crash, it was unclear what would be next for IT. Nicholas Carr, in his provocatively titled May 2003 article for the *Harvard Business Review*, "IT Doesn't Matter," made the argument that computing technology was like any other service to business, a homogenous but necessary utility such as electricity or water. The IT bubble and crash had been an exemplar for his assertion that "When the technology's commercial potential begins to be broadly appreciated, huge amounts of cash are inevitably invested in it, and its buildout proceeds with extreme speed."[8] Plenty of start-up firms survived the 1990s Internet bubble: Google, eBay, Yahoo, and Amazon among them. They reached the high ground of the information economy.

This position, what Yergin and Stanislaw in another context labeled "the commanding heights," is reserved for those firms that are able to exert global influence in their sector of business activity.[9] IT is a fundamentally important component of U.S. global economic strength.

The United States has been an innovator in information technologies for at least 150 years. During that time, a number of U.S. firms have occupied key positions in IT development. Consider the arc of four major firms: Western Union, American Telephone and Telegraph (AT&T), IBM, and Microsoft.

Western Union was the first of the American IT mega companies, with its origins in Samuel Morse's inventions in telegraph technology and syntax. Next was AT&T, which built out a national telephone system over a period of more than 50 years and was eventually subject to the largest antitrust divesture in U.S. history. One of many companies in tabulating and office machinery, IBM grew to dominate computing through the 1960s and 1970s. Running with IBM's hardware platform, the PC, Microsoft made the software to connect computers with users, and by the company's peak in the 1990s, its market share in operating systems was nearly complete on a global scale.

An overwhelming preponderance of major IT firms are based in the United States or got their start here before diversifying across the globe. IBM's name came from the international division of its one-time parent company, indicating its roots as a global multinational. The current set of IT giants is largely centered in California's Silicon Valley, a remarkable technology innovation and investment ecosystem. It is unique, because it translates ideas and concepts of science, engineering, business, and other aspects of human endeavor into lucrative businesses and brands with great regularity. At the height of the dot com boom, Michael Lewis opined, "Silicon Valley is to the United States what the United States is to the rest of the world. It is one of those places, unlike the Metropolitan Museum of Art, but like Las Vegas, that are unimaginable anywhere but in the United States."[10]

However, with regard to their security, the Valley's products and platforms are deeply flawed. *Their bugs are vulnerabilities that may be exploited and the Silicon Valley economy is dependent on the Internet, a system designed for open scholarly communication, not to serve as the global telecommunications system.* How the Valley IT innovation machine factors into measurement of U.S. power is hard to say, but cyber security appears an Achilles' heel. In cyber security, there exists a chasm between the rather large cohort of programmers, engineers, and entrepreneurs who make versus the policymakers who engage in a dialog on national and international security.[11] There is desperate need for bridging this gap, and one of the most important points of explanation for the policy crowd is what exactly computing is, what it can do, and what it represents, economically, societally, and globally. One of the critical needs for all who toil in cyber security is a shared idea of where computers came from, what they are, and what they can do.

COMPUTING

With not an inconsiderable amount of ink being spilled on the replacement of people in certain categories of jobs by computers today, it is worth reminding that up until the middle of the 20th century, a computer was a person. The Eiffel Tower, the Empire State Building, and Hoover Dam were all constructed without the aid of digital computers. Thousands of calculations in their design and construction came from people, performing operations on paper or referencing slide rules or other table-based calculation devices.[12]

Modern digital computing was born of necessity during World War II. Babbage and Lovelace's Difference Engine performed mathematical calculations mechanically. Mechanical and electromechanical computational devices advanced into the 20th century and grew more sophisticated and complicated, but the leap to entirely electronic computing was borne of the need for efficiency in the performance of calculations beyond the capacity of mechanical or human operations.

As with high-energy physics, the science of computing was pushed ahead in the United States and UK by the military demands of the Allies from 1939 to 1945. Alan Turing, for whom computer science bestows its highest award, built machines to accelerate the calculation process for code breaking of encrypted enemy messages.[13] The Electronic Numerical Integrator And Computer (ENIAC) was built by the U.S. Army at the University of Pennsylvania to calculate artillery ballistics tables. Upon his discovery of ENIAC, John von Neumann would steer its use to the postwar nuclear program.[14]

A wunderkind, polymath, and autodidact, von Neumann was credentialed as a mathematician and contributed enormously across a broad set of fields. His contribution to computing was in providing the model for a stored program computer. Writing for the Electronic Discrete Variable Automatic Computer project with Arthur Burks and Herman Goldstine, von Neumann provided a coherent model of the modern computer.

It is evident that the machine must be capable of storing in some manner not only the digital information needed in a given computation such as boundary values, tables of functions (such as the equation of the state of a fluid) and also the intermediate results of the computation (which may be wanted for varying lengths of time), but also instructions which govern the actual routine to be performed on the numerical data. In a special-purpose machine these instructions are an integral part of the device and constitute a part of its design structure. For an all-purpose machine it must be possible to instruct the device to carry out whatsoever computation that can be formulated in numerical terms. Hence there must be some organ capable of storing these program orders. There must, moreover, be a unit which can understand these instructions and order their execution.[15]

Von Neumann broke the notional computational machine into three fundamental components: a memory, a processing unit, and a control unit. *Memory* is a concept that generally is widely understood, a physical location in which binary information containing both the programs to operate and the data operated upon resides. The *processing* unit performs the mathematical calculations that each and every function of the computer must ultimately boil down to. The *Control* unit is the component of the computer that "can automatically execute the orders stored from memory."[16] From this general organization sprang forth the engineering of mainframes and today's personal computers and mobile devices.

With the engineering specifics of computers relatively fixed, Alan Turing hypothesized on what computers could do. Turing set boundaries for what could be computed by machine given an unlimited allocation of time and memory. He contended "that machines can be constructed which will simulate the behavior of the human mind very closely."[17] He suggested the possibility of a machine able to "learn by experience." He thought about such machines as a very real prospect.

Let us now assume, for the sake of argument, that these machines are a genuine possibility, and look at the consequences of constructing them. To do so would of course meet with great opposition, unless we have advanced greatly in religious toleration from the days of Galileo. There would be great opposition from the intellectuals who were afraid of being put out of a job. It is probable though that the intellectuals would be mistaken about this. There would be plenty to do, [trying to understand what the machines were trying to say,] i.e. in trying to keep one's intelligence up to the standard set by the machines, for it seems probable that once the machine thinking method had started, it would not take long to outstrip our feeble powers. There would be no question of the machines dying, and they would be able to converse with each other to sharpen their wits. At some stage therefore we should have to expect the machines to take control, in the way that is mentioned in Samuel Butler's 'Erewhon'.[18]

In our time of big data and the Jeopardy-game-show-winning IBM Watson computer, this concept, labeled *machine learning* or *artificial intelligence*, is taken quite seriously.[19] Our society has grown quite accustomed to computerized robots performing manufacturing tasks over the last several decades. Jobs once undertaken by human beings, especially highly repetitive ones, can be replaced by computer. The idea that computers are just better at some jobs than humans is now a credible one, and is also the thesis of MIT professors Brynjolfsson and McAfee.[20] Machine intelligence has far-reaching consequences.

Setting aside crypto-currencies such as Bitcoin,[21] consider how computing has changed international finance. The speed at which computer algorithms can interpret data input and deliver instructions has become incredibly lucrative. Algorithms can incorporate large quantities of data into a machine-learning decision-making structure for the purchase of securities or other assets.[22] As a colleague opined of one Texas-based quantitative analysis fund's performance through up and down markets, "those guys print money."[23] The volume of trading has grown enormously (although for a variety of reasons). In 1984, rare was the day when more than 200 million shares changed hands on the New York Stock Exchange. Now, daily volumes of 2 to 3 billion shares are not unusual.

Computers have transformed markets. Ten years ago, perhaps one quarter of all stock trades were made on the instructions of a computerized trading algorithm; five years ago that number was pegged by one analyst to fall between half and two-thirds; today we can assume it continues to rise.[24] *Algorithmic finance is but one application of the computer with profound implications, not least in the possibility that these transactions may be manipulated or subverted by outside actors.* But to understand the social forces around computing and cyberspace requires understanding how innovation in IT works, mostly in the valley south of San Francisco along the 101 Freeway.

THE INNOVATION ENGINE

In cyberspace and security politics, the dynamics of the information and computing technology industry is a key piece. This activity was in the 1990s and is again considered the high ground of the global economy. IT innovation is largely concentrated in the United States, mostly in a handful of hubs, chiefly Boston and the San Francisco Bay Area.[25] While they produce products and services of great value, these hubs are rare and hard to replicate. Irving Wladawsky-Berger's explanation for how these hubs came into being is that both are blessed with strong engineering universities, MIT in Boston and UC-Berkeley and Stanford in the Bay Area. But there's something more: an entrepreneurial culture able to take ideas from the lab and bring them to market.[26]

The Silicon Valley since the 1970s has largely been in the business of developing new software and hardware. Like many other areas of technological development, computing's growth in the United States was fueled by government investment after World War II.[27] The Intel Corporation began its rise in part by providing integrated circuits to the Department of Defense for missile technologies. This was the norm.

Government need drove computing research and development. NORAD, the Air Force's continental air defense command, worked with a consortium including IBM MIT's Lincoln Labs and the RAND Corporation to develop its Semi-Automatic Ground Environment (SAGE) computer system in the late 1950s.[28] NORAD ran the giant vacuum-tube mainframe system until 1983. When American Airlines came looking for an automated reservation and ticketing system, IBM applied lessons learned from SAGE to build SABRE (Semi-Automatic Business Research Environment), parts of which still remain under the hood of the popular Expedia website.[29] Government provided a large portion of the upfront costs for innovation, and then industry was given a base of material to commercialize in other applications.

The integrated circuit allowed electrical engineers to squeeze together components and begin to miniaturize computers. Computers constructed from integrated circuits, Gordon Moore argued, "cost less and perform better than those which use 'conventional' electronics."[30] Moore was right that the number of components that could be crammed onto a single silicon wafer could grow quite substantially.

Integrated circuits will lead to such wonders as home computers—or at least terminals connected to a central computer—automatic controls for automobiles, and personal portable communications equipment. The electronic wristwatch needs only a display to be feasible today.[31]

Moore's well-informed speculation would become the most powerful popular concept in computing, the law that bears his name. In its most simple definition, Moore's Law states that the computer processing power doubles every 24 months.[32] Today, circuit densities are measured in nanometers and the frequency clock speeds in gigahertz.[33] Raw computing performance was one of the ingredients necessary to construct cyberspace. Linking computers was the other important one.

BUILDING NETWORKS

In the early 1990s, as Microsoft was preparing to ship out the door its first copies of Windows 3.0, the leadership at the National Science Foundation took a serious look at opening the organization's university-based research network—what would later evolve to become the Internet—to anyone interested in connecting to it, even for commercial purposes. In the United States, the pieces needed to revolutionize the creation and dissemination of information fell into place. A technological explosion around Internet and World Wide Web would dramatically reorganize the distribution and eventually even the creation of information.

The impact of the Internet's development and the digital technologies that came with it may prove to be more of a once-every-few-centuries happening. Computing's intersection with global telephony was a society-redefining event.[34] J. C. R. Licklider advocated early for interconnected computing across distance.[35] Licklider moved on to become the first computer research program manager at the Department of Defense's Advanced

Research Projects Agency (ARPA, later DARPA). From there, a variety of efforts would come together in building out a mechanism by which to connect computers. These would culminate with ARPANET. The idea behind ARPANET was simple: computer engineers and scientists would be able to move programs and data around from computer to computer across significant distance.

ARPANET employed packetized communication over dedicated circuits found in telegraphic and telephonic systems. ARPANET's engineers advocated for a communications mechanism by which content of the data transmitted was divided into small pieces, packets, to be transmitted and reassembled at the intended point of delivery.[36] When ARPANET was first developed, computers were still of the mainframe variety, taking up whole rooms with massive banks of tape drives, drum memory modules, and other large pieces of equipment now found in museums and store rooms. More efficient access to mainframe computing was achieved by time-sharing schemes, and more efficient communication across phone lines or other channels could be achieved by packetized communication.

By the early 1970s, with ARPANET a growing network, Bob Frankston was completing his master's thesis on the idea of a computing marketplace. He saw that as technical barriers to entry for computers fell, systems were designed to efficiently handle heterogeneous processing requests, and rapid growth in computational power at decreasing cost was possible. He argued,

The marketplace model of the computer system is an idea whose time has come. The costs of computer hardware are decreasing so that the necessary computational power is becoming available. In fact, the major cost of computer hardware today is the overhead of new research and support personnel. As more hardware is sold, this cost can be spread thinner. Software represents a large portion of the expense of a computer system and the expertise for developing computer services is a scarce resource.[37]

These were important ideas, ones that tied the purely technical endeavors of the computation and networking research communities to the market economy found in the United States.

Throughout the 1970s, pre-Internet engineering continued, with Vinton Cerf and Robert Kahn working out the mechanics of an architecture that would replace ARPANET's Network Control Protocol.[38] Their thinking would become the fundamental building block of Internet connectivity, Transmission Control Protocol/Internet Protocol (TCP/IP). Applications that would define contemporary computing emerged. Email was developed under the leadership of Ray Tomlinson, an engineer at Bolt, Beranek and Newman.[39] Development of the Unix operating system by AT&T and UC-Berkeley's Computer Science Department gave ARPANET computers an OS that was inherently network enabled. Bob Metcalfe's creation of Ethernet at Xerox PARC enabled delivery of packetized communication to computer workstations.

Computer networks began to proliferate across more universities, labs, and agencies such as the Department of Energy, NASA, and the National Science Foundation. Network Control Protocol was replaced with TCP/IP in 1983, and "by 1985, Internet was already well established as a technology supporting a broad community of researchers and developers, and was beginning to be used by other communities for daily computer communications."[40] The Department of Defense pulled a part of ARPANET away to create MILNET, which would eventually evolve to become its classified and unclassified IP-based networks.[41]

Although U.S. government sponsorship was pivotally important to the development of networking, the community of engineers and scientists working in research and academia were equally important in working out the mechanisms by which computers could communicate with one another. The circulation of papers labeled Request for Comment (RFC) facilitated distributed development in Internet engineering. RFCs allowed those networking computers together to float ideas and generate consensus on preferred directions for development.[42]

Elsewhere, governments generally directed the development of computer networking in top-down fashion or missed the trend altogether. On the other side of the Iron Curtain, the Soviet Union built networks, but failed to interconnect them, although the Kiev Institute of Cybernetics's Viktor Glushkov proposed a Statewide Automated Management System for Collection and Processing of Information for the Accounting, Planning, and Management of the National Economy.[43] However, a central economic planning and coordination computer system was too complicated and expensive for the Soviet Union to construct. France's postal, telephone, and telecommunications ministry deployed the *Médium interactif par numérisation d'information téléphonique* (Minitel) system in 1982, providing chat, email, directory services, and online purchasing. Glushkov's system never made it off the drawing board and Minitel folded in 2012.[44]

Absent viable competitors, TCP/IP, or simply IP, rose to near-universal application in digital telecommunications. While electricity to power computers may be delivered at 120 or 220 cycles, on direct or alternating current, the mechanism by which data are transmitted or received between them is now generally the same. *IP is a global standard.* Whether YouTube videos and Twitter microblog posts or an increasing volume of telephone calls and sensitive military communications, IP is *the* technological facilitator of digital connectivity, a standard for data communication that scales to almost every computing device on the planet. Because of it, some exceptions notwithstanding, the last 20 years have been a period in which a message can be transmitted from one computer to another anywhere, in large part because the set of instructions for delivery have been open, understandable, and relatively easy to implement.[45]

BUILDING AND COMMERCIALIZING THE INTERNET

The path from ARPANET to a global Internet was an enormous technical leap, undertaken by many individuals in a deeply decentralized process. Those academic institutions not tied together via networks underwritten by the Department of Defense desired similar functionality. The capacity to pass data in a fashion to ARPANET was received in 1985 with the inauguration of the National Science Foundation Network (NSFNET).

A competitor model to TCP/IP, the Open Systems Interconnect (OSI) of networked computing, lost out to more approachable ideas forwarded via the Internet Engineering Task Force. While OSI was useful in breaking down the pieces of process in understanding how to send and receive data across communication links, it would not become the dominant set of standards, despite support for it by both the International Organization for Standardization and the International Telecommunications Union (ITU), the body responsible for international telephony policy. Throughout the 1980s and 1990s, a process resulted in the selection of a single standard for the transmission and receipt of digital data, TCP/IP. In the Internet Engineering Task Force, actors outside government performed the role of governance.[46] Formed in 1986, the IETF allowed computer scientists and engineers to meet and discuss the mechanisms by which they would interconnect the rapidly evolving computer systems of the time.

In building out the Internet, it is useful to think of the IETF functioning as a sort of *guild*. This is how Paul Twomey characterized the people who make the Internet function, those technicians and engineers of routers, switches, and other logical devices.[47] What did he mean? Typically, a guild is an association of artisans, people who make things requiring skill. Guilds grew up in medieval Europe, passing knowledge from generation to generation. They occupied a precarious space between the feudal elite and the mass of peasantry eking out subsistence from the land and underwriting the needs of the nobility, who offered martial protection in exchange for taxes. While the peasants toiled and the lords protected, *the guilds built modernity.*

As for Internet governance in the form of addressing, for years the job completely fell to Jon Postel at the University of Southern California. Postel was the heart and soul of the Internet Assigned Numbers Authority (IANA), which manages the Domain Name System (DNS) for the Internet. After Postel died in 1998, Vinton Cerf eulogized his work.

Out of the chaos of new ideas for communication, the experiments, the tentative designs, and crucible of testing, there emerged a cornucopia of networks. Beginning with the ARPANET, an endless stream of networks evolved, and ultimately were interlinked to become the Internet. Someone had to keep track of all the protocols, the identifiers, networks and addresses and ultimately the names of all the things in the networked universe. And someone had to keep track of all the information that erupted with volcanic force from the intensity of the debates and discussions and endless invention that has continued unabated for 30 years. That someone was Jonathan B. Postel, our Internet Assigned Numbers Authority, friend, engineer, confidant, leader, icon, and now, first of the giants to depart from our midst.[48]

Today, IANA manages the addressing of computer systems (known as hosts) connected to the Internet. What was once a single person's work is now a major component of the Internet Corporation for Assigned Names and Numbers (ICANN), the organizing body for Internet addressing.

FROM SELLING THINGS TO ATTRACTING USERS

Explaining what the Internet is and how it works has led to many representations of it as an amorphous cloud across which data transit. At the edges of these diagrams were well-organized and discrete maps of computers, servers, and other hardware. As computing has become more networked, the concept of a "cloud" grew to include services, storage, and applications. The contributions of a single company, Apple, are instructional in explaining the shift to a new model of computing and information commerce.

When Steve Jobs rejoined Apple in 1997, the company was perceived to be at death's door. With Apple's market share of the personal computer business in the low single digits, Microsoft handed Apple a $150 million lifeline and agreed to port its popular Office productivity software to the Macintosh computer.[49] A decade later Apple would change the landscape of the computing marketplace with the introduction of the first iPhone. Apple remained a hardware company, and a very successful one, but it gradually built up a significant portion of total revenue through its role as a vendor of digital content to mobile devices. With the introduction in 2001 of the iPod music player and its aggregate music marketplace, iTunes, Apple began its transition to a content provider. Apple was able to aggregate the music of multiple labels online, becoming the top music retailer in the United States in 2008. By that time it had sold some 4 billion song downloads from a catalog of 6 million songs to 50 million customers.[50]

While the sales numbers were impressive, a significant metric was the number of customers to which Apple sold. Roughly one in every six

Americans had downloaded a song on iTunes. That statistic brings us to an important metric upon which companies' value is computed today in Silicon Valley: number of users. Apple made impulse buying of music to a massive market unimaginably easy.[51] Users of the iTunes store opted to keep credit cards on file and need do little more than click "BUY" to make a purchase. It was friction-free retail.[52]

Beyond the selling of things, grew the rise of digital advertising. This is an area dominated by Google. The google.com Web page remains the most visited in the world after a decade of an almost uninterrupted position in the top spot. The company states, "Google's mission is to organize the world's information and make it universally accessible and useful." A useful slogan, but perhaps it's better to ask a different question: how does Google make money? In point #6 of the company's philosophy, "You can make money without doing evil," it explains:

Google is a business. The revenue we generate is derived from offering search technology to companies and from the sale of advertising displayed on our site and on other sites across the web. Hundreds of thousands of advertisers worldwide use AdWords to promote their products; hundreds of thousands of publishers take advantage of our AdSense program to deliver ads relevant to their site content.[53]

By revenue, Google is an advertising company, deriving an overwhelming preponderance of its income from ads. In 2014 it earned $59.6 billion in selling advertising, up from $51.1 billion the year before.[54]

Google is keen to bring users to its platforms, because the more user data it collects, the more specifically it can target its advertising.[55] In the 10 years since the company inaugurated its Gmail service, it has drawn 500 million users, enticing them with plentiful storage and "the power of Google's Web search in your inbox."[56] Google uses the data stored in all those mailboxes to provide focused advertising. If a Gmail user sends a message to friends about graduate school possibilities, ads for grad programs show up in the Gmail interface.[57] If this sounds like an erosion of privacy, it is, albeit a voluntary one.

Ads are showing up in a lot of other places, because today's Silicon Valley path to profitability is often paved with advertising dollars. Before IPO of their stock, companies such as Facebook and Twitter were essentially chasing after a hypothetical valuation on their websites, referred to as platforms, as well as the number of users they collected. After IPO, investors wanted to see profitability or at least revenue. This is where the valuation of users comes into play. Computer and software companies have traditionally been measured by the units they ship, but Internet companies are different.[58] The number of users on a platform or service determines their value in large part and how that number can be mone-tized in the form of ad revenues.[59]

With regard to user numbers, Facebook, the social networking appli-cation that sprang from Mark Zuckerberg's project to build an interac-tive online student directory at Harvard, is a behemoth, claiming some 1.49 billion active users as of June 2015.[60] The number of Facebook accounts exceeds the population of India or China. Over the last decade, Facebook's users have shared an incredible amount of information with the company, which uses to drive up its revenues and thus its stock val-uation. Facebook's market capitalization stands at $191.7 billion,[61] an incredible sum for a company with approximately 7,000 employees.[62]

In its acquisition of companies, user count is an obvious criterion for Facebook. In 2012, it purchased the mobile-phone picture-sharing platform Instagram, a 15-month-old company with 13 employees for $1 billion, in cash and Facebook stock.[63] In the deal, Facebook picked up a company with 100 million users at the time the acquisition was com-pleted and was adding 10 million users a month.[64] These numbers may seem staggering, but Facebook also found it in the company's interest to buy WhatsApp, an online messaging application that unbundles SMS texting functionality from telecommunications channels, for $19 billion in 2014. In the deal, Facebook got a company with a user base of 450 mil-lion that was adding new users at a rate of *1 million a day*.[65] Placing this in perspective, a commentator noted the price was roughly equal to Ukraine's short-term bond and gas debt.[66]

What enable companies like Google, Facebook, and Amazon to scale their offerings so efficiently are the breakthroughs in large-scale process-ing and storage of data on commodity hardware. Although the largest companies, such as Google, build their own proprietary systems for mas-sively scalable Internet computing, the core functionality comes from open source software developed under the Apache Hadoop project framework. Hadoop "is designed to scale up from single servers to thou-sands of machines, each offering local computation and storage."[67] It per-mits companies to dynamically grow their server infrastructure based on demand. As demand rises, additional server power may be quickly bought or even rented to cope with it. Cloud computing dynamically can shrink or grow almost effortlessly thanks to the technology.

Cloud instances running on Hadoop, or other similar software, enabled Facebook and Google to manage the growth to millions and even billions of users at relatively low cost. These advances have produced a new common computing architecture for the planet—cloud to mobile. Produc-ing revenues on these architectures have largely been drawn from adver-tising. As the communication theorist Marshall McLuhan argued, "Advertising is the greatest art form of the 20th century."[68] It is also the bedrock of Internet company revenues. But the Internet is going to more places than mobile phones. In thinking about the economics of computing, and the related cyber security issues, we must consider where computing is headed next, its role in running billions of devices from home thermostats and appliances to automated manufacturing plants and digital oilfields.

AN INTERNET OF THINGS

On August 14, 2003, a massive power blackout struck the northeastern United States and eastern Canada, leaving nearly 50 million without electricity for hours or more. The blackout was caused by transmission wires coming into contact with tree limbs, but the deeper failure was that software at the Akron, Ohio, utility responsible for the initial point of failure didn't sound an alarm, because of a previously unknown bug in its code.[69] What was a small utility's issue grew as interconnected utilities struggled to balance the load on their portions of the grid.

Issues such as the August 2003 blackout demonstrate how software failure can have unforeseen and significant consequences. Some years ago, my colleagues and I wrote an opinion piece arguing that it was not yet the time to worry about cyber events in the power grid, as load was managed by engineers and billing was handled by meter readers.[70] Things in power have changed enormously since. Computerized metering of power consumption has come to millions of households in the United States, extending a data network across the power grid.[71]

Both at the enterprise and the household level, more devices are becoming computerized and connected to the Internet. Cisco, one of the world's largest computer networking companies, has directed attention to what it calls an emergent Internet of Things (IoT), which the company qualifies as a point of time in which more devices connected to the Internet than people. Cisco estimates the number of IP-connected devices (or things) surpassed the number of people on the planet sometime in 2008 or 2009, with the estimated figure for both in the ballpark of 6.5 billion. Since then, the number of devices has grown rapidly, with Cisco's estimate that 25 billion Internet-connected devices are functioning as of 2015.[72]

Economic value of the IoT is potentially enormous. Productivity gains through automation, energy savings via smart-metered pricing, and real-time awareness of patient well-being are all current IoT applications, not years-away concepts. Consider Nest Labs, another Silicon Valley start-up, which added Wi-Fi networking connectivity and basic machine learning to the home thermostat. Bought by Google in January 2014, Nest has remained an independent brand with ambitions in other areas.[73]

Its purchase of Dropcam, a low-cost camera manufacturer, indicates it may well be moving into the home security area as well.[74] Nest owners can turn on their air conditioning or monitor their alarm by cell phone, but what are the potential vulnerabilities?

The computing of things will be built on IP. Right now, the march is on to employ IP to network computers in homes, cars, and all manners of other applications. Worrisome are the security issues that come along with the cramming of networked computing into all areas of human endeavor on a set of protocols designed for trustworthy users, not untrustworthy ones.

ASSESSING THE COMMANDING HEIGHTS

Today, the United States remains very much at the center of IT innovation and development. Computing and digital networking continue to have a profound impact on reshaping not only the U.S. economy but also those of developed and developing nations around the globe. While the vanguard of commercial activity has concentrated recently in Internet firms building platforms used by tens or hundreds of millions (or more), the Internet and its protocols have also found use in all sorts of infrastructures: financial, energy, health care, and others.

Computing stands at a new wave in its development. From 1945 to 1975, emphasis was on delivering big computing to big customers able to carry the heavy costs of what was often bespoke mainframe computing. But by 1975, the year Gordon Moore thought cramming computer power onto smaller and smaller pieces of silicon would start producing profound impact to the general consumer, personal computing was becoming a reality. Computing became commoditized and software moved to the fore, especially with regard to profitability as PC manufacturers ran prices down while Microsoft grew revenues as its operating systems became nearly ubiquitous. Starting in 2005, another change was afoot, in which interconnectivity and data collection grew in importance (although the Internet began to take off in 1995).

The phenomenon of Big Data shows how computing and information business is changing. This shift to an information focus is important. As computing has developed, functions that were once novel have become homogenous and easily replicable, first in hardware and later in software. Contemporary computing is being applied to the complex questions of science and human behavior. Consider bioinformatics, "often defined as the application of computational techniques to understand and organize the information associated with biological macromolecules."[75] It is the application of computing to biology, most spectacularly observed in the Human Genome Project, a mapping of human DNA that permits the advance of "genome-based research [which] will eventually enable medical science to develop highly effective diagnostic tools, to better understand the health needs of people based on their individual genetic make-ups, and to design new and highly effective treatments for disease."[76]

Bioinformatics can be characterized as biological inquiry enabled by computation; however, there is a larger question of computer-mediated connectivity between individuals. Consider "crowd sourcing," in which many individuals combine their effort to produce some product. The exemplar for such activity is the creation of Wikipedia. Wikipedia stands as the only website in the global top 10 operated by a nonprofit foundation, not a large Internet company. Started in 2001, the English version of Wikipedia has grown to more than 4.5 million articles.[77] Knocked for inaccuracies, vandalism, and allowance of the arcane or obscure, Wikipedia has developed and maintained its position as a global resource for encyclopedic explanation of many topics. It also has served as a model for imagination of future human organization and assembly of knowledge.

In 2006, Wikipedia conducted its first major conference in the United States, Wikimania, at the Harvard Law School. In his essay "Science 2.0," computer scientist Ben Shneiderman credited the Wikimania conference for opening his eyes to the concept of collaborative knowledge generation.[78] He argued that the combination of computing, networking, and intuitive social software would create the venue for globally interconnected collaborative problem-solving entities:

Emerging successes such as scientific collaboratories among genomic researchers, engineering innovations through open source software, and community-based participation in cultural heritage projects are early indicators of the transformative nature of collaboration. EBay, Amazon, and Netflix have already reshaped consumer markets, while political participation and citizen journalism are beginning to change civil society. Patient-centered medical information and secure electronic health records are improving healthcare, while creating opportunities for clinical research. MySpace and Facebook encourage casual social networks, but they may soon play more serious roles in facilitating emergency/disaster response. Social media platforms, such as Wikipedia, flickr, and YouTube, are also stunning success stories of web-based contributions.[79]

While some of Shneiderman's assertions are more widely accepted than others, the key concept, that the Internet permits the arrangement of human cognitive capacity and work in new and novel ways to solve problems, is an idea difficult to entirely refute. These communications are the basis for scientific advancement and economic growth, but as the following chapter illustrates, the governance of the Internet and the maintenance of trust within it, a fundamental cyber security mission, has become one of the most important global issues of our time.

CHAPTER 3

Tunis, Room 641A, and the Politics of the Information Society

With our explanation of the evolution of computing and the economics of Silicon Valley complete, we move on to governance of the Internet. Although it is obvious and often repeated: *scientia potential est* (knowledge is power). Cyberspace is fundamentally restructuring our understanding of this aphorism. Data is power as companies collect the "digital" exhaust; clicks, tweets, location pings, searches, status updates, and all of the other interactions produced by computers convert can be monetized.[1] Data is power for governments, in everything from serving as regulators of and gatekeepers to online activity as well as increasingly capable watchers of information flows. Data is power as hackers in the employ of criminal organizations and intelligence services purloin confidential information from activists, corporations, and governments.

For these reasons, how the Internet will be governed and what sort of controls can be placed upon information flowing across it has become an important political issue. There is the matter of who shall be the final arbiter of the contents of the root zone, the addressing information found on the servers of the Domain Name System (DNS), without which delivery of Internet packets could not be accomplished. Beyond DNS and other architectural issues there is the problem of digital content, the images, messages, and ideas that may offend or outrage different constituencies. Until recently, individuals and organizations largely outside of government have managed these issues.

WHO RUNS THE INTERNET?

Where government has grown heavily invested is in the area of monitoring cyberspace, primarily in response to the most significant national security issue for most of the world's countries: terrorism. Over the last 50 years, the U.S. government and U.S. firms largely built the infrastructures of cyberspace. As communication largely shifted to mechanisms enabled by TCP/IP, we were left to wonder how intelligence services would use such information to perform their missions. The 2006 revelation of an NSA intercept facility in Room 641A at AT&T's Folsom Street building in San Francisco provided some initial answers.[2] The Web was being systematically tapped by the United States and likely could be tapped by others as well. This tapping of the Web raised an important set of questions for the international community with regard to how the governance of the Internet should be conducted. The United States' enormous stature in computing and networking technologies is hard to understate.

How the Internet is governed and how the world's nations and international organizations participate in that process is now a serious area of political discourse. Only a few years ago, at the middle of the last decade, when the United Nations organized its first major conferences on the Information Society, the topic of Internet governance was a relative backwater on the policy agenda. In Washington, few cared about the workings of the Internet Corporation for Assigned Names and Numbers (ICANN), the Internet Assigned Numbers Authority (IANA), or the Internet Engineering Task Force (IETF). Today that is very different; the international affairs of cyberspace and the related security concerns are very much on the national agenda of the United States and a growing part of its diplomatic efforts.

While many government agencies, NGOs, and corporations are described throughout this book in explaining the workings of cyberspace and the politics that are evolving within it, there is an important thread illustrating that individuals matter. Remember Jon Postel, the "Numbers Czar," a single person who served as the final arbiter of allocating IP addresses globally.[3] The Internet grew up around a rather unusual entity, the IETF, in roughly a generation. These engineers created the infrastructure needed to pass an unfathomable number of messages and managed the Internet's phenomenal growth.

This process evolved from Robert Kahn and Vinton Cerf's concept of "how a protocol with suitable features might be the glue that would pull together the various emerging network technologies."[4] A community of hundreds, including professors, graduate students, research scientists, engineers, and government employees became enmeshed in the process of building the Internet. Through the 1980s, emphasis of this community was placed on achieving the fundamental goal of developing "an effective technique for multiplexed utilization of existing interconnected networks."[5] The Internet engineers developed a system that allowed data to agnostically flow across telecommunications and data networks.

Without this technological community, characterized by Twomey as a guild, the Internet would not work. But how does it exert power and how much of it does it have? Postel provided an example. In January 1998, he rerouted DNS queries from a U.S. government facility in Herndon, Virginia, to one he managed for the Defense Department at the University of Southern California's Information Sciences Institute. By sending an email that shifted the location of the root of DNS and thus the entire Internet to the parties maintaining the other DNS root servers, Postel had showed how easily DNS could be subverted.[6]

What Postel had done was to make his server, not the National Science Foundation server in Herndon, the one where the root zone file would reside.[7] Although he called the move a test, at the time Postel's word was final on numbers matters. One of his colleagues who maintained one of the other DNS root servers, at the University of Maryland's College Park campus, commented on the change in location. "If Jon asks us to point somewhere else, we'll do it ... He is the authority here."[8] Shortly before Postel's death that October, the IANA function shifted not to another person, but to an institution. The body that stood up to manage the IANA DNS function and other Internet governance issues was the International Corporation for Assigned Names and Numbers (ICANN).[9] ICANN's interim chairman said of the organization in its first press release, "Nobody should operate under the illusion that any issue has been resolved 'once and for all'. Similarly, nobody should feel that issues that are important to them and have not been addressed to their satisfaction cannot be revisited."[10]

While there was controversy over transparency and inclusion in ICANN even in its early formative stage, there was also the matter of how the Internet governance might be distinctly different from other forms of transnational governance. Lawrence Lessig asked how Internet governance might be like the process of creating open source software, asking if there was something from those projects "that would teach us something about Internet governance, and government generally?"[11]

Raising the concept of open source project governance, Lessig acknowledged that it was the U.S. government that chose to shift the IANA function to the newly formed ICANN. "It was not software that chose Network Solutions as the domain name registry – it was the United States government, by a contract that shifted the responsibility from the late John Postel."[12] ICANN was established to manage domain names, the process by which IP addresses are assigned to entities so that they may engage in communications via the Internet. It holds the *root zone*, a master list of valid Internet addresses that were held by ICANN and distributed across DNS servers around the planet. This is a confederated function, as each nation is responsible for its national top-level domain (TLD).[13]

The term "DNS root" actually refers to two distinct things: the root zone file and the root name servers. The root zone file is the list of top-level domain name assignments, with pointers to primary and secondary name servers for each top-level domain. The root server system, on the other hand, is the operational aspect—the means of distributing the information contained in the root zone file in response to resolution of queries from other name servers on the Internet ... The server where the root zone file is first loaded is considered authoritative; the others merely copy its contents.[14]

Supported by the U.S. Department of Commerce, ICANN was connected to the U.S. government, but in an ambiguous manner. "To support and enhance the multi-stakeholder model of Internet policymaking and governance" was what the U.S. Commerce Department's National Telecommunications asked ICANN to do. It also issued guidance to ICANN that it must "transition key Internet domain name functions to the global multi-stakeholder community."[15]

Multi-stakeholderism is the watchword of the Internet governance community that has grown up following ICANN's creation. Papers on the topic of multi-stakeholder governance arrangements began appearing in scholarly journals in the late 1980s. The term was applied to topics including development, environmental protection, and even management[16] and is fairly described as a progressive expression of sorts. It may be considered a process of not rowing the boat, but rather steering it.[17]

A Multistakeholder Model is an organizational framework or structure which adopts the multistakeholder process of governance or policy making, which aims to bring together the primary stakeholders such as businesses, civil society, governments, research institutions and non-government organizations to cooperate and participate in the dialogue, decision making and implementation of solutions to common problems or goals. A stakeholder refers to an individual, group or organization that has a direct or indirect interest or stake in a particular organization; that is, a given action has the ability to influence the organization's actions, decisions and policies to achieve results.[18]

What the multi-stakeholder model has meant to Internet governance issues is that representatives from government, industry, academia, and those falling under the umbrella term "civil society" convene to discuss and deliberate regularly.

This translates to not only the running of committees and conferences such as the IETF, IANA, and ICANN that might be characterized as chiefly technical in nature but also ties to international political organizations. As global interest in the Internet has grown, the debate surrounding its governance has become more political in nature (not that there aren't politics in setting technical standards or adopting them). This rise of

Internet politics became apparent at Internet governance conferences held in Geneva and Tunis at the middle of the last decade.

AN INTERNET SOCIETY

For the United States, Internet governance has not always been the highest of priorities. The Internet's phenomenal growth was managed during a transition period where the National Science Foundation opened ARPANET to non-DoD research institutions and in that process dramatically expanded the number of interconnected networks from 217 to more than 50,000 between 1988 and 1995.[19] After shutting down NSFNET and switching over to the commercialized Internet that continues to run today, that growth mushroomed.

As the commercialized Internet grew, Vinton Cerf and Bob Kahn applied their energies to a new organization, the Internet Society (ISOC). Formed in 1992, the ISOC is a chapter-based advocacy group that embodies the values of the initial Internet evangelists who spearheaded its growth.[20] With a Geneva, Switzerland, headquarters, ISOC occupies a position in connecting the technology industry with international organizations operating in alignment with the United Nations and other international governance bodies, but in international standards and governance, the ISOC is a relative newcomer.

Also in Geneva is the headquarters of the far older International Telecommunications Union (ITU), which got its start as the International Telegraph Union in 1865. A UN-specialized agency, the ITU's duties include mandates to "allocate global radio spectrum and satellite orbits, develop the technical standards that ensure networks and technologies seamlessly interconnect, and strive to improve access to ICTs to underserved communities worldwide."[21] Until the advent of the Internet, the ITU's primary role was international telecommunications infrastructure management and interconnection. But the Internet offered new issues and opportunities.

Little more than a decade ago, Internet connectivity in many countries involved porting data traffic to operate over the telephone network by modem. Points of access in many countries were limited. The concept of a digital divide, in which wealthy nations were able to provide near-universal access to the Internet and poorer ones struggled to provide much beyond limited connectivity to elites, corporations, and government entities, was very much an important agenda item of the ISOC and the ITU. There was concern that ICANN represented "Northern-led processes dominated the governance of the Internet" and this perception stood as another clear fissure between the "West and the rest."[22]

Internet penetration statistics for the world's least developed nations were often incredibly low. Discussion on Internet issues was aimed at getting connectivity to more of the planet quickly. As we will see, the march toward ubiquitous access has been fairly fast, quick enough to prompt the question whether advocacy for bridging the divide made a difference or was even necessary. Nonetheless, at the middle of the last decade, governance issues related to information technologies and the Internet beyond those of capacity development regarding infrastructure were emerging in international relations.

INTERNET GOVERNANCE GETS NOTICED

In 2003 and 2005, the United Nations held a pair of major conferences on the role of the Information Society. In 2005, the United States ostensibly could have surrendered its considerable control over the Internet.[23] That year, the second meeting of the World Summit of the Information Society (WSIS) in Tunis was convened, following a large meeting in Geneva two years before. Tunisia—Arab and Middle Eastern, yet still claiming the vestiges of a Francophone past and stable—was as interesting a spot as any to hold a conference on the future of the Internet as it would eventually be the point of origin for the revolutions of the 2011 Arab Spring.

At issue at the 2005 WSIS was the question of whether ICANN should remain the ultimate arbiter of global standards for domain names and numbers. The alternate choice would be to develop an international organization beholden not to the United States, but to an international body such as the United Nations. There had been considerable discussion undertaken by the UN Working Group on Internet Governance (WGIG) established in the wake of the 2003 Geneva meeting. Headed by Markus Kummer, the WGIG was charged with addressing four items, including formulate a working definition of Internet governance, identify relevant public policy issues to that governance, pull together common understanding among a heterogeneous group of interested parties, and prepare for the 2005 Tunis summit.

Front and center on the 2005 WSIS agenda was the role that the United States would continue to play in the governance of domain names and addresses. As a core developer of the Internet, the U.S. government had shepherded its development from a Pentagon vehicle for scholarly communication to a widely accessible infrastructure managed and operated primarily by private firms.[24] With the adoption of the High Performance Computing and Communication Act and the opening of the National Science Foundation's NSFNET research network for commercialization in the early 1990s, a series of entities—both for-profit and nonprofit—began filling the role of governing the operation of a rapidly growing Internet and World Wide Web.

Reasons other countries desired an alternative to ICANN were many. As the manager for the root, the assessor of validity at the highest level in the assignment of domain names, ICANN's U.S.-ties status annoyed or aggravated a variety of constituencies. Run on the Roman alphabet, standards promulgated by ICANN and the IETF were viewed as insensitive to the billions on the planet who read and write in Arabic, Cyrillic, Chinese, or other alphabets.[25]

Additionally, there was the issue of the "root" infrastructure, the servers distributed around the global topography of the Internet, which stood as the definitive directories of Internet addresses for the purposes of routing data around the world. Thirteen organizations, 10 of them in the United States, remain responsible for the maintenance of these servers (the other three are Swedish, Dutch, and Japanese, although synchronized duplicates of the root servers exist in many additional locations).[26] Management of DNS entries, the tables of stored data that match the Web address lexicon represented in text with IP address information, was managed from these servers with overall direction coming from the United States.[27]

With a successor for ICANN not at hand, the world did not wrestle control of the "root" away from the United States at the WSIS in Tunis. On June 30, 2005, the National Telecommunications and Information Administration (NTIA), which reports to the U.S. Department of Commerce, issued a single-page set of principles regarding the domain name and addressing system for the Internet. In it, the NTIA stated that it would: (1) preserve the security and stability of the DNS; (2) recognize the national interest regarding their top-level domains; (3) maintain the position that ICANN was the "appropriate technical manager of Internet DNS"; and (4) support the continued dialogue on Internet governance in multiple fora.[28]

While shifting of ICANN from U.S. sovereign control to international management was not demanded at the 2005 WSIS, the United States failed to achieve its goal of bringing a comprehensive initiative on information security out of the conference.[29] The *Tunis Commitment* drafted out of the conference merely mentioned security, but contained firm language regarding a continued effort to bridge the digital divide between Internet-connected haves and have-nots, as well as other Internet governance issues. On governance emerged a framework for talks and meetings, what would become the Internet Governance Forum (IGF).[30]

At issue in the Geneva and Tunis WSIS summits was the manner in which the Internet governance would be undertaken through input from a variety of stakeholders. But also at play was the issue of digital convergence, as global telecommunication has grown increasingly dependent on the Internet's standards and protocols. For the ITU, the UN-affiliated international organization for telecommunication, the phenomenon by which Internet traffic would supplant or even entirely replace traditional telephony, represented an inconvenient reality. Considering this issue some time later, Organization for Economic Co-operation and Development (OECD) researchers observed:

Convergence between traditional voice networks and the Internet has the potential to produce conflicts between the existing framework for the exchange of voice traffic, which is largely regulated, and the Internet model of traffic exchange based on voluntary agreements.[31]

The Tunis WSIS took place only a few weeks after Web auctioneer eBay purchased the Skype Internet telecommunications software. Skype was a clear rival to conventional long-distance and international telephone services, employing the Internet to complete calls between computers. While ITU regulated international calls, its role regarding services like Skype was largely unknown.[32] It was a telecommunications regulator ostensibly managing a declining set of issues.

The WSIS process demonstrated that pulling together a global community of states, NGOs, corporations, and others required bridging significant gaps in understanding of issues and basic definitions. There was a divide between technical and semantic roles of the Internet. At WSIS, "some delegates envisaged a 'narrow' or restricted definition of governance 'Of' the Internet." This view embraced a dialogue on technical issues, of the sort that ICANN, the IETF, and IANA had undertaken as the Internet grew from its research network past to its commercializing present. "Others took a broader or extensive view of governance 'On' the Internet, relating to what the Internet carries."[33] Here a set of ideas stretched into an agenda on access, ameliorating the issue of uneven deployment of ICTs in the developing world.

Governance could be exerted through government and others. National laws and policies of countries shaped the basic rules for the global community. A second governance flow came from "formalized rules, procedures and related programs that are collaboratively defined by the private sector, including both for profit and not for profit entities."[34] WSIS demonstrated a growing politicization of the Internet and cyberspace. What had been largely run by a small group of technicians, academics, and engineers only a decade earlier was now drawing the attention of a much larger group of interested parties, both inside and outside of governments. With a larger group came a broader set of issues.

Barely mentioned, however, was the matter of information or cybersecurity. Tunisian president Zine al-Abidine Ben Ali avoided addressing security in his remarks at WSIS, choosing instead to focus on ameliorating the digital divide and pushing for openness of the Internet. This openness

would eventually draw his wrath as Tunisians rose up against his
government in December 2010.

Network security is already attracting a lot of interest from governments in the
industrialized world as an arena ripe for enhanced international cooperation.
One could imagine an effort to move toward broader multilateral instruments that
would put teeth into the "global culture of security" that has already been
endorsed by the UN General Assembly and the December 2003 WSIS Summit.
But on current trends, the WSIS process would probably play a supporting rather
than a leading role in catalyzing any such activity.[35]

WSIS's reticence about security might be explained in part because, in
2005, the world was focused on countering violent extremism. Al Qaeda
and other Islamic groups were still very lethal well outside the Middle
East. July 2005 saw multiple bombings in London, killing 56 and wound-
ing more than 700. In the prior year, Russia suffered through Beslan
school siege, which eventually claimed 334 lives, half of them children,
after security forces moved in. WSIS took place before the Iraq Study
Group offered its guidance on a United States mired in Iraq. Bin Laden
remained at large and Afghanistan was largely forgotten. As a result, for
the U.S. government and those of its allies, Internet governance and
cybersecurity were niche issues. They simply didn't resonate.

POLITICS OF INTERNET GOVERNANCE

The political maneuvering over the World Summit of the Information
Society demonstrated the emergence of an international politics over
Internet governance in which U.S. authority could be challenged. For the
United States, opposition to the Internet governance model it had put into
place only a few years ago represented an important harbinger of the
future. IANA, once a person, then an institution, became part of an
international debate over what role ICANN should hold in managing
the evolution of the Internet.

Although the outcome of the WSIS was largely inconclusive, there
remained after it a fundamental question of how ICANN of Marina del
Rey, California, could be at the center of Internet governance. That said,
few advocated a migration of functions to the ITU or any other UN-
affiliated agency. ICANN worked and had successfully managed the
incredible growth of the Internet. The IGF was a practical stopgap on
discussion of radically altering how Internet governance was performed.
The United States had built the Internet and, to most of the nations concerned, remained a reliable steward for its management and continued
cultivation.

For the time being, however, the United States had kept challenges to its dotted line authority between the Commerce Department and ICANN at bay. To most leaders of the world's more developed, democratic nations, the status quo worked. The United States had built the Internet and appeared a reasonably good steward. Arguments from the People's Republic of China and Russia, both nations viewing the topic of information security as how to shield their publics from information unpopular with the regime that might form the seeds of discontent, could be easily dismissed. Those views clashed with ideals regarding openness and freedom of speech held by many multi-stakeholder participants in Internet governance. The actions of the U.S. Intelligence Community to employ cyberspace as a collection tool for its missions in pursuing terrorists would eventually strain the patience of those who had seen a U.S.-sponsored ICANN as the best answer to governance problems.

QUESTIONING U.S. BENEVOLENT HEGEMONY: INTELLIGENCE IN CYBERSPACE

Thirty miles north of Palo Alto came the first significant allegation on how the U.S. signals intelligence program had evolved from 9/11. In December 2005, a news story appeared in the *New York Times* on warrantless wiretapping being undertaken by the U.S. government, ostensibly directed at not only foreign parties but also the communications of U.S. citizens abroad and potentially at home. After reading warrantless wiretapping stories, an AT&T employee, Mark Klein, decided to reach out to the media regarding the operation of a "secret room" at the company's 611 Folsom Street facilities in San Francisco. Klein, who had retired from AT&T in 2004, detailed how NSA had developed a locked and secure facility, Room 641A, inside 611 Folsom Street that was producing a copy of the data and telephone traffic transiting AT&T's facilities in San Francisco via fiberoptic link.[36] Additional secret rooms existed at other points where long-haul fiberoptic cables made landfall in the United States. Klein's allegations added up to an NSA capability to tap not only all international phone calls but potentially every bit of data transiting via the Internet across switches and through cables on U.S. soil.

Despite Secretary of State Henry Stimson's assertion in 1929 that "gentleman do not read each other's mail,"[37] intercepting the communications of one's adversary became an enormously useful form of intelligence collection as military forces embraced telegraphy, radio, and telephony to communicate at global distances and coordinate the actions of widely distributed forces. Since 1947, this mission has fallen on the shoulders of the NSA, the successor to U.S. military signals intelligence

(SIGINT) services that grew impressively during World War II and included a special relationship with the British service, Government Communications Headquarters (GCHQ).[38]

After 9/11, the NSA's capabilities were considerably upgraded and the agency's surveillance powers expanded. Revelation of Room 641A became a political issue in Washington. In his run for the presidency, then-senator Barack Obama modified his views on the highly controversial warrantless wiretappings undertaken by the NSA directed at U.S. citizens and persons. A previous ardent critic of the Bush administration's use of electronic means to collect intelligence in its campaign against transnational terrorism, the junior senator from Illinois changed his mind before assuming the nation's highest office, ceasing his high-profile criticism of warrantless wiretapping programs.[39]

As the long ordeal to locate Osama bin Laden testified, the intelligence agencies of the United States and its allies struggled to break into the top ranks of tightly knit terror groups. As a result, intelligence agencies focused more on technology for answers regarding the collection of actionable intelligence in terror and criminal networks. Indonesia's Abu Sayyaf, Colombia's FARC, and Mexico's Sinaloa Cartel, although radically different organizations in ideology, all share a common need: they must communicate at a distance. This entails using technology, from cell phones to chat rooms, to communicate and deliver messages. The best hope for collecting intelligence on most of these groups often has been in intercepting those communications.

During the Cold War, the United States' Intelligence Community built upon its World War II electronic surveillance and code-breaking successes to penetrate the Iron Curtain when human agents could not. Wiretapping grew more sophisticated, as exemplified by the *Ivy Bells* program, which installed recording devices on Soviet submarine communications cables that transited the bottom of the Sea of Okhotsk.[40] The U.S. intelligence enterprise constructed sites around the globe and developed means to collect signals bouncing off the moon to get transmissions. Concomitantly, the haul of information from electronic eavesdropping grew exponentially.[41] With the development of ARPANET, the packet-switching technology that would evolve into the Internet, a vast new terrain in the area of electronic surveillance and signals intelligence sprang forth. As the Internet grew to span to globe, so did the capacity to monitor it.

The digitization of telephone communications and later the mass adoption of other digital technologies like the mobile computer, cell phone, and smart phone[42] changed the game of signals intelligence collection. In the analog period, wiretapping was a resource-intensive activity generally requiring access to the phone infrastructure in close proximity to the targeted telephone. Computing technology markedly changed this.

PRIVACY AND INTELLIGENCE

On the domestic side, U.S. law enforcement tapping the telephone system for the collection of evidence stretches back a century. Early on, the legality of such activity came to the U.S. Supreme Court in 1928's *Olmstead v. United States*. The Taft court heard the case of Roy Olmstead, declared the wiretap evidence regarding his bootlegging activities collected against him admissible.[43] It was Supreme Court Justice Louis Brandeis's prescient dissent that spelled out concerns of future telecommunications eavesdropping. Co-author of what is likely the first significant scholarly article advocating for a right to privacy nearly 40 years before *Olmstead*, Brandeis argued:

The progress of science furnishing the government with means of espionage is not likely to stop with wiretapping. Ways may someday be developed by which the government, without removing papers from secret drawers, can reproduce them in court, and by which it will be enabled to expose to a jury the most intimate occurrences of the home.[44]

Brandeis saw a future in which the most intimate information about individuals could be easily known by the investigative powers of government. The advance of technology would enable broader capacity for government to spy on the citizenry.

Although Brandeis's position would be vindicated in the overturning of *Olmstead* in 1967's *Katz v. United States*, organizations took up the charge of asserting the right to protection from unconstitutional surveillance as the level of intrusiveness of counter-subversive programs undertaken by the FBI and other agencies came to light, particularly during the hearings of the Church Committee during 1975–1976.[45]

CYBERINT: TAPPING THE WEB

The transition to computerization in telecommunications allowed emplacement of equipment at the point of digital switching from the local phone network to the national telecommunications grid with minimum effort. Moving from electromechanical to computerized switching, phone companies opened a new avenue for simplifying the business of phone wiretapping. Analog signals traveled over copper wire to switching offices, but when it arrived, the analog signal was converted to digital data, routed by computer to the eventual connection.

In the early 1990s, guidelines and rules for electronic surveillance were still very much directed toward an analog telephone network.[46] With the advent of packet-based telephony, the U.S. government realized that if tapping could be undertaken at the computerized switch offices, federal agents didn't need to splice taps up telephone poles anymore. The enactment of

Communications Assistance for Law Enforcement Act (CALEA) after a contentious debate in the 1990s required U.S. telecommunications providers to streamline the wiretapping process. A feature of digital switching, conference calling, in which multiple parties could participate in a single telephone conversation, provided the avenue for simplified telephone wiretapping. Digital telephone switches offered a conference call capacity, which enabled wiretapping, with the wiretapper serving as a silent party to the conversation.[47] Law enforcement seized upon this capability and quickly realized they wanted to monitor many more conversations than the conference-calling technology permitted.

Aware of the conference call feature, the FBI initiated "a massive lobbying effort" in support of the Digital Telephony Proposal: new wiretapping legislation designed to facilitate wiretapping of digital telecommunications.[48] In a battle to convince Congress of the importance of new telecommunications-monitoring legislation, then FBI director Louis Freeh made repeated visits to Capitol Hill to lobby on its behalf. "Mr. Freeh had devoted considerable personal time to lobbying for the bill and made it his agency's highest legislative priority. He repeatedly argued that the FBI could not fight crimes like terrorism, foreign espionage and international drug dealing if telephonic technology continued to outpace eavesdropping abilities."[49] But CALEA was very much a pre-Internet piece of policy, and with the proliferation of Internet connectivity and mobile telephony over the next several years after its enactment, the powers specified were increasingly viewed as insufficient by the Department of Justice.[50]

Dramatic overhaul of wiretapping and digital surveillance powers came in October 2001, with the passage of the Uniting and Strengthening America by Providing Appropriate Tools Required to Intercept and Obstruct Terrorism Act, known by its household name, the Patriot Act. It updated wiretapping law to the digital age. Revision of the pen register function (the process of collecting dialed telephone numbers) was considerably amended. The text, "electronic or other impulses which identify the numbers dialed or otherwise transmitted on the telephone line to which such device is attached," was replaced with the significantly more exhaustive, "dialing, routing, addressing, or signaling information transmitted by an instrument or facility from which a wire or electronic communication is transmitted, provided, however, that such information shall not include the contents of any communication." In addition, the term "or process" was tacked onto the term "device" wherever it appeared in the statute.[51]

Wiretapping was no longer about phone calls, and sometime after the 9/11, signals intelligence began growing into *cyber intelligence*, the capacity to analyze a massive number of data streams. Looking to the NSA, hypothetical capabilities came to light in an article from a former director of Central Intelligence that revealed the NSA's Echelon program.

Allegedly, the NSA used Echelon "to search through collected signals intelligence, using key words via a computer" allowing "more material to be searched and exploited."[52] This capability, previously imagined but never publicly acknowledged, gave strong indication that the U.S. government held the capability to use computers to selectively listen in on phone conversations in a sophisticated manner.[53]

By 2005, much of what is considered phone calls had become delivered by Voice over Internet Protocol (VoIP) services employing the Internet. As one researcher opined, "using Internet telephony, almost anyone can be a telecommunications carrier, including Google, Skype, Vonage and Yahoo."[54] With widespread adoption of VoIP, wiretapping targeting moved beyond the telephone company and its circuits and on to anyone providing communication services via the Internet. Of course telephony, including VoIP, is not the whole picture in the world of digital communications.

In the converging world of IT, the phone call is but one avenue for communication. New modes for relaying information proliferated as social networking websites—Twitter, YouTube, and Facebook—took off.[55] The U.S. government's signals intelligence program, often encapsulated in a debate on warrantless wiretapping, was growing the capacity to monitor the planet's interconnected digital communications networks. Wiretapping outgrew simply listening to the phone. *Really, wiretapping became webtapping, listening to (and reading and watching) everything transmitted in digital form. It is, at heart, splicing into the planet's digital nervous system.*

What that meant was massive communications monitoring of content sent via voice, text, and video, to analytical offices of the U.S. Intelligence Community. Mark Klein's revelation to the press for the first time brought the idea of massive eavesdropping on the Internet into the public light in a significant fashion. While Europeans had complained of Echelon and its capabilities for years, suddenly there was much more significant evidence to back their claims.

SIGINT INTERCONNECTING WITH CYBERSECURITY

Klein's disclosures regarding the NSA's burgeoning IP packet capture capability provided evidence that U.S. leadership on the Internet was not necessarily without problems. Those concerned with warrantless wiretapping were principally preoccupied with protections for American citizens at home. Organizations such as the Electronic Frontier Foundation and the Electronic Privacy Information Center were focused on individual liberties extending into cyberspace, but it was a niche issue. The ACLU was just awakening to how important protections for data transmission might be.

However, the idea that U.S. cyber intelligence activities might bring about a deep cleavage on its legitimacy as the ultimate arbiter on Internet governance was a long way off. The 611 Folsom Street story died down, the telecommunications companies named in the incident were granted immunity,[56] and the matter forgotten and dismissed as an excess of the scary days immediately following 9/11. But why would the United States wish to give up such a capability? As the fifth anniversary of the Al Qaeda attacks ticked by, Bin Laden remained at large while the United States and a shrinking coalition of allies fought on in Afghanistan and Iraq. Worries on webtapping fell down the national political agenda as a small party of committed organizations sued government agencies and others in an attempt to stop what they viewed as unconstitutional.

CHAPTER 4

The Great Cyberwar of 2007

Since the 1990s the discussion on cyberwar has been akin to virgins talking about sex: everybody says they're doing it but nobody really knows what it is. Although recent events have demonstrated that cyber techniques can be employed by militaries to aid in achieving operational goals,[1] the idea of war or military action by computer remains abstract. Nonetheless, by the mid-2000s, a conversation was intensifying on how computer network attack and exploitation (CNA and CNE) could be employed by the U.S. military in their campaigns.

The actions against Estonia during April 2007 changed the discussion on cyber conflict. After the Estonians displeased their Russian minority and Moscow by relocating an Unknown Soldier monument, the country's IT infrastructure was attacked, not by Russia, but by hackers. This non-attributed attack stands as an important signpost in the evolution of cyber conflict.

In cybersecurity, there are numerous lexical and definitional issues that have yet to find satisfying resolution or consensus either within narrow technical or legal communities, or in larger discussion on national or global policy. In computational circles, cyber attacks are when an unauthorized actor is able to compromise a system via vulnerability. That seems fairly pedestrian in comparison with terms like "terror attack" or "air attack," where bombs go off and bullets are fired. But after Estonia, the lawyers of armed conflict wrestled with the tough problem as to when a cyber attack merited a kinetic (i.e., armed) response. We wonder, "When do bits require response with bullets?"

Despite these unresolved issues, the U.S. Department of Defense (DoD), particularly the Air Force, has marched forward with an aggressive building campaign regarding the development of a cyber force, including the establishment of U.S. Cyber Command. This activity has included turf battles, political horse-trading, and resource grabs, despite a weak understanding of exactly what cyberwar or cyber warfare might be. Ultimately, the DoD chose to call cyberspace a warfighting domain. What this means to international peace and stability should be anyone's guess.

THE FIRST NATIONAL HACK ATTACK

In the spring of 2007, Estonia, marvel of the newly invigorated former Soviet bloc for its economic revitalization and transformation, became the target of a massive cyber attack against information systems of the nation's public and private institutions. Websites for government ministries and the country's largest financial institutions were knocked offline, victims of distributed denial of service (DDoS) attacks, which overwhelmed the computer hardware upon which the websites ran with an avalanche of false data requests. The attacks, which bombarded Internet servers with a massive avalanche of false data traffic, shut down many of the online services upon which the country's citizenry had grown incredibly dependent. Estonia became a "slash-dotted" nation.[2]

Ostensibly the 2007 attacks on Estonia's computer systems began with the move of the Soviet-era Bronze Soldier statue, which memorialized unknown soldiers of the Great Patriotic War. The shift of the Bronze Soldier's location on April 26, 2007, from downtown Tallinn to a military cemetery a few kilometers away tapped deep anger and resentment among the country's sizable ethnic Russian minority, sparking riots and an attack by youths on the Estonian embassy to Moscow. While the real disturbances peaked and waned in a few days, the attacks upon the computer networks and services at the core of Estonia's modern infrastructure went on for weeks. The contents of Estonia's public-facing government websites were replaced with pro-Russia propaganda defacements, with the government able to do little more in the short term to combat the problem than power its systems down and cut off connectivity to the outside world. Then, the work of seeking aid began.

Joining the European Union (EU) and NATO in 2004, Estonia has shifted away from the former Soviet sphere and established firm ties to the West, particularly Scandinavia. With a population of roughly 1.3 million, Estonia rapidly became a highly "wired" or Internet-connected nation and stood as a model for IT adoption. The number of cellular phones in use exceeded the number of citizens,[3] an overwhelming of government and banking transactions were Internet-mediated, and in the February 2007 national elections, more than five percent of the population voted online.[4]

Influenced and aided by its Scandinavian neighbors, Estonia developed a robust technology sector under the *Tiigrihüpe* (Tiger's Leap) project begun in the 1990s. Estonia rapidly reached a GDP level found in most developed nations. IT was the key attribute as "the economic success of the tiny former Soviet republic is built largely on its status as an e-society, with paperless government and electronic voting. Many common transactions, including the signing of legal documents, can be done via the Internet."[5]

Electronically disconnected by DDoS, Estonia's vibrant economy was suddenly imperiled. Websites and services of the Estonian presidency, parliament, most of the government ministries, the major political parties, the largest news organizations, two of the largest banks, and several firms specializing in telecommunications were knocked offline.[6] Putin's Russia, increasingly assertive in protecting the rights of ethnic Russian minorities in its former Soviet republics, publicly condemned the Bronze Statue move. Moscow Mayor Yury Luzkhov announced that Estonia's leaders appeared "as people who justified and abetted fascism."[7] Estonia's leadership pointed the finger at the Kremlin for initiating what many in the Western press characterized as a cyberwar, with one member of parliament stating, "there are strong indications of Russian state involvement," alleging a tie between the DDoS attacks and a Russian government official's Internet Protocol (IP) address.[8]

In response, security firms from the West worked to stave off "botnets" of networked computers hijacked by unauthorized parties and then used to send direct massive quantities of data at a particular website, email server, or Internet address.[9] The botnets were the vehicle for conducting the DDoS attack and were composed of compromised computers residing in locations as far away as Egypt, Peru, China, and the United States. For NATO, Estonia's predicament produced a thorny issue: were the attacks a martial act? Fortunately they were not, but NATO and the United States dispatched observers to Tallinn, while Scandinavia's formidable academic and commercial computer security community pitched in to aid in cleaning up the mess.[10] Systems were restored, software updated, and by June Estonia's e-society was once again up and running, about two months after the first attacks.

ELECTRONIC PEARL HARBOR: PART I

As access to the Internet has broadened, cybersecurity has become a subject of debate on the potential vulnerability of a society increasingly dependent on networked computing systems. With Internet access nearly ubiquitous in much of the world and rapidly moving to every corner of the globe, a dependency upon it has grown. Absent digital connectivity, global supply chains jam, financial institutions are paralyzed, and the general population is soon massively inconvenienced at best. Nearly a decade ago the U.S. Department of Labor asserted that soon, "half of all U.S.

workers will be employed in industries that produce or intensively use information technology, products, and services."[11] That fraction likely continues to grow.

This dependency acknowledged, many fret over an "electronic Pearl Harbor" crippling national communications, transportation, and financial systems; effectively paralyzing the United States; wrecking its economy; and rendering it unable to mobilize or project military forces to meet the aggressive actions of enemies abroad. In the first decade of the 21st century uncertainty prevailed in ascertaining the possibility of a catastrophic attack on the information infrastructure of the state. Computer-based attacks producing changes to objects in the physical environment were relatively unknown. One such attack had taken place before 2005, however, and was consistently mentioned by U.S. officials. There was a real case of an unauthorized user producing physical damage via digital means. It happened in Australia, in a sleepy beach town of the Gold Coast called Maroochy Shire.

On April 23, 2000, police in Queensland arrested Vitek Boden, a computer software developer. He was eventually convicted for instructing the Maroochy Shire computerized waste management system to spill millions of liters of raw sewage into rivers, parks, and the grounds of the Hyatt Regency hotel. As a result, "marine life died, the creek water turned black, and the stench was unbearable to residents," according to an official of the Australian Environmental Protection Agency.[12] An employee of the company that had installed the system, Boden apparently conducted the attack after the local council passed on hiring him to stay on in a support capacity. Armed with a laptop computer, wireless equipment, and intimate knowledge of the computer system's design, he acted alone to produce what is perhaps the first environmental cyber attack.[13]

The Boden case illustrated that a computer attack on physical infrastructure could happen. It also reinforced a lesson that has been painfully learned by the U.S. Army and the National Security Agency in years since. Perhaps the greatest vulnerability to networked computer systems is those individuals who hold or may have at one time had access to the targeted system.

MILLIONS OF ATTACKS

By the middle of the last decade, reports of break-ins, disruptions, and attacks perpetrated against computer networks became increasingly common in the popular media. These activities, labeled "hacking" or as being undertaken by "hackers," rose concomitantly with the broader adoption of IT globally and its employment in entirely new purposes or to overhaul existing processes. Internet-mediated cyber attacks, a reality since the Morris Worm of 1988,[14] had become far more common by 2007, the year of the Estonia cyber affair.

As the number of information security incidents rose, a community of security practitioners and academics attempted to categorize the types of threats. While the U.S. military had considerable experience in how it identified, classified, protected, transmitted, processed, and destroyed information, outside of government such knowledge was scarcer. Study of security produced a characterization of three categories in which information or information systems could be compromised: *confidentiality, integrity,* and *availability*. Into these categories, supplemented by a few others that often are subject to debate, almost any security can be placed. In computer and information security, any "single unauthorized access attempt, or unauthorized use attempt, regardless of success" carries the label of "attack," a word with many applications in the English language, from verbal dispute to acts of war.[15] This is an incredibly problematic term especially when it is employed outside the computer and information security community. We all know a military attack or a terrorist attack is an event that carries with it the likely loss of life and destruction of property, but what the policy crowd didn't have a firm grasp upon was what sort of damage a cyber attack could do.

Important is to remember that an attack under this definition is merely an attempt, neither a successful theft of information nor reorganization of data nor disruption of a system. Indeed, the antecedents of cyber attack are largely drawn from "cryptanalysis," the process of attacking the mechanism by which text is encoded.[16] Cryptographic attacks as part of cryptanalysis are activities of espionage, undertaken in both war and peace. While cyber attacks are like warfare, they also may well not be. There is a lexical problem in that, "compromising a system to steal data or blow up an oil refinery is an attack, but only the explosion would likely be an act of war."[17]

The daily chore for the Internet-connected organization in the late 2000s was in sifting through lots of data and detecting attacks from the large number of real processes undertaken by computer systems. Each process is a discrete item, which we identify as an *event*. This process of distilling attack from event remains the focus of significant resources today. On an information system, for example the computer network of an organization, billions of events may occur each day, but it is hard to determine which of them may indeed be unauthorized attempts to access, change, or disrupt a system. Then there is the matter of knowing an attack has occurred or is ongoing. Multiple attacks may compose an incident, "a group of attacks that can be distinguished from other incidents because of the distinctiveness of the attackers, and the degree of similarity of sites, techniques, and timing."[18]

Cyber attack phenomena are often difficult for those outside of the technical community to understand. Trojan horses, viruses, worms, DoS attacks, and logic bombs are just a few of the more commonly invoked terms in computer and network security. Information security professionals know each of these items generically as a type of attack, much in the way the national security community identifies attacks such as air strike, commando raid, or naval bombardment as different applications of military force. Cyber attacks may be employed in combination within a single cyber incident designed to produce a desired outcome.

Much can go wrong to complex computer systems without any outside intervention. Then there are deliberate systems abuses. As the Internet was just beginning to achieve widespread adoption, Martin Libicki saw six general forms of abuse of computers and information systems, which could be conducted through the utilization of hacking skills or tools. They were: (1) theft of service; (2) acquisition of objective data; (3) acquisition or alteration of subjective data; (4) theft of assets; (5) corruption of data in storage or motion; and (6) disruption of information service.[19] While the crypto crowd embraced the themes of confidentiality, integrity, and availability, policy thinkers attempted to categorize actions of theft, alteration, or disruption.

HACKERS

"People attack computers."[20] Cyber attacks are the product of human endeavor and the term most often used to label those who perpetrate them is "hacker." This is a tough piece of language to throw around because it means many things to different constituencies. In computer science departments and software engineering groups, "good hack" is a compliment of élan and innovativeness, but hackers and the very term "hacked" have both acquired a decidedly negative quality in public perception. Going back to those with pre-Internet investment in shaping computing, Guy Steele and Eric Raymond's definition of hacker from their light-hearted dictionary of computing slang provides clues to how multifaceted the term is. They contend,

hacker: [originally, someone who makes furniture with an axe] n. 1. A person who enjoys exploring the details of programmable systems and how to stretch their capabilities, as opposed to most users, who prefer to learn only the minimum necessary. 2. One who programs enthusiastically (even obsessively) or who enjoys programming rather than just theorizing about programming. 3. A person capable of appreciating hack value. 4. A person who is good at programming quickly. 5. An expert at a particular program, or one who frequently does work using it or on it; as in "a UNIX hacker." (Definitions 1 through 5 are correlated, and people who fit them congregate.) 6. An expert or enthusiast of any kind. One might be an astronomy hacker, for example. 7. One who enjoys the intellectual challenge of creatively overcoming or circumventing limitations. 8. [deprecated] A malicious meddler who tries to discover sensitive information by poking around. Hence "password hacker," "network hacker." See cracker ... This term seems to have been first adopted as a badge in the 1960s by the hacker culture surrounding TMRC and the MIT AI Lab. We have a report that it was used in a sense close to this entry's by teenage radio hams and electronics tinkerers in the mid-1950s.[21]

Before Estonia, we knew that spies broke into computers primarily for information of political or economic reasons; criminals stole information of financial value; vandals caused damage for personal satisfaction, to demonstrate political beliefs, or simply to display talent. Estonia showed that countries might wish to massively disrupt the computing infrastructure of other countries to provide a signal, falling between diplomatic or public admonishment and military threat or action.

Of national cyber motivations, one CIA official offered the following concerns regarding the application of hacking skills in geopolitics in 1998:

Potential attackers range from national intelligence and military organizations, terrorists, criminals, industrial competitors, hackers, and disgruntled or disloyal insiders. Each of these adversaries is motivated by different objectives and constrained by different levels of resources, technical expertise, access to a target, and risk tolerance.[22]

It seems as if "and hackers" is always a good term to add in any discussion of cyber threat actors, but perhaps it is better to just let hacking be a skill and hackers be those who have acquired a skill that may be used for purposes from the international to the personal.

Despite this, usage of the term "hacker" in a negative light persists. Defining the hacker as its own class of potential attacker is a recurring theme. Hundley and Anderson described hackers as "individuals satisfying a variety of personal agendas, which in their view do not include criminal motives."[23] Individuals without malicious intent often find security flaws. When a flaw is discovered, the hacker often reports it. A minor industry of software vulnerability detection has grown up around fees paid by some of the largest companies in IT to hackers reporting security-related bugs or issues.[24] Indeed, a preferred method for verifying system security involves the use of "red teams" of hackers employing various techniques to discover faults and provide advice on their repair to organizations.

Skill is the medium by which hacking efficacy is measured. Producing quality software that achieves the desired results is generally accepted in computing to be a form of engineering, but one with an artistic component. Like other texts, software code has a style. It will be viewed as elegant if it performs the desired functions in the most efficient manner possible. Programmers toil inside a hierarchy of skill, where few are very good, many are competent, and many more capable but often producing workable but flawed software.[25] These flaws are the vulnerabilities that hackers can exploit to access or disrupt systems.

For those exploiting systems, the hackers, a hierarchy of skill is also present. In their pyramid, a few individuals are uniquely talented and a growing number are good, but the efforts of others may be mobilized via dissemination of malicious software as easy to run as a spreadsheet application or diagnostic tool. There are other skill sets of value as well. Social engineering, the process of getting information of utility to pulling off an attack, is one. System penetration, which involves knowing how to manipulate systems to gain unauthorized access, is another. Guessing the right password may boil down to solid research of the targeted parties acquiring likely answers to password reset questions.[26] Achieving results is accomplished by whatever means work.

OFF WE GO . . . CYBERSPACE, THE AIR FORCE, AND THE CYBER TURF BATTLE

During the second term of the George W. Bush administration, while the U.S. Army and Marine Corps were deploying brigade after brigade for counterinsurgency operations in Iraq and Afghanistan, the U.S. Air Force announced its intent to conduct military operations in cyberspace.[27] Air Force Secretary Michael Wynne delivered a message that the service understood the information dimension of conflict. He discussed Cursor on Target, the framework for easily passing data from different surveillance and intelligence platforms to those employing lethal force in ongoing counter-terror operations. Wynne made the point that the Air Force was extensively engaged in understanding the "information mosaic" of contemporary warfare, and knowledge in that area was applicable to cyber operations. Furthermore, the Air Force was preparing itself doctrinally for the job. Wynne reminded, "In December 2005, General Moseley and I restated the Air Force Mission Statement to include Cyberspace as a Domain where the Air Force delivers Sovereign Options."[28] These options would be delivered by a new Air Force element, Cyber Command, an organization that could eventually stand on par with other major Air Force components such as Air Combat, Global Strike, and Special Operations Commands, as well as its training, support, and reserve components.

After the announcement, the Air Force's assistant secretary responsible for basing solicited input from 18 governors in selecting the optimal location for USAF Cyber Command's headquarters.[29] Perhaps, seeking to enlist the maximum level of support spread across congressional districts around the country, Air Force Cyber's leadership team assembled a large organization in less than two years, tapping active and reserve units around the United States and overseas, three of them in the San Antonio, Texas, area at Lackland AFB, and another unit at nearby Brooks AFB. With so much of Cyber Command's mass concentrated in San Antonio, it made sense that a headquarters there would be a logical choice.

The Air Force kicked off its 2008 recruiting campaign with a cyber television commercial at the same time the Army and Marines recruits were signing on for what was likely to be an enlistment with multiple combat deployments to Iraq and Afghanistan.[30] The other services had developed cyber capabilities of their own and the Air Force's announcement was labeled as "a dollar grab" in the inter-service struggle over resources. The Air Force was behaving rationally; according to one unnamed source, "with an estimated $30 billion being spent on cyber capabilities, who can blame them?"[31] A memorandum placing the independent Air Force initiative on hold was leaked to the Associated Press.[32] As one intelligence blogger opined, "CyberCommand [sic] looked more like a jobs and dollars program than a military effort. Apparently that didn't set well with DoD leadership."[33]

WAR AND CYBERSPACE

Despite the hold placed on the Air Force cyber initiative, evidence of growing foreign capabilities continued to accumulate. In the summer of 2008, a year after the Estonia hacking episode, Russia was again flexing its muscles in its near abroad, this time on its border with Georgia. Unlike the cyber attack against Estonia, the 2008 Russo-Georgian War was a conventional conflict precipitated by the activities of pro-Russian separatists in South Ossetia and Abkhazia and the Georgian state response to them. During the second week of August 2008, Russian forces quashed a Georgian attempt to reassert control over South Ossetia, bombed targets across the country, and sank most of the country's navy.

While major fighting in Georgia ended in less than a week, the conflict also included a significant cyber and information campaign undertaken by Russia. In attacks, "reminiscent of other coordinated campaigns against Estonian government Web sites in April and May 2007," Georgian government websites were compromised while DoS attacks disrupted Internet traffic for the national top-level domain (.ge).[34] Russia-leaning hacker groups, including the Russian Business Network (RBN) hacking organized crime syndicate, were fingered as perpetrators of much activity.[35] In addition, a significant propaganda campaign was waged against Georgia in traditional and online media operated or supported by Moscow. All manner of tools were used by Russia against Georgia in

2008: air strikes, commando raids, combined arms ground attacks, as well as cyber attacks and a broad information campaign in support of Russia's grievances with its increasingly Western-leaning neighbor.[36]

For more than a decade before bombs fell on Tbilisi, a small community of defense academicians considered the rise of cyberspace and the possibility of conflict within it. The harbinger of many books and articles was a 1993 journal article written by John Arquila and David Ronfeldt, two social scientists affiliated with the RAND Corporation: "Cyberwar is Coming!"[37] Deeply impressed by the role of information technologies as a force multiplier and decisive advantage to the allied coalition in the 1991 Gulf War, the pair considered how such capabilities could be extrapolated and exploited in the future. The Georgia conflict appeared an example of the scholars' theory.

In their joint work, Arquila and Ronfeldt considered two concepts, Netwar, "information related conflict at a grand level between nations or societies," and Cyberwar, conduct of "military operations according to information-related principles." Theoretically, Netwar could be seen as conflict between ideas and ideologies, while cyberwar was the conduct of information technology–related operations to degrade or distort an enemy's capacity to assimilate information, produce valid situational awareness, and effectively command and control their forces.[38] Earlier in his career, Ronfeldt pondered, "Recent political events, in particular the historic international political changes of 1989-1991, suggest that modern information systems and capabilities . . . have been major factors in what many take as positive changes in the world."[39]

Over time, the pair delved more deeply into the consideration of how information technologies might change the political processes of a globalizing world. They discussed the concept of a *nöosphere*, the total of human thought, an idea formulated by Pierre Teilhard de Chardin, a French Jesuit priest and paleontologist, and Vladimir Vernadsky, a Ukranian mineralogist and geochemist, during the first half of the 20th century. This idea of global thought was intriguing in the 1990s as the world's computers became interconnected and the barriers on international communication receded. It aligned with the concept of *soft power* described by Joseph Nye, regarding the influence of ideas and images in international relations.

Concepts of global thought or soft power were a long reach from the demands of a U.S. military seeking to establish a capability of pursuing military goals in cyberspace. Perhaps the *éminence grise* of cyber conflict theory, Martin Libicki, explained the breadth of doctrinal thinking in the United States relevant to cyberspace some years later. As new technologies and desired capabilities arrived, the U.S. armed forces had created different administrative and bureaucratic entities to support them. Computing and the advent of cyberspace blurred the lines between many of them. Information warfare, psychological operations, and other forms of propaganda or influence activity were increasingly computerized activities. Signals intelligence, electronic warfare, and other forms of denial and deception also became more computerized. What Arquila and Ronfeldt saw on the horizon 20 years ago was beginning to play out in independent cyber campaigns and cyber actions between countries. But the other force they saw at work, beyond the technological, was that of the other potential combatants of cyberspace: terror groups, criminal organizations, and political activists with a talent for hacking.

Arquila and Ronfeldt viewed cyber weapons as significant in future war, arguing, "It seems clear that a cyberwar doctrine will give its able practitioner the capability to defeat conventional regional aggression between nation-states decisively, at low cost in blood and treasure."[40] They were less certain how cyber arms could fare against unconventional adversaries—insurgents, jihadist groups, and transnational criminal syndicates.

PLACING CYBER CONFLICT IN INTERNATIONAL RELATIONS

Although this is very much a text of exposition on what has happened rather than an attempt to theorize the geopolitics of cyberspace, we require an occasional visit to theory-making on the international system. In seeing the international system as an anarchic system of states, we may perceive cyberspace as an anarchic system of networks. The states in which the networks reside may choose to adopt policies to curb the anarchic nature of the cyberspace, but such policy would fail to recognize that states have ceased to be the sole body of stakeholders in matters pertaining to the security of the networks. We may begin to recognize the high-level theoretical concepts at work in the information security issue. States, software firms, nongovernmental organizations, educational institutions, and telecommunications providers have all constructed the networks that are largely interconnected.

Argument in international relations swirls around the fundamental issue of whether the answer to the state's security dilemma resides in the capacity to protect itself and deter the attacks of others or the collaborative effort between states to reduce security threats through the mechanisms of international agreements and regimes.[41] Looking at cybersecurity, how each state builds up the means for self-defense is a new problem.

Applying liberal or neoliberal theories of international relations to cybersecurity, we would expect international action in a world in which nation-states cooperate to form international regimes on cyber attacks.[42]

But under such conditions, signals intelligence agencies as the National Security Agency or the British Government Communications Headquarters might be prevented from engaging in electronic espionage in cyberspace. It is hard to accept that countries like the United States would be interested in truncating what is formidable cyber intelligence capability that it is developing.

Through the lens of realist or neorealist theory, we would see a world in which states deploy defenses in cyberspace.[43] National institutions for information defense would spring up to stand alongside armies, navies, and air arms in the defense ministries. Information-age national security would rest not only on the merits of air or sea power but also on the cyber power to protect one's own networks and damage the networks of attacking adversaries. From this position emerge the views of those who develop current conceptualizations of cyber power as an analog to early forays on the application of another revolutionary technology, the aircraft.[44] This school of thought revisits ideas conceptualized after World War I by Giulio Douhet and appears to be making more headway.[45]

Application of realist and liberal interpretations of the international system get bogged down in the problem of making an effective application of sovereignty in the information-age state. States may sign agreements or attempt to build electronic fences, but that does not mean their citizens will adhere to the boundaries and rules, let alone their corporations. In such a security environment, we must accept a wider band of stakeholders engaged in conflict beyond states. Instead of continuing to hold paramount a system of states, one must instead consider a system of networks, human and computer. States likely cannot assure the security of networked information systems alone.[46]

MILITARIZATION ADVANCING IN CYBERSPACE

The 2007 cyber attack against Estonia demonstrated that, despite all positive intentions regarding the governance of cyberspace as a global commons of value to all, conflict had arrived. For readers of William Gibson's *Neuromancer*, this should have come as no surprise.[47] The book's central character was a damaged veteran cyber soldier of unconventional conflicts living in a world dominated as much by criminal syndicates and powerful corporations as any government. The cyberspace of science fiction was a venue in which battles or fortunes could be won or lost. By 2007, the world's militaries were beginning to arrive at that fact as well.

The actions of Estonia in moving its memorial displeased the Russian leadership, but looking back at the incident years later, it was a fairly benign expression of displeasure. No tanks rolled on Tallinn, nobody was killed, and even NATO ultimately deemed the actions against Estonia failed to necessitate an alliance-wide response under *casus foederis*, the binding grounds for military action contained within Article 5 of the organization's treaty. Fairly quickly, Estonia bounced back, receiving aid and assistance from its technologically sophisticated Scandinavian neighbors. Eventually it landed the opportunity to host NATO's Cooperative Cyber Defense Center of Excellence. As the first NATO member to be explicitly targeted in cyber attack, Estonia embraced the incident and incorporated it into the nation's ongoing strategy of technological-driven economic and societal advance. Despite the Russian sanctioned onslaught on the national information infrastructure, in very little time Tallin's leaders could return to touting E-Stonia, a technical powerhouse with a tiny population.

For Russia, the cyber attack against Estonia represented an important move to inconvenience an annoying neighbor. Remember, the stage setter for the attack was little more than a tiff. But there was a lesson to be learned in that parties with something to gain from using cyber means to disrupt adversaries or enemies, might very well do so. And this is an important point to consider. Then, cyber attacks of significant impact were rare events. Criminally engineered data breaches were occurring, and there was certainly a good deal of espionage going on, but breaking things with digital technologies was still the fodder of imagination.

In September 2007, the Department of Homeland Security (DHS) added an item from the theoretically possible to probable column. DHS released information regarding a test conducted at the Department of Energy's Idaho National Lab.[48] In the test, dubbed Aurora, a computer-controlled generator was hacked and instructions fed to it that caused its catastrophic failure. The context in which the Aurora test was released was that if the Department of Energy engineers could break significant pieces of the critical infrastructure, so could others. If big pieces of the electricity infrastructure were broken, it might be weeks or months until replacement hardware could be bought, built, and installed. How DHS would assemble the resources to meet the cybersecurity issues of the United States, particularly its critical infrastructure systems, would be a daunting challenge across the Bush and Obama presidencies.

CHAPTER 5

Securing Cyberspace in the Homeland

In the Bush administration's last year, Rod Beckstrom, a highly accomplished entrepreneur, thinker, and organizational leader, was appointed to be the first director of the Department of Homeland Security's (DHS) National Cybersecurity Center (NCSC), an institution created to "coordinate all government cybersecurity efforts."[1] Less than a year later, Beckstrom tendered his resignation to Janet Napolitano. He did so not on grounds of party allegiance. Longevity in position for DHS cyber officials has often been short, in part because lucrative private sector computer security executive posts are available to these public servants, and also because of frequent complaints of extreme difficulty in making meaningful progress at the agency.[2] Beckstrom was already well off, so his reasons fell into the second category, but he used his departure as an opportunity to publicly present a political issue that American politics is only now beginning to understand.

Beckstrom's letter of resignation made its way to the public eye within hours of its submission, published alongside a story in the *Wall Street Journal* by Siobhan Gorman,[3] a long-time NSA watcher. The letter pulled back the veil on the interagency cyber politics of the Washington Beltway and the sprawling signals intelligence complex at Ft. George Meade, headquarters of the NSA. He made quite clear to Secretary Napolitano that the NCSC was coming up short and offered his opinion as to why.

"As Secretary of DHS, you have direct responsibility for the nation's cybersecurity," he reminded. But DHS was unable to achieve that mission. Beckstrom explained why. "NSA effectively controls DHS cyber efforts through detailees, technology insertions, and the proposed move of NPPD [National Protection and Programs Directorate] and NCSC to a

Fort Meade NSA facility."[4] He explained the NSA's massive footprint in cybersecurity and provided his fundamental concern.

NSA currently dominates most national cyber efforts. While acknowledging the critical importance of NSA to our intelligence efforts, I believe this is a bad strategy on multiple grounds. The intelligence culture is very different than a network operations or security culture. In addition, threats to our democratic processes are significant if all top level government network security and monitoring are handled by any one organization (either directly or indirectly). During my term as director we have been unwilling to subjugate NCSC underneath the NSA. Instead, we advocated a model where there is a credible civilian government cybersecurity capability which interfaces with, but is not controlled by, the NSA.[5]

Considering Beckstrom's points, while this chapter contains a narrative of DHS confusion, missteps, and borderline ineptitude, it is the author's opinion that the need for it to succeed in becoming a capable and competent lead agency for cybersecurity efforts remains an imperative. DHS cybersecurity is essentially a story in two parts, that which happened before the election of President Obama and that which came after.

PROTECTING THE HOMELAND

As a result of the 9/11 attacks, the issue of domestic security—customs, immigration, border management, and internal intelligence—fell under intense scrutiny. DHS was created to meet the terror threat, but powers enunciated in legislation related to DHS's establishment touched cybersecurity as well. The Patriot Act gave new authorities to intelligence and law enforcement agencies to more effectively monitor, track, investigate, and prosecute terror groups often falling afoul of civil liberties critics.[6] DHS pulled together agencies and offices from all over the federal government and attempted to refocus them on a set of domestic security missions, but the agency has often been viewed as dysfunctional, mismanaged, and bereft of organizational culture.[7]

In 2002, while Congress and the Bush administration were hammering out what DHS would do, one of the items that fell on the agency was that of cybersecurity, an embryonic activity distributed across all of government. Specialized organizational cybersecurity pieces came from multiple civilian departments including Treasury and Justice. Also included in the DHS amalgamation was the National Communication System, an office established following the Cuban Missile Crisis to foster more resilient communications in the event of a major national emergency. DHS was charged with big swathes of cybersecurity response capability, but how capable the agency was or could be on protecting information systems—its own, those of other federal agencies, and those found in the private sector—was in doubt. How DHS would evolve to incorporate these functions across the end of the Bush administration and into that of President Obama was punctuated by inconsistency, high personnel turnover, and fluid institutional mandate.

THE ORG CHART

Figuring out exactly what cybersecurity is at DHS and how it has grown can be explained by where that function sits in what has grown to be third largest in the federal government. During its creation, DHS amalgamated 22 agencies from 11 departments. Cyber components came from several areas, and new offices were rapidly created for emerging problems and new powers issued to the agency. But despite the considerable budget now dedicated for cybersecurity efforts at the agency, some $1.25 billion for the 2015 fiscal year,[8] the answers to questions exactly what it does, how it does, and what it will do remain unclear. The problem of securing information systems is a widely distributed one, and for the federal government, pulling together cybersecurity missions or even creating the pathway to implement strategy enunciated by the president was a tall order when DHS stood up in November 2002.

Early in its development, DHS was assigned roles in securing cyberspace. It is not clear that anyone in Washington had a clear idea of what that meant as the department grew into its responsibilities under the leadership of secretary Tom Ridge. One Government Accountability Office report assessing just how the broad set of federal agencies responsible for homeland security roles repeatedly mentioned the need to "secure cyberspace," but emphasis was placed more concretely on improvement of information sharing, creation of an enterprise architecture for homeland security, and overall improvement of IT in government.[9]

Cybersecurity at DHS and much the rest of the federal government was largely the outgrowth of activity in critical infrastructure protection (CIP). Concern grew during the 1990s that CIP targets were ripe for terror attack, and in July 1996, Bill Clinton signed into effect Executive Order (EO) 13010.[10] In it, he described the importance of critical infrastructure, its vulnerability, and the physical and cyber threats to it. EO 13010 initiated the work of a commission on protection, which ultimately led to Presidential Decision Directive (PDD) 63.[11] PDD 63 created several institutions including a Critical Infrastructure Assurance Office (CIAO) in the Department of Commerce and the National Infrastructure Protection Center (NIPC) at the FBI. Also contained within PDD 63 were the provisions for creation of Information Sharing and Analysis Centers in each of the major infrastructure areas, such as water, energy, banking, health care, and telecommunications. This element has grown significantly relevant to cybersecurity efforts undertaken in the United States today.

In a summer 2002 plan, six offices, including the NIPC and CIAO as well as the National Communications System (Defense), the National Institute for Standards and Technology's Computer Security Division (Commerce), the National Infrastructure Simulation and Analysis Center (shared between Defense and Energy), and the Federal Computer Incident Response Center (General Services Administration), were to be rolled into a single Information Analysis and Infrastructure Protection division at DHS.[12] New iterations of the organization chart for the DHS appeared at a regular interval through the 2000s.[13] Cybersecurity was a DHS role, but it had no prior agency identity in the way that the Secret Service, Coast Guard, or Border Patrol did.

There was no cyber agency to build upon, and instead until the creation of Beckstrom's NCSC, the cyber function resided on a bureaucratic rung in DHS considered far away from the secretary's office. By 2008, the same year the NCSC was established, criticism of DHS competency on cybersecurity had become a steady drumbeat. James Lewis, who convened a commission on cybersecurity for President Bush's successor in the 2008 election year, argued, "While DHS has improved, oversight for cybersecurity must move elsewhere."[14] The CSIS report's suggestion was that only the White House could assert leadership on the issue.[15]

A PLAN

Absent a monolithic Soviet threat, in the 1990s, the primary national security concern to the United States and the American people became terrorism. Although terrorist groups had targeted U.S. companies, facilities, and military forces in the 1980s and before, terror attacks assumed new prominence. Bombings of the World Trade Center (1993), the Murrah Federal Building in Oklahoma City (1995), the Khobar Towers (1996), the U.S. Embassies in Nairobi and Dar-es Salaam (1998), and the destroyer *Cole* in Aden demonstrated the lethality of domestic and foreign terror plots.

As the United States learned from these incidents, in the 1990s the U.S. Government Interagency Domestic Terrorism Concept of Operations Plan (CONPLAN) was developed.[16] In CONPLAN, the heads of the Departments of Justice, Defense, Energy, and Health and Human Services, as well as FEMA and the FBI, established the mechanisms by which authorities and responsibilities would be exercised in the United States in the event of an imminent terror attack or after occurrence of such an attack.

Lessons learned were codified within the CONPLAN in a manner in which powers were enumerated and pathways to action clearly identified.

For instance, the FBI was designated lead agency for crisis management; in doing so, the agency was charged with managing "a crisis situation from an FBI command post." The local Special Agent in Charge (SAC) would run the command post, and if he or she needed assistance, for instance from the DoD, such requests would come "from the Attorney General to the Secretary of Defense through the DoD Executive Secretary."[17]

After 9/11, the scope of preparation for major terror events rose. The DoD established Northern Command to more effectively deliver military support to civil authorities in cases of domestic crisis.[18] Further consideration regarding disaster response and concerns regarding pandemic disease outbreaks contributed to the creation of a government-wide Homeland Security National Response Framework (NRF) in which scenarios for human-made and natural disasters were mated to strategic plans, national-level concept plans, and individual agency operations plans based on their responsibilities in each particular type of incident.[19] The 15th and last item in the inventory of scenarios was cyber attack.

Produced for the NRF in 2004 was a Cyber Incident Annex, describing "the specialized application of the National Response Plan (NRP) to cyber-related Incidents of National Significance."[20] For the first time cyber incidents were labeled "an actual or potential high-impact event that requires a coordinated and effective response by and appropriate combination of Federal, State, local, tribal, nongovernmental, and/or private-sector entities in order to save lives and minimize damage, and provide the basis for long-term community recovery and mitigation activities."[21] Only the president or secretary of Homeland Security possessed the authority to declare incidents, including cyber ones, to be of that magnitude.

An interagency planning document, the cyber annex identified purpose, scope, and policy for the marshaling of resources across the federal government in the event of a major cyber incident. Roles for federal agencies, other layers of government, and the private sector were identified, but in rather general terms. Clearly identified, however, was the important role of DHS's National Cyber Security Division (NCSD). The annex stipulated:

DHS/IAIP/NCSD is a focal point for the security of cyberspace for purposes of analysis, warning, information-sharing, vulnerability reduction, mitigation, and aiding national recovery efforts for critical infrastructure information systems. It facilitates interactions and collaborations (with the exception of investigation and prosecution of cybercrime, military operations to defend the homeland, or other activities identified below) between and among the Federal departments and agencies; State, local, and tribal governments; the private sector; and international organizations. Other Federal departments and agencies with cyber expertise collaborate with and support DHS in accomplishing its mission.[22]

Released in 2004, the Cyber Annex appears to remain the openly available guidance with regard to U.S. government response on cyber attack.[23]

TRANSITION

In 2009, the Obama administration arrived in Washington with significant ambitions for the application of information technologies in government and also a strong interest in cybersecurity issues. This made sense; in the 2008 campaign Obama raised large sums of money through Internet-based donations, some $778 million, almost double that of his Republican challenger, John McCain. The campaign had an iPhone app only a year after Apple had brought the product to market, and was steeped in election data analytics.[24] The Obama campaign also had been hacked, allegedly by the Chinese government, as had McCain's.[25]

Deeply reliant on IT in its electoral campaign, the Obama administration installed the federal government's first chief information officer and chief technology officer, Vivek Kundra and Aneesh Chopra, respectively. It also conducted an extensive review of cybersecurity issues within a 90-day window and placed emphasis on IT issues and technology-driven government transparency initiatives.

One of the initiatives suggested in the White House's 2009 Cyberspace Policy Review, spearheaded by Melissa Hathaway, was preparation of a "cybersecurity incident response plan."[26] While a draft version of the National Cyber Incident Response Plan (NCIRP) was released in 2010, it never was adopted. Prepared by DHS to serve as a concrete set of guidance for the U.S. government in the event of a major cyber incident impacting the information systems of the United States, the NCIRP was employed in the 2010 Cyber Storm III exercise and quietly shelved. The document was called "a sound framework," but "the supporting processes, procedures, roles, and responsibilities outlined in the Plan require[d] maturity."[27]

Much like the 2004 Cyber Annex, the NCIRP was to cover all levels of government, from international to local, as well as the purveyors and users of IT in the private sector. The document covered four key components: (1) a national concept of operations; (2) the organization of the National Cybersecurity and Communications Integration Center (NCCIC); (3) an outline of the incident response cycle; and (4) the roles and responsibilities that cut across federal agencies and other stakeholders in the national cybersecurity enterprise. In line with other DHS efforts to identify steps of risk or threat, the NCIRP identified four National Cyber Risk Alert Levels (NCRAL), regarding risk and desired level of response (Table 5.1).

Table 5.1

U.S. National Cyber Alert Levels

National Cyber Risk Alert Levels[28]			
Level	Label	Description of Risk	Level of Response
1	Severe	Highly disruptive levels of consequences are occurring or imminent.	Response functions are overwhelmed and top-level national executive authorities and engagements are essential. Exercise of mutual aid agreements and federal/non-federal assistance is essential.
2	Substantial	Observed or imminent degradation of critical functions with a moderate–to-significant level of consequences, possibly coupled with indicators of higher levels of consequences impending.	Surged posture becomes indefinitely necessary, rather than only temporarily. The Department of Homeland Security secretary is engaged, and appropriate designation of authorities and activation of federal capabilities such as the Cyber UCG take place. Other similar non-federal incident response mechanisms are engaged.
3	Elevated	Early indications of, or the potential for but no indicators of, moderate-to-severe levels of consequences.	Upward shift in precautionary measures occurs. Responding entities are capable of managing incidents/events within the parameters of normal, or slightly enhanced, operational posture.
4	Guarded	Baseline of risk acceptance.	Baseline operations, regular information sharing, exercise of processes and procedures, reporting, and mitigation strategy continue without undue disruption or resource allocation.

While perhaps logically pleasing to the cybersecurity bureaucracy, differences between the four levels were difficult to identify. As the review of Cyber Storm III offered, "To increase NCRAL effectiveness, the thresholds that precipitate an alert level change, the communications and messaging that accompany a level change, and the recommended security posture and actions at each level must be further defined, widely distributed, and incorporated into" other plans.[29] At first view, the NCRAL looked like other measures of security the U.S. government knew well, such as the THREATCON force protection index[30] for counter-terrorism risk or the Defense Condition (DEFCON) scale that indicated the level of hostility between the United States and the Soviet Union during the Cold War, but the basis for determining the difference between levels was not obvious.

At the close of 2010, the draft NCIRP was placed in limbo. Despite many cyber attacks and incidents since, no comprehensive unclassified playbook on the civilian/U.S. government response to major cyber events or attacks appears to exist. A top-down civilian capability for cyber response is obviously difficult to order and construct. For this reason, it is worthwhile to look at more specific, bottom-up approaches to particular kinds of cybersecurity undertaken at DHS over the last decade.

EDIFICE

While DHS was unable to establish the sort of unified guidance on responding to cyber attacks through the early years of Barack Obama's presidency, it did continue making major investments in cyber defense capabilities. While the bureaucratic placement of cybersecurity in DHS and indeed the entire matter of civil-military cybersecurity relations could be seen as problematic, DHS was able to marshal resources to achieve results through three creations: the U.S. Cyber Emergency Readiness Team (US-CERT), the NCCIC, and the EINSTEIN technology projects.

Of the three major DHS initiatives, the US-CERT concept stretches decades before DHS's establishment to the creation of the Computer Emergency Response Team (CERT) at Carnegie-Mellon University after the Morris worm crippled much of the not-yet-commercialized Internet in 1988. A DARPA-funded creation of Carnegie-Mellon's Software Engineering Institute (SEI),[31] the CERT concept evolved during the 1990s, with SEI's CERT evolving into the CERT Coordination Center (CERT/CC) and eventually the CERT Division at SEI. Its role, however, has been fairly constant. CERT was "established to coordinate response to internet security incidents."[32]

Since its creation, the Carnegie-Mellon CERT has developed relationships and practices for a growing community of organizations carrying the label, Computer Security Incident Response Team (CSIRT), "a team that responds to computer security incidents by providing all necessary services to solve the problem(s) or to support the resolution of them."[33] It has held a role in building of an association of CSIRT organizations, the Forum of Incident Response and Security Teams (FIRST), which coordinates communications between national and other CSIRTs around the world. FIRST is an international organization of growing relevance as cybersecurity issues rise on national and international agendas.

US-CERT was stood up as the operational arm of DHS's NCSD with an organizational mandate to "lead efforts to improve the nation's cybersecurity posture, coordinate cyber information sharing, and proactively manage cyber risks to the Nation while protecting the constitutional rights of Americans."[34] In cybersecurity, the CSIRT mission undertaken by US-CERT had evolved over time and stood as generally accepted, but US-CERT's bureaucratic placement has evolved over time. It was eventually placed under the authority of the NCCIC, a body created in 2009. While the US-CERT can very much be seen as a group of people, the NCCIC is very much a place. It "serves as a central location where a diverse set of partners involved in cybersecurity and communications protection coordinate and synchronize their efforts."[35] NCCIC is the location where all cybersecurity information and effort on cybersecurity, from DHS, "other government agencies, the private sector, and international entities" is pulled together. The NCCIC "analyzes cybersecurity and communications information, shares timely and actionable information, and coordinates response, mitigation and recovery efforts."[36]

While DHS has built or taken on a number of tangible programs and institutions on or related to cybersecurity, its major technical activity is largely centered in one area, the EINSTEIN intrusion detection and prevention system. EINSTEIN was established to build out a unified intrusion detection system for locating anomalous and malicious events in data traffic coming from the open Internet to government agencies and the reverse. Intrusion Detection Systems (IDS) are a widely deployed network security tool typically employing a set of signature information, such as known dangerous IP addresses or digests of malicious software. When a signature is detected, the IDS system produces an alert and prompts human intervention regarding the item.[37] EINSTEIN was envisaged to distribute IDS protection across all of the civilian agencies of the federal government.

In its first iteration, EINSTEIN was considered to be somewhat of a disappointment, but EINSTEIN 2 incorporated a set of additional features, including real-time, automated alert functionality that gave it a much greater practical utility. EINSTEIN 2 changed the way federal agencies access the Internet by passing outgoing and incoming data traffic to the Internet via a Trusted Internet Connection (TIC). By passing data through the TIC, EINSTEIN IDS machines could flag suspicious items within the flow of Internet data traffic to and from federal agencies. The effort was clearly in line with the first objective of President Bush's Comprehensive National Cybersecurity Initiative (CNCI) to "Move towards managing a single federal network."[38] EINSTEIN 2 met this objective by providing a uniform network intrusion detection capability for all federal agencies.

But DHS began to expand the EINSTEIN capability to its critical infrastructure mandate under EINSTEIN 3. Currently being designed and deployed, the EINSTEIN 3 system is designed to stand as a barrier between computers and computer networks employed in running the nation's critical infrastructure and the Internet. It would serve as a variation of "an electronic fence,"[39] a term invoked by several of the most serious thinkers on Internet security and policy as a reminder of DHS's other massive technology project, the Secure Border Initiative (SBI) and its technology component, SBINet, both referred to frequently by DHS secretary Michael Chertoff as "the virtual fence."[40]

Because so much of the U.S. critical infrastructure is operated by entities within the private sector, the figure of 85 percent is commonly cited, the process of securing that infrastructure from cyber attack is an inherently public-private process.[41] What DHS has advocated is probably less an electronic fence than a great firewall of sorts, but firewalls are merely a part of a security program, not the entirety of it. For this reason, the technology solutions envisaged under EINSTEIN 3 would be deployed into a much larger programmatic space in which the sharing of information between the private sector and the government take place.

While the term "private-public partnership" may sound appealing and represent a path to progress, the reality of such efforts, never mind their programmatic implementation, is fraught with difficulty. In combining efforts of government agencies and multinational corporations on cybersecurity, all manner of issues arise involving everything from sovereign agreements to industry-specific regulations. The grand scheme of how to share cybersecurity threat and vulnerability information remains an elusive accomplishment.

COLLABORATION AND PREVENTION

Response to the terrorism threat after 9/11 was translated to federal agencies in a mandate to shift from the "need to know" culture of information management to a "need to share paradigm." The grand problem for DHS in achieving its larger cybersecurity mandate remains in getting the right information regarding threat and vulnerability to those who need it in a timely manner. In counterterrorism, the concept of an ever-compressing

intelligence-implementation-decision cycle was acknowledged as a fundamental concern. The CIA's preeminent thinker on the problem explained.

US policymakers, war-fighters, and law-enforcers now operate in a real-time,
worldwide decision and implementation environment. Information about a new
development in Baghdad is known in Washington within minutes. Decisions
about a response are made in Washington within minutes. These decisions are
implemented in Baghdad within minutes. The total "intelligence-decision-
implementation" cycle time can be as short as 15 minutes. While this is an extreme
example, it highlights the tremendous compression of the response time required
by all involved compared to previous generations. This severe compression not
only affects the highest priority issues, but also ripples back into the most routine
intelligence, decision, and implementation processes.

DHS's capacity to effectively engage in cyber defense likely functions on
an ever more compressed time cycle.

Major cyber attacks against industrial targets, such as the cyber attack
on Saudi Aramco in 2012, take place in minutes. As the *Shamoon* worm
propagated across the company network and hard drives were being
deleted on Aramco computers, those companies linked to Aramco's network had to determine if, what, and how to disconnect from it very
quickly or face massive data destruction themselves. This example
illustrates the compressed nature of the cyber intelligence-decision-
implementation cycle. Temporally, it may be more akin to the time sensi-
tivity found in missile defense than anything else.

While EINSTEIN's critics invoked the image of DHS's failed "virtual
fence" project, the larger problem of intelligence acquisition, analysis,
and dissemination was distributed across multiple federal agencies as
well as a massive number of companies in IT and IT security. This speaks
more to the problems faced in the establishment of fusion centers across
the United States where intelligence, law enforcement, and public safety
staff across the tiers of government work to manage the risk of terror threats
to their communities. Such centers were to facilitate a collaborative effort of
two or more agencies that provide resources, expertise, and information to
detect, prevent, investigate, and respond to criminal and terrorist activity.[42]

Experience with the fusion center model in the United States has been
varied above all else. With 77 of them established around the country, they
have become a fixture in intelligence and homeland security. They were
designed to be a venue for the intermingling of classified intelligence with
observations of police forces or other local resources on countering terrorism. "Fusion is about focusing our intelligence and information collection
systems, and about the speed of responding to the task, precision in
addressing the problem with the best available capability, and understanding what the expected outcomes should be."[43]

Ideally, fusion centers were to be bidirectionally beneficial to both state and local authorities and to federal authorities. Moreover, the centers were designed to be a defined DHS entry point across the United States. In reality, they were often decried as "confusion centers" that rarely did what they did in a manner similar to one another.[44] But despite the criticism, the intelligence fusion function was perceived as important, and perhaps more importantly the fusion centers were a driver for the National Information Exchange Model (NIEM), a set of standards to make intelligence information portable and machine readable. Interoperable standards for intelligence sharing are also highly desirable in cybersecurity.

This idea of interoperable intelligence information for cybersecurity is at the heart of the still developing DHS NCCIC. The NCCIC is DHS's and thus the entire U.S. federal government's hub for civilian cybersecurity preparedness and response. Its vision and mission statements, which are virtually identical, lay out its daunting responsibilities.

To operate at the intersection of government, private sector, and international network defense communities, applying unique analytic perspectives, ensuring shared situational awareness, and orchestrating synchronized response, mitigation, and recovery efforts while protecting the Constitutional and privacy rights of Americans in both the cybersecurity and communications domains.[45]

The roles the NCCIC has taken up include the lead role in protecting U.S. civilian federal agencies, working with critical infrastructure providers on their cyber vulnerability and risk, collaborating with state and local governments, cooperating with international partners, coordinating national response, analyzing threat data, coordinating major incident response, disseminating threat and vulnerability information, and carrying critical communication support roles in the event of a national emergency.

The massive information clearinghouse role undertaken by the NCCIC has begun to push beyond its boundaries into the critical infrastructure providers by a variety of mechanisms, including analytic reports and sector specific outreach. For those in critical infrastructure industries, the most desirable NCCIC function is to pass intelligence from U.S. government sources to sector-specific Information Sharing and Analysis Centers (ISACs).[46] These ISACs were one of the Clinton administration's counterterrorism security responses later revised through President Bush's Homeland Security Presidential Directive-7 in 2003.[47]

In their operation, the ISACs have stood as a vehicle for passing threat and vulnerability information to entities that are in similar areas of endeavor. While operating under government authority, they are nonprofit private entities. There are ISACs for financial institutions, the electricity industry, medical IT, institutions of higher education, and state and local agencies. They derive their operating income from membership fees and pass information among members employing a traffic light protocol (TLP). The TLP attempts to overcome the grand problem of cybersecurity information sharing by providing a rule set for protecting the interests of institutions providing that information.

How the ISACs function with government is another matter. As one ISAC association document has argued, "The ISACs have a track record of responding to and sharing actionable and relevant information more quickly than DHS and doing so in an accurate manner."[48] That such information sharing would be viewed as more effective makes since as there is doubtlessly value in matching general cyber intelligence data with the particular needs of institutions within each business sector.

RESULTS

Assessing the efficacy or success of DHS in confronting the cybersecurity problems of the U.S. government and the entirety of the nation and its people is likely asking the impossible. Since DHS's inception, cybersecurity has become a grander problem for government. Despite all of the attention paid to the issue by the Obama administration, the most serious cyber incidents to hit the U.S. government would occur first at the State Department and later the NSA. But what could DHS have done about those?

Ultimately DHS found itself in the midst of multiple powerful agencies, those concerned with fighting crime, collecting and analyzing intelligence, and preparing to wage war by cyber means. Two of DHS's attorneys asserted after leaving their federal appointments that "The cybersecurity system is not working." As to why it wasn't, they explained,

[T]he Obama administration must confront and resolve two thorny issues before its cybersecurity program can be successful: (1) the problem of bureaucracy – that is who is ultimately responsible to the President and the public for implementing the program effectively and lawfully; and (2) the question of acceptance – that is, what technical tools are the American people comfortable having the government deploy, and what level of government involvement and interaction with the private sector will the people allow.[49]

And the two lawyers provided a set of six actions DHS needed to lead or at least coordinate to begin overcoming the systemic obstacles present in cybersecurity. DHS had to coordinate cybersecurity functions across agencies, shore up its own systems, provide the space for collaboration with the private sector, develop private sector standards, reduce liability, and promote transparency. But perhaps most important was a prescription for getting the desired products of the U.S. Intelligence Community to pass along the unrivalled cybersecurity knowledge held in the NSA to DHS and allowing DHS to engage with Congress and the American public on issues of oversight and privacy.[50]

Meeting any of these goals is a tall order, but the federal government has considerable experience in the development of standards, and an entire segment of the Commerce Department's National Institute of Standards and Technology to help. Other items, such as liability, can be removed legislatively, as was accomplished with extension of immunity to the relevant telecommunications firms after the revelation of NSA's massive data collection effort by AT&T's retiree Mark Klein in 2006. Getting federal agencies to work effectively together is and will always be an inherent issue of bureaucracy, and one must hope that some progress is being made in consolidating cybersecurity efforts to put the government's own house in order.

Finally, that so many of the security firms derive profitable income from generating good security intelligence or offering reasonably secure platforms means that divulging the "secret sauce" of a product or process may lead to swift financial demise. For these reasons, an ongoing, productive conversation on security among all of the builders and users of IT, just at an organizational level, remains elusive. That is because figuring out how to have an open conversation on vulnerability still remains as anachronistic as it sounds.

CHAPTER 6

A Commission, a Review, but Little Policy

By the close of the Bush administration, cybersecurity had become a significant policy issue in the United States. The term appeared in no less than 50 resolutions or amendments proposed by members of the U.S. House of Representatives and Senate in the 111th Congress. Support for policy to improve national cybersecurity efforts was and remains largely bipartisan, a common ground issue in an increasingly fractious federal politics.[1] Before the 2008 elections, interest in doing something about cybersecurity issues spurred not only the Congress but also an increasing number of actors in academia, think tanks, corporations, government agencies, and the IT sector.

But beneath the veneer of bipartisan support for cybersecurity initiatives lay some very complex questions.[2] For instance, where should the dividing line of responsibility fall for industry and government in responding to cyber incidents? What were the roles or responsibilities of the information technology industry in building more secure software, hardware, and platforms? And what were the roles of civilian defense, judicial, and law enforcement bodies versus those of intelligence and national security? For at least a decade, these questions have needed answers, but all too often, straightforward ones were not easily found. In enacting cybersecurity policy, whether through legislation, executive order, or agency rulemaking process, the answer to hard questions was often a vexing, "It depends."[3] What the attacker is after, who he or they represent, how effective the attack is, and the collateral damage produced by the attack all factor into organizational and government response to cyber attack.

Here we consider why it is difficult to make headway on the cybersecurity issue in the United States. Despite the growth of awareness on the issue; the enormous sums spent on security programs, staff, and technologies; and the national and international debate surrounding what should be done to make cyberspace more secure and who should do it, there remains a reality that cyber attack appears to work and the capacity for the attacker to achieve desired results increased as the 2000s became the 2010s. While there existed a sentiment in Washington to do something about cybersecurity, it remains unclear that anything already mandated or stipulated has produced results on order of those desired for the last decade.

THE POLICY ANTECEDENT: FISMA

The atmosphere of crisis following 9/11 opened a window for major legislation on cybersecurity.[4] Enacted in 2002, the Federal Information Security Management Act (FISMA) instituted U.S. government-wide direction for federal agencies to secure their information systems. It mandated that agencies would send reports to the Office of Management and Budget (OMB) and then receive feedback regarding performance. The process, grossly simplified, involved: (1) creating an inventory of systems; (2) categorizing information on the systems and determining its importance; (3) conducting risk assessment; (4) creating a security plan; (5) certifying and accrediting systems; and (6) engaging in continuous monitoring of systems.[5] With FISMA, OMB, in theory, could deny an agency funding if it failed to take adequate measures to secure its computer systems.

But FISMA did not solve the government's information security problems. To an outside observer, it appeared that much or even most federal activity on the security of information systems emphasized preparedness and not understanding of systems operations.[6] It is a law that "requires U.S. federal agencies and their partners to procure information systems and services only from organizations that adhere to the specific requirements."[7] Over time, it has depended on a set of standards produced by the National Institute for Standards and Technology (NIST) to guide agencies in securing information systems. NIST set to work on multiple fronts, addressing risk management, policies, awareness, evaluation, incident response, and remediation.[8]

Implementation of the law was largely a process of agencies certifying and accrediting systems as adequately prepared to face security threats.[9] FISMA put the task of implementing the law's provisions upon the agencies themselves, with OMB standing as a reviewer. To some degree, the law reduced cybersecurity in government agencies to a paperwork process, primarily undertaken through the ongoing need to certify and accredit systems as meeting requirements that ostensibly added up to being well-prepared to face some sort of an attack.[10]

But to a systems administrator focusing upon security, the idea that an annual review or multi-year certification would say much of anything about systems security was incongruent with the continuously evolving nature of threats to information systems.[11] For instance, due to the discovery of a previously unknown security bug, a so-called "zero-day" vulnerability, a properly certified system could become vulnerable at any time. Accreditation did not necessarily provide a guarantee of trouble-free operation, but rather offered a basic level of certainty that the system was operating in a manner that security practitioners would find to be acceptable.

Initially, systems security staff in federal agencies filled out certification and accreditation (C&A) reporting templates as a part of the FISMA process, but the gap between OMB evaluations and real levels of vulnerability was difficult to grasp. Adding to the dire assessment of government cybersecurity through much of the first decade of the 21st century was the federal information security report card produced by Representative Tom Davis.[12] Davis, whose northern Virginia district contained a variety of technology companies (including one-time giant AOL), spent much of his congressional career working on and eventually chairing the government reform committee. Davis's committee released a cybersecurity report card every year between 2000 and 2007.

The report card included dismal grades for many agencies and a terrible overall average, while often reserving the worst for agencies with large staffs, a variety of organizational missions, and a large number of heterogeneous information systems.[13] Defense, State, Justice, the Veteran's Administration, and the newcomer, Homeland Security, usually scored poorly, but with each year, critics of the report card became increasingly difficult to ignore. Amit Yoran, the first director of US-CERT, said, of FISMA "This is more an audit of agency paperwork than it is jacking into the networks and looking at the systems and actual performance of an agency's security technologies."[14] While FISMA was flawed, Davis's report card appeared caustic.

With time, the desire for new approaches to meeting the FISMA mandate emerged. In May 2010, NASA's deputy CIO for IT security, Jerry Davis, argued in an agency-wide memorandum that the fiscal year 2010 FISMA instructions from OMB were "clear regarding a shift away from cumbersome and expensive C&A paperwork processes, in favor of a value-driven, risk-based approach to systems security."[15] What was unclear, however, was how such an approach to cybersecurity would be undertaken. This remains the case. There are few measures of agencies or the entire government achieving desired results on cybersecurity, but systems are continually subverted, breached from within, or knocked off-line by malicious parties.[16]

As consensus that the certification and accreditation process had become undesirable or even perhaps counterproductive, a campaign to fix the FISMA law gained adherents. Under FISMA, OMB could withhold funding for agencies failing to improve, dictating that struggling agencies should produce more with less and get back on track.[17] This was a perfectly rational strategy for killing off bad IT projects, but was analogous to cutting hospital budgets for institutions in a region with a failing record on public health. Needed instead was an approach to determine which federal cybersecurity projects didn't work and find new initiatives that might. As the 2008 elections approached, Congress was beginning to accept that it had a role in overhauling federal cybersecurity policy.

THE COMMISSION

Increased concern over cyber threats spurred the creation of the Commission on Cybersecurity for the 44th president, a body co-chaired by Representatives James Langevin, Democrat from Rhode Island, and Michael McCaul, a Republican from Texas, to provide new thinking on how to better cope with the security problem. Announced in November 2007, the commission would eventually produce a report that was a key input for the comprehensive review of cybersecurity issues by the Obama administration.

From their positions of chairman and ranking member of the House Homeland Security Committee, Langevin and McCaul, respectively, were commencing a push to place cybersecurity back on the national security agenda. One item important to the commission's work was the realization that so many of the major incidents up to 2007 were perpetrated by actors exploiting vulnerabilities that had much more to do with lax IT management and operation than the guile and sophistication of the attacker. As a former OMB official stated after the announcement of the commission's formation, "nearly every example of something bad that happened — even the Chinese having their way with defense systems — has not been rocket science but poor security practices."[18]

For more than a year, the commission, managed by the Center for Strategic and International Studies (CSIS) senior fellow James Lewis, convened meetings and solicited expert input. Incorporated into the project were co-chairs from industry, Scott Charney, head of Microsoft's Trustworthy Computing Group,[19] and retired U.S. Air Force Lt. Gen. Harry Raduege, who had taken up an industry position with the consultancy Deloitte. CSIS prepared a report that challenged assumptions in declaring the process of cybersecurity inherently broken and calling for a national strategy on the issue.[20]

The Commission Report argued that the White House, not a single agency or the OMB, should lead on cybersecurity, creating a National Office for Cyberspace. Needed were new public-private partnerships, updated government authorities, improved authentication, addition of security requirements in federal acquisition, and overall capacity development. In addition, the report called for regulation in cyberspace, an incredibly controversial idea contested by the multi-stakeholder constituencies of Internet governance and engineering as well as the technology companies building cyberspace's components.

The authors asserted, "It is undeniable that an appropriate level of cybersecurity cannot be achieved without regulation, as market forces alone will never provide the level of security necessary to achieve national security objectives."[21] Argued for was abandonment of the anti-regulatory position found in the 2003 National Strategy to Secure Cyberspace. Instead, regulation was viewed as necessity. The commission's authors stated:

In pursuing the laudable goal of avoiding overregulation, the strategy essentially abandoned cyber defense to ad hoc market forces. We believe it is time to change this. In no other area of national security, do we depend on private, voluntary efforts. Companies have little incentive to spend on national defense as they bear all of the cost but do not reap all of the return. National defense is a public good. We should not expect companies, which must earn a profit to survive, to supply this public good in adequate amounts.[22]

The winner of the 2008 election, Barack Obama, the former junior senator from Illinois, would inherit this mandate and others. For him the problem was already growing all too apparent. As with the agencies of the federal government, major U.S. firms, and a variety of other actors, the Obama campaign had fallen within the sights of China's cyber espionage machine.

AN IMPERATIVE

Immediately following the 2008 U.S. presidential election, news reports emerged of a computer-hacking incident that occurred the prior summer at the campaign headquarters of Barack Obama, then the Democrat holding the largest number of delegates from the primary process and presumptive candidate for the presidency. After malware was detected, agents of the FBI and Secret Service visited the Obama offices in Chicago. The hack was far worse than the campaign staff assumed. "You have a problem way bigger than what you understand," said the responding FBI agent. "You have been compromised, and a serious amount of files have been loaded off your system."[23] While the public was interested in how the new president-elect would be able to continue using his BlackBerry while holding the nation's highest office, the security incident prompted serious questions about hacking of the presidential campaigns.[24]

There was an international dimension to the hack. David Plouffe, Obama's campaign manager, received a call from Josh Bolten, George W. Bush's chief-of-staff, stating that he believed the network had "been penetrated by a foreign entity."[25] Once again, at China the finger was pointed. Eventually, a hacking unit reporting to the Chinese government was identified as the most likely culprit.[26] While the Obama campaign had used the Internet to both raise money and drive up voter turnout in 2008, the Obama administration went into office aware that the insecurity of computer networks was an Achilles' heel. Equipped with the Commission Report, the Obama transition team began putting together the pieces to dramatically revamp how the federal government would handle cybersecurity.

THE REVIEW

Evidence of the extensive nature of breaches of U.S. government unclassified computer systems became increasingly difficult to refute. Personal information for 26.5 million Americans on a laptop computer belonging to a VA data analyst went missing after the computer and an external hard drive were stolen.[27] During the build-out of IT infrastructure for DHS's rapidly enlarged Transportation Security Administration (TSA), Unisys installed an intrusion detection system that was bypassed for months, likely by Chinese actors. Despite the systems being certified and accredited by both the contractor and DHS, they failed to shield TSA's unclassified computer network.[28] Hackers also were able to interfere with the operation of NASA Landsat and Terra satellites via the Svalbard Satellite Station in Spitsbergen, Norway. Disturbingly, the hackers gained full control of the Terra satellite's functions.[29] Despite increasing security spending and awareness, when Barack Obama entered the White House, plenty of U.S. government systems were being hacked.

Obama came to the presidency in a period of economic crisis, inheriting two wars, and with an intelligence community still on the hunt for Osama bin Laden. There were plenty of issues he could and would address besides cybersecurity, but he did nonetheless. On February 9, 2009, John Brennan, President Obama's assistant for counterterrorism and homeland security, announced a *60-Day Cyberspace Policy Review*. Tapped for the job of leading the effort was Melissa Hathaway, a former Bush administration cyber official and Booz Allen Hamilton consultant. As with the CSIS effort, relevant documents were considered, opinion from industry solicited, and existing and proposed federal law studied. The Guardian opined, "Although any report is likely to suggest increasing the level of partnerships with private companies to help the government, the Hathaway report could also prove something of a boondoggle for the technology industry."[30] Federal cybersecurity spending was likely to rise, perhaps considerably.

In May, President Obama presented a completed report, *Cyberspace Policy Review: Assuring a Trusted and Resilient Information and Communications Infrastructure*, which stated, "America's economic prosperity in the 21st century will depend on cybersecurity."[31] Once again, public-private partnerships were touted, as well as definition of a new strategy, new avenues for collaboration, research and development, and increased awareness. One item was radically different from the CSIS Commission Report. While the commission had advocated for some form of regulation, on this Obama backed away, stating, "So let me be clear. My administration will not dictate security standards for private companies."[32]

Abandoned in Obama's address and absent from the *Cyberspace Policy Review* was any specific consideration of new regulation for industry, particularly the IT industry. A lengthy annex, Growth of Modern Communications Technology in the United States and Development of Supporting Legal and Regulatory Frameworks, was provided with the review. It detailed the evolution of telecommunications regulation from the Radio Act of 1912 straight through to Patriot and Homeland Security Acts. But the annex was not prescriptive in any way, but rather a reflective document detailing the existing powers of the Federal Communications Commission, DHS, and other relevant federal agencies. Its concluding remarks were particularly hazy.

The history of electronic communications in the United States reflects steady, robust technological innovation punctuated by government efforts to regulate, manage, or otherwise respond to issues presented by these new media, including security concerns. The iterative nature of the statutory and policy developments over time has led to a mosaic of government laws and structures governing various parts of the landscape for information and communications security and resiliency. Effectively addressing the fragmentary and diverse nature of the technical, economic, legal, and policy challenges will require a leadership and coordination framework that can stitch this patchwork together into an integrated whole.[33]

What the review did not make clear was whether there was any need for new regulation. Obama's statement that "The Federal government also must be careful not to create policy and regulation that inhibits innovation or results in inefficiencies or less security"[34] made it appear that the call for regulation from the CSIS Commission Report had been dropped until the right leadership and coordination framework could be found.

While much touted, the review appeared so much more ballyhoo to critics. Eric Greenwald, then the chief counsel to the House Permanent Select Committee on Intelligence (and later the cyber adviser to President Obama), chronicled Washington policy discourse on cybersecurity extending back to 1998's Presidential Decision Directive 63. He observed a repetitive pattern of concern answered with relative inaction and fuzzy objectives. Greenwald saw the review as more of the same. "Every few years, a proposal has come along in the form of a cybersecurity strategy and a promise of leadership from the White House or DHS, but the implementation has always fallen short."[35] While the Obama administration demonstrated great interest in cyberspace and cybersecurity, it would be Congress's job to deliver on new policy. That process soon devolved to sour debate on the legislative and technical feasibility of emplacing an Internet "kill switch" able to be thrown in time of cyber crisis. Congressional movement on comprehensive cybersecurity policy would appear more minefield than legislative process.

GRIDLOCK

Its review complete, the Obama administration began the process of communicating on cyber issues with congressional leaders, many who had their own ideas on what policy was needed. Langevin and McCaul mobilized members of the House of Representatives via the Congressional Cybersecurity Caucus.[36] A number of long-serving and influential senators also took a significant interest in cybersecurity, perhaps the most visible being Jay Rockefeller.

Rockefeller introduced sweeping legislation, S.773, the Cybersecurity Act of 2009 (later 2010). Co-sponsored by Evan Bayh, Barbara Mikulski, Bill Nelson, and Olympia Snowe, the sole Republican sponsor, S.773 called for creation of a cybersecurity advisory panel and a cyber threat clearinghouse, providing resources for workforce development, and facilitating public-private cybersecurity partnerships. But the bill drew vociferous criticism for its consideration of federal powers in a "cyber emergency" declared by the president.[37] The powers were summarized as offering the White House a "kill switch" capability that could quickly bring Internet communications to a halt. If that could actually be accomplished is another matter. Opponents of the bill rallied in opposition to the kill switch concept. Languishing through the 111th Congress, it failed to make it to the floor of the Senate for a vote before the end of the session. The same was true of 13 other cyber-related bills introduced in either the House or the Senate during the session.[38] The forces arrayed against the Rockefeller cyber bill were primarily civil liberties organizations.

Despite the Democrats' loss of the majority in the House of Representatives during the 2010 mid-term elections, cyber bills continued to emerge. Like the 111th Congress, the 112th also drafted cyber-legislation. While the 111th Congress's most controversial item was the "kill switch" item thought to be in the Rockefeller bill, the great controversy of the 112th was SOPA, the Stop Online Piracy Act, and a companion bill of sorts, PIPA, the PROTECT (Preventing Real Online Threats to Economic Creativity and Theft) Intellectual Property Act. Introduced in the House of Representatives on October 26, 2011, by Lamar Smith, a Texas Republican, SOPA (H.Res 3261) was aimed at curbing of online copyright violation and the sale of counterfeit items, primarily pharmaceuticals. PIPA was directed at achieving similar goals.

Both bills fell onto snags in the Internet technical engineering community and were problematic to Silicon Valley technology firms, especially those social media sites that might serve as pointers to content shared in violation of copyright or vendors for counterfeit goods. Yes, theft of copyrighted works and sale of counterfeit goods were a problem, but the proposed solution, the "blacklisting" of certain DNS addresses by the U.S. government or by order of the U.S. government to ISPs or other Web companies, was potentially menacing.[39] It smacked of censorship. But more worrisome to the Internet engineers was language in the legislation that could be interpreted to order the banning or dismantlement of the Domain Name System Security Extensions (DNSSEC) features employed on Internet Protocol (IP) networks to protect the integrity of DNS data, a capability not envisaged as necessary in the formative phases of Internet development.[40] Petitions were widely signed by influential technologists, policymakers, academics, and artists asking for the bills to be withdrawn.[41]

Technical issues aside, the debate on SOPA and PIPA soon was largely reduced to a political argument between the San Francisco Bay Area technology firms and the major entertainment companies, many of them headquartered in Los Angeles. To a degree, the debate was Silicon Valley versus Hollywood. Ultimately, the tech companies spoke out more loudly with their one-day blackout January 18, 2012, campaign against the initiative. Although most websites, such as those for Mozilla, Google, and Craigslist, placed only black banners on landing pages, Wikipedia largely removed its content from the Web for the day.[42]

The SOPA/PIPA lesson was clear. The U.S. government could attempt to exert control over cyberspace, but if enough interested parties who were requisite in making the whole thing work disagreed, the government could be thwarted. In the debate on SOPA and PIPA, a connection was made to the alleged massive theft of corporate intellectual property regarding proprietary interests and research and development activities, not just media such as software, music, or film.[43] The property theft message did not catch on and was still fairly poorly understood as major reports of corporate cyber theft by Chinese and other actors had only recently begun to appear in public. Without a clear path to passage, like so many other cyber bills, SOPA faded into obscurity. After markup by the House Judiciary Committee in late 2011, the bill was dropped from the legislative agenda in the House of Representatives, effectively dying in committee. On January 20, 2012, PIPA also stalled after Senate majority leader Harry Reid announced the delay of a vote on the bill.

With SOPA and PIPA off the table, Congress continued to work on other cyber legislation. In the first days of August 2012, the U.S. Senate introduced new legislation designed, among other things, to improve the level of security for the networks of computer systems used by government, the private sector, and other public sector agencies. After a series of bills failed, a new piece of legislation, the Cyber Security Act of 2012 (CSA2012), was introduced in the Senate in July, following the issuance and passage to committee of earlier drafts across the span of the 112th Congress. Sponsored by Sen. Joseph Lieberman and co-sponsored by four other senators, including Republican Susan Collins of Maine, CSA2012 was at root an effort to provide the federal government, through DHS, a way to take on the perceived problem of an insecure cyber infrastructure —an infrastructure that is the pivotal component of almost all commercial, public health, and government activities in the United States.[44]

Moved to the floor of the Senate for debate, the bill's sponsors were unable to assemble the 60 votes required to advance the legislation. A group of lawmakers, led by Sen. John McCain, argued against its passage. McCain stated, "There are those that believe any legislation is better than no legislation ... I've been around long enough to know that isn't true."[45] McCain argued in favor of legislation he co-sponsored with fellow Republican Sen. Kay Bailey Hutchison—the SECURE IT Act, an effort to improve information sharing between government and industry on cybersecurity matters. Pivotal in the debate against CSA2012 was the U.S. Chamber of Commerce who argued the "bill would have imposed debilitating pressures on businesses to establish cybersecurity measures."[46]

Once again, cybersecurity legislation for 2012 was pushed to the following year. The U.S. Congress put off sweeping legislation that would have impacted industries across the country—including the energy industry, from oil and gas firms, and services companies to electricity producers and distributors. What eventually emerged was the proposed legislation still under consideration as of March 2015, the Cyber Intelligence Sharing and Protection Act (CISPA). Introduced in the House of Representatives by Mike Rogers in 2011, CISPA was designed to incorporate cyber issues into the provisions of the National Security Act of 1947. It was drafted to provide authorities for enhanced sharing of cybersecurity information between government and industry, and bring the Office of the Director of National Intelligence (ODNI) into information-sharing activities on cybersecurity.[47]

Creation of the Cyber Threat Intelligence Information Center came in early 2015. Since its formation, ODNI has become a home for interagency information sharing and analysis centers that had once existed in individual agencies. At least two of them, the National Counterterrorism Center (NCTC) and the Office of the National Counterintelligence Executive (ONCIX) would appear to have some cyber component involved in their areas of operation, defending against terror attacks and preventing theft of sensitive information held by both government and private industry. NCTC grew out of the CIA's counterterrorism center and ONCIX presides over a function in which the FBI stands as the lead agency. The new center for cyber intelligence was established and will initially be sited at Ft. Meade, home to the headquarters of both the National Security Agency and the DoD's Cyber Command.[48]

But where cybersecurity legislation in the vein of CISPA has bogged down is in consideration of how government and the private sector can effectively collaborate. As we have seen, when the security of cyberspace is considered, the prescription is peppered with discussion of public-private partnership. Such efforts exist for the security of communications networks, principally under the banner of the National Security Telecommunications Advisory Committee (NSTAC). "The NSTAC's goal is to develop recommendations to the President to assure vital telecommunications links through any event or crisis, and to help the U.S. Government maintain a reliable, secure, and resilient national communications posture."[49] Established in 1984, under a reorganization of the Kennedy-era National Communication System, NSTAC has become the focal point of the industry-government cooperation on communication in times of crisis. But NSTAC is a construct for coping with a worst-case scenario, disruption of critical communications needed by the U.S. government in time of grave crisis, not the daily flow of incidents that flare up across the national cyber infrastructure.

UNLEGISLATED POLICY

The disconnect between the reality of a day-to-day previously unknown vulnerabilities and potential worst-case scenarios means that policy is often flustered by rhetoric misaligned with potential incident consequences. Cyber war, cyber terrorism, and catastrophic incident imagery are often invoked in public discourse on cybersecurity policy. Societal dependence on cyber infrastructure is great and growing. As critical systems are "internetworked,"[50] real-world functionality, such as delivering electricity, water, or fuels, may be opened to subversion by digital means.

As the impact of cyber attacks grew, the U.S. government was unable to clearly legislate how response to incidents should function. Many major pieces of cyber legislation have been proposed since FISMA, but none has passed. Several cyber laws of more limited scope have been enacted, however. For the policymaking on cyber, one lesson is clear: *legislating away cyber vulnerabilities is no more possible than seeking technological remedy to them.*

CHAPTER 7

Hard Cyber Power, from Stuxnet to Shamoon

THE IRANIAN BOMB

By 2007, Iran, particularly its nuclear program, began to assume a greater presence in U.S. national security concerns. Beyond Washington, there was general consensus among leaders across the Middle East, in Europe, and those dependent on oil exports from the Persian Gulf that an Iranian bomb would be an enormously destabilizing factor in global geopolitics.[1] It would jeopardize security for the Saudis and other Gulf States, present an existential threat to the state of Israel, and represent a significant potential shock to world energy markets, further complicating the U.S. position in the region. North Korea's nuclear tests in 2006 demonstrated that even a regime as straightjacketed by international sanctions as Pyongyang's could still put together the materials and knowledge to assemble and test an atomic weapon.

For Iran's leaders, assembly of a nuclear arsenal no doubt appeared a necessity in 2006 and likely remains so. Saddam Hussein's Iraq hadn't had the bomb and largely dismantled its chemical and biological weapons programs, making the country's capacity to deter a U.S.-led invasion in 2003 negligible. After Ba'athist Iraq fell, Moamar Gadhafi entered into talks with London and Washington on abandoning his weapons of mass destruction (WMD) program.[2] By December 2003, when Gadhafi renounced WMD development, Libya had already hosted inspectors and was on the way to normalized relations with the United States.[3] North Korea had gone the other way, detonating a marginally successful nuclear device in 2006 followed by missile tests closely watched by the U.S., South Korean, and Japanese intelligence establishments.

Of George W. Bush's Axis of Evil, that is, Iran, Iraq, and North Korea, by 2007 Iraq was off the list but wracked by insurgency and civil conflict, while North Korea had gone nuclear. Iran had no bomb, but was still very much a "state of concern" and sponsor of terror activities.[4] Iranian support of Shia insurgents in Iraq was an unquestionable reality and the head of the State Department's Bureau of Intelligence and Research, among others, asserted Iranian anti-armor weapons were often responsible for the improvised explosive device attacks that were the leading cause of casualties for allied forces in-country.[5] Iran's behavior was far more than a nuisance, but the case for any military action against it was predicated upon the need to prevent it from acquiring a nuclear capability.

While some within the Bush administration clamored for immediate action,[6] a comprehensive study of the intelligence on Iran's bomb was requested. With longtime intelligence analyst and former director of central intelligence Robert Gates running the Defense Department, a National Intelligence Estimate (NIE) on Iran's nuclear program was assembled. The analysis of this NIE would influence the U.S. position on military action aimed at damaging or ending Iran's nuclear program. Unusual for an NIE, the estimate, *Iran: Nuclear Intentions and Capabilities*, was produced with an unclassified summary for release to the public.[7]

It was a rarity. Although a handful of NIE summaries were made publicly available after 2006, many in the Intelligence Community viewed the practice of public dissemination of such information as out of scope. Tom Fingar, chairman of the National Intelligence Council, stated that he and his colleagues "pushed back" on congressional demands for declassifying other such analyses.[8] But the Iran nuclear program was of critical importance, and the unclassified summary of the document released to the public stated that Iran was not rapidly developing its nuclear *weapons* capability, which would diminish the impetus for immediate military action. Impact of the Iran NIE on the U.S. national security establishment and foreign policy apparatus was seismic.[9] That a top-level analysis from the IC characterizing Iran's program as not swiftly moving toward the assembly of a nuclear arsenal had emerged was almost entirely unexpected.

[The] apparent turnaround [on Iran's nuclear program] prompted the *New York Times*, on the day after the unclassified NIE's release, to begin its front page "news analysis" article with the observation that "rarely, if ever, has a single intelligence report so completely, so suddenly, and so surprisingly altered a foreign policy debate [in Washington]."[10]

Fingar, who also served as the first chief intelligence analyst at the Office of the Director of National Intelligence, opined after retirement that the Iran NIE was the one the U.S. Intelligence Community had gotten right on WMD proliferation (Iraq was the one gotten wrong).[11] It asserted that

"Iran made significant progress in 2007 installing centrifuges at Natanz, but we judge[d] with moderate confidence it still face[d] significant technical problems operating them."[12] How the IC knew this was ostensibly a detail not meant for release in the unclassified digest of the NIE. Sources and methods needed to be protected.

But there was a clue. An article published in the *New York Times* almost two years later stated that U.S. cyber intelligence had been a significant factor in determining when Iran attempted to advance its enrichment activities.

"They have cheated three times," one senior administration official said of the Iranians. "And they have now been caught three times." The official was referring to information unearthed by an Iranian dissident group that led to the discovery of the underground plant at Natanz in 2002, and evidence developed two years ago—after Iran's computer networks were infiltrated by American intelligence agencies—that the country had sought to design a nuclear warhead.[13]

That U.S. cyber intelligence capabilities, manifested in the infiltration of Iran's computer networks, offered visibility into the Iranian nuclear program was now public knowledge. What was not yet known was how a cyber tool could be used not only to spy on the program but also to disrupt or damage Tehran's nuclear project, until a rather peculiar worm began traversing the Internet.

SPINNING

In the summer of 2010, security researchers discovered a new self-replicating worm that contained a unique payload and one not seen before in the computer security space. The new worm, first detected by VirusBlokAda, a Belarusian antivirus software company, eventually drew the attention of Symantec, arguably the world's largest independent computer security company. It was labeled W32.Stuxnet, or *Stuxnet* for short.[14]

The more security researchers investigated Stuxnet, the more interesting it became. It was a self-propagating piece of malware. It copied itself from system to system automatically once it detected the opportunity to do so. This was nothing new, as Robert Tappan Morris's worm of 1988 held the same functionality. What *was* interesting was where those replications occurred. Symantec researchers queried systems around the globe and found an unusually large concentration of Stuxnet infections on computers within the .id, .in, and .ir top-level Internet domains. Stuxnet copies were concentrated on computers whose IP addresses were allocated to Indonesia, India, and Iran. Furthermore, nearly 60 percent of all Stuxnet infections were registered in a single country: Iran.[15]

The more we learned about Stuxnet as a piece of software, the more interesting it became. It employed multiple previously unknown zero-day vulnerabilities within the Windows operating system to gain access to systems and elevate permissions. It held the pathway to complete system compromise by an outside actor. Stuxnet contained three previously unknown vulnerabilities in the Windows operating system known as "zero-days," each having escaped the attention of cybersecurity researchers and the larger software development community for years. In addition, Stuxnet was made to look authentic. It contained a stolen digital certificate. When queried, Stuxnet looked like valid device driver software from a reputable developer.[16]

If Stuxnet's propagation pattern was interesting, its payload was even more so. Most worms compromise systems to surreptitiously employ them for other means—sending lots of spam email, launching DDoS attacks, or sending along financially useful pieces of information about user transactions. Not so Stuxnet. It provided instructions to a very particular model of computer, the Siemens Simatic Series 7 of programmable logic controller (PLC) computers. It was able to rewrite instructions on the Siemens computers, which are the brains of supervisory control and data acquisition (SCADA) process control systems.[17]

This was important because PLCs in SCADA applications deliver instructions to real pieces of hardware on pipelines, production lines, and electrical grids opening valves and flipping switches. They do work that used to be done by human beings, much like telephone calls used to be completed by human operators at switchboards but now are handled by computerized switches.[18] PLC computers take people out of the loop; they collect data from sensors and then activate resources in response. They are used to automate tasks that may be mundane or even hazardous. PLCs are also extremely useful in running machines within very specific parameters of performance with little tolerance for variation or fault. Machines like centrifuges.

THE STUXNET DETECTIVES

Figuring out what Stuxnet was and what it did fell to a distributed set of actors who work, largely in private firms but occasionally in academia and often as freelancers, who engage in the businesses of malware analysis and cyber threat intelligence.[19] Two researchers in particular, Liam O'Murchu, a Symantec employee, and Ralph Langer, an independent consultant, shed much light on Stuxnet: what it was, what it could do, and the sorts of targets at which it could be or had been aimed.

O'Murchu and his colleagues at Symantec released their comprehensive report on Stuxnet on September 30, 2010.[20] It detailed how Stuxnet replicated itself and sent copies by exploiting three previously unknown, zero-day vulnerabilities in the Microsoft Windows and Windows Server operating systems. Employment of these vulnerabilities to clandestinely self-copy and transmit Stuxnet meant that it could move from Windows computer to Windows computer *so long as those bugs remained undiscovered.* The bug that allowed Stuxnet to copy itself had likely existed in the Windows operating system since the release of the Windows XP variant in October 2001, or roughly nine years between creation and detection. That bug remained in revisions of Windows through the Windows Vista and Windows 7 operating systems and was detected by VirusBlokAda.[21] The other two Windows zero-day vulnerabilities were identified by Microsoft, and all were mitigated by the company via patches provided for the relevant operating systems.[22]

Called "600 kilobytes of War 2.0" by one blogger,[23] Stuxnet could get to many computers via the three security bugs it exploited in Windows. Once installed, it had the capacity to interact with an outside command and control server and receive instructions.

Moving beyond its capacity to self-replicate and hide, there were many guesses as to where process controllers (PLCs) attacked by Stuxnet might be, but once the payload was understood, the target became far more obvious. Stuxnet's payload issued instructions to the Siemens S7 PLCs. Langer connected the dots on S7 controllers being present at Natanz.[24] Later a journalist would locate the presentation from a 2008 conference in which researchers from the Department of Energy's Idaho National Lab and Siemens gave a presentation at a Chicago conference on vulnerabilities within the Siemens process controller. Stuxnet exploited those vulnerabilities.[25]

Stuxnet's payload caused two types of failures in the centrifuges found at Iran's Natanz nuclear enrichment facility. As opposed to mature enrichment facilities found in the West, at Natanz, operations were highly unstable. Natanz was built on the model of the Pakistani nuclear enrichment program, one that substituted size of operation for reliability. At Natanz, centrifuges broke regularly and in ways not readily understood by the engineers and technicians maintaining them. Once on the S7, Stuxnet subverted either the operation of the centrifuge isolation and exhaust valves or the rotor drives, causing centrifuge overpressure or excessive rotor speed, respectively.[26] Either outcome damaged the centrifuge, necessitating its replacement and disrupting enrichment operations.

Stuxnet made an unreliable operation more unreliable. Worse, unbeknownst to the Iranians, the visits of President Mahmoud Ahmadinejad filmed and broadcast on Iranian television showed to any interested party the status of operations at Natanz. Langer and others could see the control system operations on computer screens captured in screen grabs from the news video. While the United States had made much hay over Saddam

Hussein's efforts to acquire the aluminum tubes necessary for enrichment, Ahmadinejad was happy to show his enrichment infrastructure off in press photo opportunities. Worse, he was recorded in front of SCADA system control screens and the images could be captured and magnified, a critical error. Langer explained,

While no Western plant manager would have cleared such photographic material for publication, Iran didn't seem to bother to hide that fact from the media. To the contrary, there might have been a sense of pride involved by showing a technological achievement that allowed for tolerating centrifuge failure.[27]

The photos and screen grabs showed that many Natanz centrifuges were broken much of the time, or at least operating in a less-than-optimal manner.

By the autumn of 2010, the best working theory on Stuxnet was that it subverted the operation of centrifuges at Natanz. Rumors swirled in the computer security community that the Iranian government was actively seeking talent familiar with the configuration and deployment of the process control computer systems.[28] While Iran cleaned up the Stuxnet mess, the computer security research community moved on to new malware and the Fourth Estate worked to seek confirmation on what had actually happened beyond the clues provided in Stuxnet's source code.

Although hypotheses continued to compete on Stuxnet, David Sanger's June 2012 article for the *New York Times*, "Obama Order Sped Up Wave of Cyberattacks Against Iran," provided an enormous amount of detail about what had actually happened at Natanz.[29] Sanger interviewed American, European, and Israeli officials involved with the centrifuge cyber attacks, a program code-named "Olympic Games," for 18 months before publishing his story. Much additional detail on the matter was contained in his book *Confront and Conceal: Obama's Secret Wars and the Surprising Use of American Power.*[30]

Sanger stated that Olympic Games commenced in 2006, with the Bush administration holding few options for reigning in the Iranian nuclear program. Stuxnet was considered effective by the Bush administration, and when Obama was elected, he chose to continue the program after being briefed on it. Olympic Games involved deep collaboration between the NSA and the Israeli Defense Forces' Unit 8200.[31] Cooperation was viewed as a hedge against Israeli independent military action against the Iranian nuclear program. Israel had bombed Syria's nuclear facility at Deir ez-Zor in 2007 as well as the incomplete Iraqi *Osirak* nuclear reactor in 1981. Furthermore, its agents had allegedly killed as many as five Iranian nuclear scientists in the last decade.[32] *Stuxnet was a nonlethal alternative to military action and the incapacity to persuade Iran to forgo enrichment*

through diplomatic means. It represented an unorthodox third option between use
of force and nonviolent attempts at persuasion.

In summary, Stuxnet was the first cyber-physical attack. It propagated
to where it could find industrial control system computers and then produced a physical outcome on a particular motor or valve.[33] Security
researchers had long conjectured about such an attack. Before it, the clos-
est thing to Stuxnet in the record of computer security incidents was the
previously mentioned 2000 incident in Maroochy Shire, Australia, in
which a disgruntled developer of a municipal sewage SCADA system
subverted its operation.[34] But Stuxnet was an outsider attack. Former
NSA and CIA director Michael Hayden said of it, "This is the first attack
of a major nature in which a cyberattack was used to effect physical
destruction."[35] The Rubicon had been crossed.

NATION-STATE MALWARE

After Stuxnet came the detection of Duqu, the next computer worm
possessing sophistication commensurate with the capabilities found in a
major nation-state cyber attack malware.[36] It held the capacity to remove
and delete data from infected computer hosts, but its role was described
as "a reconnaissance drone," designed to find SCADA system targets for
Stuxnet or other malware like it.[37] Equipped with another Windows zero
day, it appeared to be a close relative to Stuxnet as well.[38]

Duqu's discovery represented a new process for finding sophisticated
malicious software. Knowing what Stuxnet looked like, antivirus firms
and computer security labs could find its stable mates. These corporate
labs were distributed all over the world, representing competing commercial interests yet often collaborating. The chief researcher at one of these
firms, F-Secure's Mikko Hypponen of Finland, himself a veteran of the
effort to restore Estonia's computer networks in 2007 following the cyber
attack allegedly orchestrated by Russia, opined of the process, "I can't
think of any other IT sector where there is such extensive cooperation
between competitors."[39]

Research continued. Next discovered was Flame, a Remote Access
Toolkit (RAT) surveillance software designed to purloin data, including
via the clandestine operation of built-in webcams and microphones found
within many of the world's computers. Flame had been found throughout
the Middle East, including on computers at the Iran's Kharg Island oil ter-
minal and at the Iranian oil ministry.[40] It was bespoke malware with a
purpose, standing as distinctly unlike the prior generation of widely
distributed malware, the likes of Conficker and Code Red.

Upon discovery, the Iranians brought Flame to the International
Telecommunications Union (ITU).[41] ITU officials tapped Kaspersky Lab,

a Russian security company, to study Flame.[42] Kaspersky, based in Moscow, put out an FAQ on its findings on its website, but not a full malware analysis report containing extensive documentation regarding Flame's source code and how it functioned.[43]

The Iran-ITU-Kaspersky linkages represented a new politics of collaborative cybersecurity intelligence undertaken outside the United States and its network of allies. The ITU had "found a willing ally in Kaspersky."[44] Eugene Kaspersky's political allegiances, his past as a KGB-educated cryptographer and computer engineer, and his ties to Russian intelligence raised questions of his role as a servant of the Russian government. Once Kaspersky's company released its summary findings on Flame, the Iranians were quick to castigate Israel as Flame's source.[45] Arguments circulated on the Web that Flame's code was written during the Jerusalem time working hours and not on days of the Jewish Sabbath.[46] Again a Microsoft zero day was detected and patched.[47]

Equipped with the analysis from Kaspersky, the ITU announced plans to issue its first ever cyber warning.[48] This came in advance of the organization's World Conference on International Telecommunications (WCIT), which took place in Dubai in December 2012. At Dubai, details were provided as to how the ITU intended to expand its role in international Internet governance, the job undertaken by ICANN. The message was clear. *The more the United States allegedly employed cyber espionage and attack tools, the more Russia, Iran, and other adversaries would push for the shift of Internet governance away from ICANN and to an international organization, preferably the ITU.*

Beyond the increased pressure on a new mechanism for Internet governance, a new concern emerged regarding the world after Stuxnet. One key distinction between Stuxnet and commercial malware was the ease by which its code could be accessed and retrieved. Criminal malware authors are growing as cognizant of the need to protect their revenues from the problem of unauthorized reuse of their software much in the way that Microsoft would be.[49] The question arose as to when something like Stuxnet would be shot back at the United States or someone else by another party.

RETURNED FIRE

While Stuxnet, Duqu, and Flame were all sophisticated pieces of malware, they were not designed with the sort of protections that would restrict their reuse increasingly found in commercial cybercrime malware. The code in each of them, once discovered, could be easily reused, although the zero-day vulnerabilities employed by them were discovered and mitigated through patches fairly quickly. The portability of this set of malware code led to the natural concern that Stuxnet-like attacks would begin to impact SCADA systems in the United States and elsewhere.

Allegedly produced by enormously sophisticated cyber intelligence agencies in Israel and the United States, Stuxnet represented a tremendous jump from theoretical possibility to real capability. While the security industry has long studied national source of origin for attack traffic,[50] the cyber offensive capabilities of nation-states are much more difficult to measure. The United States, Israel, and the UK were widely considered to be in a top tier of states in regard to cyber attack capability. Down the list, but perhaps not by far, are Russia, China, and France. A decade ago, India, Iran, Pakistan, and North Korea were developing the underpinnings of cyber warfare capabilities including doctrine, training, exercises, and information warfare units.[51] How they stack up is hard to assess.[52] Nonetheless, in August 2012, the first such attack occurred.

On one of the holiest days of Ramadan, the Lailat al Qadr, the day of celebration for the Koran's revelation to Muhammed, a computer worm was activated on the computer network of Saudi Aramco, the world's largest oil producer. As some 55,000 of the company's employees stayed home for the holiday, the worm replicated itself across more than 35,000 Windows-operating system computers and began deleting the contents of every hard drive in which it came into contact.[53] The company's CEO, Khalid al-Falih, stated the process control systems performing production were not compromised.[54] In a post on Facebook, he declared, "we addressed the threat immediately, and our precautionary procedures, which have been in place to counter such threats, and our multiple protective systems, have helped to mitigate these deplorable cyber threats from spiraling." In another announcement, the company declared, "Aramco's oil production operations [were] segregated from the company's internal communications network."[55]

The worm did not stop at the boundaries of Aramco's network. Copies of it showed up on computers at RasGas, a joint venture between the nation of Qatar and ExxonMobil.[56] Concern regarding the worm's spread rapidly consumed the attention of computer security professionals throughout the oil and gas industry. Baker Hughes, a services firm hit by a significant cyber attack in 2010, struggled to disconnect itself from networks possibly compromised by the worm.[57] For the next two weeks, Aramco struggled to bring computers back online and purge the worm from its systems. An indiscriminate data destruction attack, it is reputed to have deleted valuable drilling and production data.[58]

As mitigation efforts geared up, the question of attribution came to the fore. On the Pastebin website a group calling itself Cutting Sword of Justice claimed credit. Its announcement stated, "we penetrated a system of Aramco company by using the hacked systems in several countries and then sended [sic] a malicious virus to destroy thirty thousand computers networked in this company. The destruction operations began on Wednesday, Aug 15, 2012 at 11:08 AM (Local time in Saudi Arabia)."[59] Even as Aramco was making its initial announcements on what had happened to its network, the malware analysis community began its study of the new worm, called *Shamoon*. Symantec, Kaspersky, and Israeli security firm Seculert performed initial studies. A Kaspersky researcher offered that Shamoon appeared to hold similar "wiper" data deletion capabilities found in Duqu and Flame, but that it was likely an inferior attempt to replicate the functionality in those pieces of malware.[60]

Beyond the questions of what Shamoon could do, the issue of attribution arose as well. Who would want to crash out Saudi Aramco and damage its capacity to produce and market petroleum? The simple answer was any country exporting into the market, but speculation quickly bore in on Iran. After roughly two months of investigating Shamoon, U.S. officials began making statements to the effect that Iran was likely behind the attack, but little conclusive evidence was offered.[61] Other hypotheses pinned Shamoon on the actions of a single Aramco employee who had been logged in on a company workstation to launch the attack. The RasGas attack was possibly a copycat event by another insider. And then there was the matter that Shamoon was written in a fairly sloppy manner.[62]

What we learned from Shamoon was that cyber attacks could be fired in both directions.[63] Oil and gas firms had been on the receiving end of cyber attacks before, but those were largely aimed at stealing confidential corporate data, in the case of the Night Dragon campaign, "project-financing information with regard to oil and gas field bids and operations."[64] But actually breaking company operations was a new phenomenon. Aramco recovered and the oil and gas industry dedicated additional resources to cybersecurity functions and pursuing the development of an Oil and Natural Gas Information Sharing and Analysis Center (ONG-ISAC).[65] Far less significant than Shamoon was the Anonymous hacker collectives Op Petrol campaign against oil companies in June 2013. But other sectors were vulnerable.

BREAKING THE BANKS AND THE NEWS

Although confirmation of Iranian responsibility for Shamoon remains inconclusive, cyber campaigns and events linked to both Iran and Syria have shown the vulnerability of the United States and its allies. Borrowing a term from computer security, massive societal dependence on IT in the United States makes it a target for attack with an enormous attack surface. We are just beginning to learn how the adversaries and enemies can exploit that attack surface.

Iran is reputed to be behind a major DDoS campaign directed at the on-line portals of major U.S. banks. Much like the earlier generation of DDoS attacks used to overwhelm websites, as was seen in Estonia in 2007, the DDoS attacks on the banks beginning in September 2012 and continuing into 2013 doubled the amount of downtime on the banking portals of the 15 largest U.S. banks as compared to the previous year.[66] Those launching the DDoS attacks, the al-Qassam Cyber Fighters, scaled up the amount of traffic usually seen in traditional, botnet-derived attacks.

The attacks were much larger and ostensibly required state support. Senator Joe Lieberman commented on attribution: "I think this was done by Iran and the Quds Force, which has its own developing cyberattack capability."[67] It made sense inasmuch that the ejection of Iranian financial institutions from the Society for Worldwide Interbank Financial Telecom-munication (SWIFT) global money transfer system in March 2012 had sig-nificant impact on the country's capacity to engage in international trade.[68] Indeed, after the election of the Rouhani government, lifting the SWIFT ban was rumored to be a top priority.[69] Gradually, the banks have mitigated the DDoS problem, although not without prompting from government regulators.[70]

The next major cyber event to demonstrate how even false informa-tion could bite back was the report of an explosion at the White House on the Associated Press's (AP) Twitter feed on April 23, 2013, after the account was hacked. AP's account reported, "Breaking: Two Explosions in the White House and Barack Obama Is Injured."[71] This precipitated a "flash crash" with varying impact across the financial markets. In approximately two minutes, some $121 billion fell out of the New York Stock Exchange before buying canceled out the loss. The Dow Jones industrial average was up one percent for the day, as were the S&P 500 and NASDAQ.[72] The false information had caused a panic of sorts for the computerized trading algorithms widely used throughout the financial sector. It also showed just how much Wall Street's quantitative traders were looking to social media platforms to search for clues on mass human behavior upon which they could exercise lucrative trades.

The Syrian Electronic Army (SEA), an organization that had gradually grown in prominence since the start of Syria's civil war in 2011, took responsibility for the AP Twitter account hack.[73] It was a new player in the geopolitics of cyberspace, ostensibly linked to the Assad government. Its hackers preferred to target purveyors of news, including major American and European outlets Forbes, CNBC, the *Guardian*, *Le Monde*, and others. Whether it was behind the hacking of Aramco's Twitter account on the day Aramco CEO Khalid al-Falih spoke at the 2013 CERA Week energy conference is anybody's guess, however.[74]

What seems to have been a fairly clear case of SEA activity was the hacking directed at the *New York Times*'s website in August 2013. The attack came on the heels of information from Médcins Sans Frontières (MSF) that chemical weapons, including nerve agents, had been employed in at least two neighborhoods in the outskirts of Damascus. According to MSF, more than 3,600 Syrians had been treated for neurotoxic symptoms and some 355 had died.[75] Following the report, attention turned to the issue of a Western response if Bashar Assad had indeed used chemical weapons on the Syrian people. The United States, UK, and France considered military options, with punitive strikes, a likely choice.

But as the West considered how to move forward, an attack was launched against the *New York Times*. Altered were an Australian DNS register reseller's "DNS records of several domain names on [a] reseller account ... including nytimes.com." SEA took credit for the hack.[76] The bogus DNS records propagated across the global DNS system, placing incorrect routing information on the location of the *New York Times*'s websites, making it disappear for much of August 27, and causing intermittent outages afterward.

While the SEA attack on the *New York Times*'s DNS records was not terribly damaging, it came at a critical time in the discussions on whether or not to proceed with punitive strikes against the Assad government. The SEA was able to censor the chief news outlet for those working in or supporting the current party in power in the United States. It took the breaking news content of the paper away for a relatively short period of time at a key moment in an international crisis when use of force was being considered.[77]

SOME HARD CYBER GEOPOLITICAL REALITIES

From Stuxnet to the actions of the Syrian Electronic Army, we can see an evolving record of how cyber tools may be used in international disputes and conflicts. Each time a new piece of malware or politically relevant hack takes place, analysts must put together information regarding forensics, malware functionality, target selection, and a host of geopolitical factors to answer not just what happened or how it happened, but why it happened and, ultimately, who did it. We know that on August 27, 2013, the *New York Times* website was knocked offline. We learned that a DNS issue was the culprit. We understood the context of the attack, coming during a significant international crisis with Syria, and that the pro-Assad hacker group happily took credit for it. Despite these facts, we are left with other questions. How did the SEA know to take down an Australian DNS reseller? Did SEA have help? Did Russia, one of Syria's few remaining allies, provide assistance? Did Russia wish to intervene to prevent punitive strikes?

These are the sorts of questions that use of cyber tools and techniques to achieve political goals in the international system provoke. Cyber attacks remain fairly easy to accomplish, hold low risk of attribution, and do not fit neatly into the norms of international conflict that have evolved within the Westphalian system.[78] Despite the considerable attention already dedicated to the justness regarding use of force in response to a cyber attack by international lawyers and diplomats, a clear-cut case of knowing when a state may "respond to bytes with bullets" has yet to appear.[79] *We are seeing acts of cyberwarfare, we just don't know exactly how they translate to real war.*

CHAPTER 8

Diplomacy, Social Software, and the Arab Spring

Characterizations of power relationships in cyberspace tend to cover espionage, covert action, and cyber attacks perpetrated in aims of military goals. In themselves, these events are significant; however, power dynamics in cyberspace are not well understood. Cyber power is very much an ideational concept and coheres with Nye's concepts of soft power as well.[1] While the United States develops an increased cyber defense and offense capability, there is a diplomacy of cyberspace afoot as well.

The Internet held a significant role in the events of the Arab Spring revolutions, with the Facebook, YouTube, and Twitter platforms, as well as blogs, serving as a medium for political communication and coordination. In addition, the impact of a major data breach, the passing of classified and sensitive diplomatic cables by Chelsea Manning to WikiLeaks and subsequent news reporting on their contents, was likely significant in providing evidence to protesters in Egypt and Tunisia of the corruption in their governments.

As most of the world's largest Internet firms are headquartered in the United States, they represent a significant facet of U.S. economic power. However, divisions between those firms and the U.S. government have grown more pronounced as their business interests diverge from its military, intelligence, and diplomatic objectives. Nonetheless, the Hillary Clinton State Department made considerable use of social media and the IT sector, building upon Internet activities of her predecessors. In coping with cyber threats, hacking matters, but so does the proliferation of ideas. This translates to a cyber diplomacy undertaken by nations as well as the largest IT firms. How that diplomacy is undertaken will increasingly depend not only on how American diplomacy manages bilateral and multilateral relationships with states but also on the tech companies at the vanguard of global business.

TRANSFORMING DIPLOMACY

When former national security adviser Condoleezza Rice succeeded Colin Powell as secretary of state, she searched for a theme upon which to construct her institutional strategy as secretary of state.[2] Powell's tenure at the State Department had largely looked inward with regard to information technology and policy. A self-described IT enthusiast and former board member for one-time Internet titan America Online (AOL), Powell had arrived at the State Department shocked to find an information organization without any significant connectivity to the Internet.[3] One of his top institutional priorities for the Department of State was simply to push Internet connectivity to all of its employees.

At an address given at Georgetown University in January 2006, Rice employed the term "transformational diplomacy" to describe a set of fundamental shifts in how the United States would employ its diplomatic resources. While transformational diplomacy was largely related to shifting resources toward conflict areas and emerging world powers such as Brazil, China, and India, one technological element was incorporated into the strategy—the concept of "virtual presence." Rice described the initiative:

Perhaps the newest and most cost effective way to adopt a more local posture is through a Virtual Presence Post. Here one or more of our young officers creates and manages an Internet site that is focused on key population centers. This digital meeting room enables foreign citizens, young people most of all, to engage online with American diplomats who could be hundreds of miles away.[4]

First conceived to support U.S. outreach into the cities surrounding the U.S. Consulate in Yekaterinburg, Russia, the Virtual Presence Post (VPP) was developed "to combine virtual presence through an embassy-hosted Web site with coordinated outreach, programming, and travel targeted at a particular city or region."[5]

Virtual presence represented an important change in the way diplomacy, particularly public diplomacy, could be undertaken. Even before getting noticed by Rice, it had been identified as a potentially valuable diplomatic innovation.

The concept, launched by Tom Niblock, the former U.S. Consulate General of Yekaterinburg, Russia, has the potential to stream germane and time sensitive information to audiences in major cities and remote regions where the United States has no physical presence. Additionally, initial anecdotal evidence from

Russia suggests that a virtual consulate may be able to perform up to 50 percent of the work of an actual consulate and do it in a timely and cost effective manner.[6]

Beyond virtual presence, the expanded development of public diplomacy enabled by information and computing technology (ICT), particularly in the Arab world, was identified as a potential opportunity during Colin Powell's tenure as secretary of state.

In 2003, a Middle East strategy report prepared for the U.S. House of Representatives Appropriations Committee by the Advisory Group on Public Diplomacy for the Arab and Muslim World identified five key policy planks in ICT development in the Middle East: (1) programs to develop sustainable access to ICT and the Internet; (2) widespread dissemination of computer hardware and software; (3) expanded information resources in languages of the Muslim world, including those that would benefit women and bolster public health; (4) incorporation of foreign nationals in U.S. digital outreach efforts; and (5) a push for wider access to information resources and curbs to state censorship efforts.[7]

During Bush's second term, Karen Hughes was appointed as undersecretary of state for public diplomacy and public affairs. Heading up public diplomacy efforts,[8] she inherited the task of enhancing outreach in the Middle East. Hughes's tenure at the State Department was generally viewed as unsuccessful, with her Middle East travels sounding a particularly sour note.[9] Hughes did, however, observe how information revolution was changing the business of public diplomacy. In remarks to the Council on Foreign Relations in 2006, she said:

During the Cold War we were trying to get information into societies that were largely closed, where people were hungry for that information. Well, today in places like the Middle East there's an information explosion and no one is hungry for information. What we are competing for there is for attention and for credibility in a time when rumors can spark riots, and information, whether it's true or false, quickly spreads across the world, across the internet, in literally instants.[10]

Public diplomacy for the Middle East was bolstered through newly established digital outreach teams, producing "Arabic language blogs and forums to provide information about U.S. policies and to counter misinformation and myths posted on the [other] blogs."[11]

State also funded research on the Iranian/Persian blogosphere.[12] Resources were aimed at blogs in the Middle East, but interaction on the Internet was undergoing a dramatic change. While virtual presence had forged the concept of diplomacy via websites and blogs were offering the ability for many individuals to publish political content to the Web, new platforms were radically transforming online interaction.

ANOTHER INFORMATION REVOLUTION: WEB 2.0, THE PARTICIPATORY INTERNET

As the U.S. military engaged in relearning the art of counterinsurgency (COIN) operations and redeveloping its repertoire for winning the support of local populations,[13] the U.S. armed forces were forced to cope with the use of new information technologies by its terrorist and insurgent adversaries. The most deadly weapon in the insurgent arsenal, IED attacks were being video recorded and posted to the Internet within minutes of happening. A valuable recruitment tool for terror groups, the videos showed that these adversaries had great capacity to use the Internet.[14] Indeed, Al Qaeda's legacy of operational successes and capacity to influence potential recruits online led to the observation that "Al Qaeda is a brand to protect."[15] That brand extended to the Internet and did so during a particularly interesting point in the development of the cyber ecosystem—the period of development for Web 2.0, the participatory Internet.

Web 2.0, a term coined by Internet and computer book publisher Tim O'Reilly, represented a redefinition of Internet experiences.[16] New software platforms, delivered via an Internet browser, often described under the heading social media, changed the pattern of interpersonal interaction on the Internet. Web 2.0 was a concept predicated on the idea that almost anyone could publish text, images, video, or other content onto the Internet with minimal effort. The first of these technologies, the weblog, or blog, was in many ways the first Web 2.0 technology. Blogging platforms such as WordPress, Movable Type, and Blogger allowed individuals to quickly set up their own multimedia websites for producing articles, usually fairly limited in length. Blog platforms also featured the capacity for readers to respond to posts through moderated or unmoderated comment fields. They were not just published documents, but a conversation.

Beyond blogs, three additional platforms transformed the way online conversation was taking place on a global scale: Facebook, YouTube, and Twitter. Facebook, the social network, linked individuals to one another and to topics, themes, events, and causes.[17] YouTube permitted the posting of video to the Internet by a highly intuitive, user-friendly method. The videos were then indexed by the Google search engine.[18] Twitter is a micro-blog, a publishing platform that restricts the length of posts to 140 characters. Twitter posts, or tweets, typically include free text, hashtagged metadata, other Twitter identities (handles), and links to Web pages, images, and other resources.

In the United States during the second half of the 2000s, blogging challenged traditional news publications, while as was mentioned in Chapter 2, Facebook, YouTube, and Twitter changed the definition of what made a leading firm in Silicon Valley. Within a few years of their creation, Facebook,

YouTube, and Twitter were among the world's top 10 most popular websites.[19] These technology platforms had a pivotal role in U.S. electoral politics, and lessons learned there would eventually be incorporated into American foreign policy.

DIPLOMACY FOR THE 21ST CENTURY

Obama's arrival in Washington brought more political clout to information technology in the federal executive branch. Among the top technology questions for the new president was whether a federal chief information officer (CIO) position should be created.[20] Interested in an agenda of innovation, the Obama administration created positions for both a federal CIO and a federal chief technology officer (CTO). Those officers, Vivek Kundra and Aneesh Chopra, respectively, brought with them new ideas about how to run federal IT, the business of government, and *also the level of transparency afforded the public regarding the function of government*.

At the State Department, the politics of the Internet assumed a new prominence. Jared Cohen, a Rhodes scholar who had written on youth in the Middle East and member of Condoleezza Rice's policy planning staff since 2006, found an important collaborator and ally in Alec Ross, a key figure in Obama campaign's mobilization of support from the U.S. IT sector. Secretary of State Hillary Clinton installed Ross as her senior adviser for innovation. Ross and Cohen's shared efforts bore fruit in new initiatives to reach a technologically savvy audience.

They heavily employed both Facebook and Twitter to connect with others as part of their duties as Clinton's Internet gurus. Traveling widely and often in the company of senior executives from technology companies, the pair came to public prominence. Chronicling the mobile smartphone Twitter postings of both men, and their propensity to intersperse substantive policy views with ordinary pabulum, their actions made argument for the future of statecraft undertaken via blogs, Twitter, YouTube, and Facebook.[21] Perhaps Ross and Cohen's harshest critic, Evgeny Morozov, framed the other side of an argument regarding one of Secretary Clinton's key foreign policy initiatives, regarding Internet Freedom as naïve and sophistic.[22]

While Condoleezza Rice had attempted to put her mark on the State Department and international relations via her transformational diplomacy initiative, Hillary Clinton staked out her goals for the State Department through an initiative titled "21st Century Statecraft." Her October 2010 speech on the topic, given to the Commonwealth Club in San Francisco, mentioned several major initiatives for a State Department that was entangled in the realities of working closely with the Defense Department in a number of conflicts and that was in need of institutional retooling. The precepts of 21st Century Statecraft were in part underwritten by then–Secretary of Defense Robert Gates, who argued for expanded funding and resources to flow to State rather than the DoD in coping with the soft power tasks in which the United States engaged as it coped with counterinsurgency and counterterrorism around the globe.[23]

Replicating DoD planning, the State Department and the U.S. Agency for International Development (USAID) produced a Quadrennial Diplomacy and Defense Review (QDDR) in 2010. The QDDR was built around the identification of important new trends in international relations. Among those was an acceptance that "The information age has accelerated the pace of international affairs and facilitated a new era of connectivity."[24] In the QDDR, the U.S. diplomatic establishment recognized the forces at work in the relationship between digital connectivity and international politics.

The communications revolution that has swept across the world has had a profound impact on the attitudes, behaviors, and aspirations of people everywhere. Public opinion is influencing foreign governments and shaping world affairs to an unprecedented degree. The advance of democracy and open markets has empowered millions to demand more control over their own destinies and more information from their governments. Even in autocratic societies, leaders must increasingly respond to the opinions and passions of their people. And the tools of technology create unprecedented opportunities to engage foreign publics and advance jointly the interests we share with them.[25]

Remember, this assessment was written in 2010, before the series of events that have come to be known as the Arab Spring. The Clinton State Department was laying the groundwork for diplomatic engagement via the Internet, even as it was about to be buffeted by the largest breach of classified material since the Vietnam War, the WikiLeaks episode (covered in the following chapter), and the tumultuous events across the Middle East in beginning with the uprising against the Tunisian government in December 2010.

HACKING AND FREEDOM

While Hillary Clinton's State Department was forced to largely react to the political upheaval of the Arab Spring, it did have a strategic plan for the Internet. How that plan came to be had more to do with the increasingly contentious issue of cyber espionage undertaken by China against U.S. firms than any grand strategic goal enunciated by the president. There was little publicly available information about how foreign hacking groups subverted the confidentiality of privately held information systems. A 2009 report on hacking aimed at civil society organizations changed that.

After receiving a request to analyze computers used by the Dalai Lama organization, researchers at the University of Toronto's Citizen Lab had detected extensive hacking activity aimed at computers used by the Dalai Lama's staff as well as computer systems used by governments and other NGOs. The compromise of the Dalai Lama's computer network was part of a large effort the Canadian researchers dubbed GhostNet. Nart Villeneuve, the technical lead of the GhostNet project, said of the activity, "Close to 30% of the infected hosts are considered high-value and include computers located at ministries of foreign affairs, embassies, international organizations, news media, and NGOs."[26] Led by Citizen Lab Director Ronald Deibert, they stated that the systems employed in the campaign were located in China, but declined to directly finger the Chinese government for the hack.[27]

Less than a year later, in January 2010, Google would be less ambiguous about identifying the hacking directed against it by Chinese sources. In a statement posted by David Drummond, Google's chief legal officer, on the company's official blog, he stated that it too had fallen victim to Chinese hacking and that "a highly sophisticated and targeted attack on our corporate infrastructure originating from China ... resulted in the theft of intellectual property from Google."[28] Beyond the theft, Drummond alleged that the attack was aimed at accessing the Google Gmail accounts of human rights activists in China. In response, the company was considering its options for remaining in the world's largest emerging market. "These attacks and the surveillance they have uncovered—combined with the attempts over the past year to further limit free speech on the web—have led us to conclude that we should review the feasibility of our business operations in China."[29] Google was fed up with Chinese hacking of its services, theft of company IP, and the requests for censorship by the Chinese government of Google search results for its google.cn Chinese search engine.

Google CEO Eric Schmidt met with Secretary Clinton soon after the official blog post regarding China. The State Department convened a major dinner discussion of Silicon Valley leaders from other established firms such as Microsoft, Cisco, and Twitter as well as several start-up CEOs and NGO directors.[30] On the agenda was Clinton's upcoming address on the topic of Internet Freedom. It was an opportunity for the United States to shape its Internet politics agenda, and the tech leaders could doubtlessly provide useful input.

Hillary Clinton gave her address on Internet Freedom at the Newseum in Washington, D.C., on January 21, 2010.[31] In it, Mrs. Clinton made a clear statement in support of free movement of information around the world unfettered by state censorship. The address was rich in issues and facts, mentioning, for instance, the potential for mass mobilization by IT, including State's recent initiative to direct relief donations to Haiti by telephone text message.[32] In the speech was the clear message that freedom of speech and expression is considered by the United States to be a global value and one to be universally applied to the Internet. Secretary Clinton argued, in essence, that the First Amendment was potentially applicable to every corner of the globe.

Regarding China's hacking, Clinton did not mince words, demanding, "We look to the Chinese authorities to conduct a thorough review of the cyber intrusions that led Google to make its announcement." Beijing was not pleased. Chinese press response to Clinton's remarks was universal in its hostility. The editors of *Global Times*, a subsidiary of the Chinese Communist Party's *People's Daily*, criticized the Americans for their global dominance of information.

The free flow of information is a universal value treasured in all nations, including China, but the US government's ideological imposition is unacceptable and, for that reason, will not be allowed to succeed. China's real stake in the "free flow of information" is evident in its refusal to be victimized by information imperialism.[33]

Hong Junjie of Shanghai's *Jiefang Ribao* relayed an almost conspiratorial tone.

The US is controlling core technology in the internet realm and is occupying the vast majority of internet resources, and has to a certain extent turned this weapon for benefiting mankind, disseminating knowledge and maintaining peace into a tool for regime infiltration and wanton interference in other countries.[34]

In much the rest of the world, Clinton's remarks on Internet Freedom were seen with far less concern or controversy.

There was scant mention of the Clinton speech in most world capitals. In *Le Monde*'s brief dispatch "Clinton menace la Chine à demi-mot," the French paper hinted that the remarks were a veiled threat.[35] The Internet Freedom address, while not by any means barnburning oratory, was a generally useful policy plank. As an observer remarked, Internet Freedom "should be part of the national brand" of the United States.[36] How it would be viewed after the United States' cyber intelligence activities became widely known to the public would lead many to wonder if it was mere rhetoric.

FACEBOOK, YOUTUBE, TWITTER, AND REVOLUTION

In late 2010, five years after the WSIS, the world's attention again fixed upon Tunisia—but far more intensely than during the 2005 World Summit on the Information Society. Pressures building across the Middle East likely since the departure of colonial powers exploded with the protracted suicide of a single produce vendor, Mohamed Bouazizi, who set himself on fire to protest political corruption in Tunisia and his inability to make a living. Suddenly, discontent in the government and institutions of the Middle East boiled over from Libya to Bahrain.[37] In just a few weeks, a tectonic political shift, labeled the Arab Spring, radically changed the political complexion of the region.

While leaders across the Arab world had flirted with ideas of reform, democratic representation, and economic liberalization, to the man on the street, the pace of change appeared glacial. Between demographic pressures of populations growing far more rapidly than their economies could possibly produce jobs, the rise of social service institutions largely outside the auspices of the state[38] (which in many cases appeared ineffectual at providing them), and the outright kleptocracy of ruling families, a recipe for discontent morphed into uprising on a massive scale. Presidents Zine al-Abidine Ben Ali (Tunisia), Hosni Mubarak (Egypt), Moamar Gadhafi (Libya), and Bashar Assad (Syria) held between them nearly a century of executive power. Those they ruled were left to wonder whether their successors would provide a path for increased prosperity or expansion of democratic institutions.

Corruption, rising prices for staple goods, and the lack of economic mobility all contributed to the overthrow of regimes in the Middle East in 2011. But the uprisings have been labeled Facebook, Twitter, or social media revolutions. Social media and its utility to the youth at the core of the Arab Spring movement was recognized by American diplomacy. In a February 2012 town hall meeting with students in Tunis, Clinton considered the hyperconnectivity available to them:

[Y]ou are living in a world that your parents, and certainly your grandparents, could never have imagined—satellite television, the Internet, Facebook. My late mother used to say, "What is this about faces on the Internet?" ... And new communications technologies shrink your world but expand your horizons. Now everybody can see how others are living—living in prosperity, dignity, and freedom, and they rightly want those things for themselves.[39]

Facebook did matter in Tunisia as individuals organized resistance movements against the Ben Ali government. It appears fairly clear that the Ben Ali regime was threatened by the use of Facebook by those who opposed the ruling government. In early January 2011, thousands of Facebook accounts accessed in Tunisia were compromised. Facebook's information security team realized that "the country's Internet service providers were running a malicious piece of code that was recording users' login information when they went to sites like Facebook."[40]

As discontent spread, first to Egypt and then elsewhere in the Middle East, the speed at which political discontent morphed into viable and sustained protest movements overtook the capacity of well-established regimes to maintain order and isolate opponents. Where the Ben Ali government had attempted to monitor discontent on social media by logging ISP data, Egypt went for a wholesale shutdown of Internet connectivity on January 26, 2011.[41] Despite the shutdown, protests continued unabated. Social media–based organization was surpassed by raw people power exercised in the streets. Internet tools and mobilization tactics had served a purpose, but were unnecessary to maintain sustained pressure on the Mubarak government with tens of thousands of protesters camped out in Cairo's Tahrir Square.

A 2012 conversation with Egyptian university students, all of whom had actively participated in the protests against the Mubarak government pursuing degrees in either engineering or science, had a set of very intriguing views on how they received information, what information they trusted, and how they passed it along. Of the Egyptian state-run media, they found the contents absurd. But the students could access the international news networks. What of them? They saw Qatar's Al Jazeera as holding a clear political bias and rerunning what they viewed as sensationalistic video clips unnecessarily often. The BBC's service in Arabic was perhaps a bit too Western. Nobody watched the State Department–backed Al Hurrah. Preferable to all was the Saudi-owned, but Dubai-based Al Arabiya, principally because the network's offices are sited at Tahrir Square. They had a bird's-eye view of the protests, and ran coverage hour after hour.

More trusted by this small sample of Egyptians was the information they received via their social circles on the Web. Every one of the visitors was an active Facebook user. Many had Twitter accounts. They all were well acquainted with YouTube. It was through these platforms that the students got the information they trusted *most*. The judgment and observations of those they knew trumped anything the journalists could say. But the link to the Internet was severed on January 26, 2011, as the government realized the protesters were using social media to mobilize and organize.

What followed was a surprise to the Mubarak government, the protests intensified. Whole families, cut off from their most trustworthy source of information, went into the streets to get it, and to keep an eye on one another. And gradually, technologists began to route around the barriers to Internet access and restore data communications inside and beyond the country. The Internet did what the Internet is supposed to do: route around damage and deliver data. And on February 11, 2011, Mubarak stepped down and the foreign news media and our collective attention moved on.

When Egyptian Vice President Omar Suleiman announced Mubarak's resignation, the Arab world tilted. Further resistance in the Middle East became bloodier, subject to far more harsh state responses and international intervention. For those regimes that survived, censoring the Internet became a priority, as open communication was perceived as a pathway to instability and eventual overthrow. Mass mobilization had been enabled by the social media platforms of Silicon Valley, and despite the efforts of government to circumvent these platforms in the case of either the Tunisian hacking of Facebook or the Egyptians cutting off Internet connectivity altogether, the popular uprisings were not put down. But in little time, governments across the Middle East were buying cybersecurity tools to perform Internet content monitoring and censorship in an effort to quell domestic distress. Many factors led to Mubarak's removal from power, from a jump in local wheat prices to discontent with the prospects of Gamal Mubarak taking his father's place as the nation's leader, but the Internet was a catalyst for change.[42]

INTERNET LEGACIES IN U.S. FOREIGN POLICY

With the onset of the Arab Spring, the United States was tested enormously in managing a shift in how online platforms and social media technologies impacted international relations. American diplomacy attempted to erect a sovereign response to issues produced by a global infrastructure that is, at times, difficult to confine to the sovereign boundaries of an international system assembled in Europe in the wake of the last information revolution, which was spurred by the development of the printing press.

Nonetheless, the United States responded. In diplomacy, a significant transformation occurred. Official statements from U.S. embassies around the globe were increasingly transmitted by Twitter, a tool of seemingly great value in crisis situations where the information picture may be highly fluid and filled with incorrect or specious inputs. The March 2012 coup d'etat in Mali was yet another case of such activity, with the Twitter feed from the U.S. embassy in Bamako serving as perhaps the definitive information tool for the U.S. government. The post's first tweet during the crisis was on point. "Contrary to rumors, #Mali's president #ATT is not at @USEmbassyMali."[43] The State Department found itself rapidly moving to practice a new form of digitally mediated engagement.[44]

The growth of international cyber policy raised items to consider. A common refrain is that cyber issues represent an erosion of state power and the decline of effective sovereignty as well as an amplification of non-state actors' capability.[45] Furthermore, there is a blurring of lines between the state, the individual, the NGO, and the corporation. Consider Jared

Cohen, the de facto Internet expert on the policy-planning staff at the State Department, who left that institution in 2010 but brought with him more than 200,000 Twitter "followers" to his new position as the head of Google Ideas (a corporate-run policy think tank) and to a parallel appointment at the Council on Foreign Relations.[46]

Because of the ambiguities of digital diplomacy, we are left to wonder what is the policy of states, the sentiments of individuals, or the behavior of corporations. With more horizontal, nonhierarchical networks rising as a prevailing form of organization, preexisting norms, rules, and models will likely change. Finally, there is the issue of making international policy in an atmosphere of profound technologically driven disruption. With the term "disrupt" a mantra for Silicon Valley's innovation class, the task of updating diplomatic practice to keep pace appears incredibly daunting.

CHAPTER 9

Espionage, Radical Transparency, and National Security

HEY CHINA!

When Xi Jinping visited the United States for his summit with Barack Obama in June 2013, a variety of items, including the People's Republic of China's peaceful rise, the value of its currency, North Korea, and global climate change, were on the agenda.[1] But the item that appeared foremost on the agenda in advance was that of cybersecurity. Tensions between the United States and China on economic and military espionage activities had been growing for years.[2] Several significant counterintelligence cases had been prosecuted by U.S. federal authorities since the 1990s,[3] but by 2013, it was painfully apparent that China or computer hackers in China working for either the Chinese government or other concerns were engaged in coordinated, concerted, and apparently effective cyber operations designed to purloin data from U.S. corporations as well as those in other Western nations.

The indicators of China's ambitious cyber espionage campaign were many. While Google had called out the PRC in 2010 for its theft of the company's intellectual property and compromise of Gmail accounts of opponents to the Chinese government, the level of economic espionage became clearer as systematic efforts to copy massive quantities of data from dozens of multinational corporations were discovered. Although defense firm Northrop Grumman produced an extensive report on Chinese cyber espionage aimed at the United States,[4] corroborative evidence found by companies in the computer security sector made the case against China more convincing.

McAfee, with its large install base of computer antivirus software and cybersecurity services portfolio, produced a comprehensive report on Chinese cyber espionage in 2011. Dmitri Alperovitch, then the company's head of threat intelligence, studied a newly discovered piece of malicious software detected after viewing the logs of a command and control server used to manage espionage efforts on targeted networks. Alperovitch's method was strikingly similar to the one employed by the University of Toronto researchers and summarized in the 2009 GhostNet report.[5]

Part of microprocessor giant Intel since early 2011, McAfee's report described a malware agent installed on compromised computers and managed by an offsite command and control server. It called the enterprise "Operation Shady RAT," and detailed what it called the most extensive cyber espionage campaign to target corporations (as well as governments and international organizations). Among those targeted were the governments of the "United States, Taiwan, India, South Korea, Vietnam and Canada; the Association of Southeast Asian Nations (ASEAN); the International Olympic Committee (IOC) . . . and . . . companies from defense contractors to high-tech enterprises."[6]

Shady RAT referred to the type of software emplaced on targeted systems. The RAT was one or more variants of Remote Access Toolkit, not unlike Duqu or Flame, in that once installed it could be employed to search for, collect, copy, and exfiltrate data to servers outside the enterprise network. Shady RAT was yet another sophisticated attack tool, found not because copies of it were detected on individual systems, but because of its communication patterns. After GhostNet, it became clear that detecting data traffic between compromised hosts and the command and control server or servers was more effective than locating individual pieces of increasingly customized and hard-to-find client-based malware. McAfee employed that method and traced traffic to 71 organizations in 14 countries (Table 9.1).[7]

Shady RAT came on the heels of another McAfee report, Night Dragon, which detailed a campaign of cyber espionage activity directed at companies in the energy sector. McAfee's Night Dragon report went as far as the company was likely willing to go in making attribution as to the source of that campaign. As remedy for compromise via the RAT employed in the Night Dragon campaign, it recommended the following action:

[C]onfigure intrusion detection system (IDS) rules to detect the noted signatures . . . and monitor DNS for outbound communications to dynamic *DNS addresses resolving to or pathed back as suballocated to servers in China,* where the company's name or common abbreviation forms the first part of the address. (author's italics)[8]

As with Night Dragon, culpability for Shady RAT also appeared to rest with China. Some targets were similar to those in the Citizen Lab Ghost-Net project. There was a considerable effort in the campaign to target the International Olympic Committee, the World Anti-Doping Agency, and

Table 9.1

Organizations Targeted in Shady RAT Campaign

Shady RAT Targets		
Country	Number of Victims	Type of Organization(s)
United States	49	Real Estate; Federal, State, and Local Government; Defense; Electronics; Accounting; Think Tank; IT; Nonprofit; Communications; News & Media; Energy
Canada	4	Government; IT; International Sport
Taiwan	3	Electronics; Government; International Sport
South Korea	2	Steel; Construction
Japan	2	Undisclosed
Switzerland	2	International Sport; International Organization
United Kingdom	2	Computer Security; Defense
Indonesia	1	International Sport
Vietnam	1	Electronics
Denmark	1	Satellite Communications
Singapore	1	Electronics
Hong Kong	1	News & Media
Germany	1	Accounting
India	1	Government

Source: Alperovitch, Dmitri. *Revealed: Operation Shady RAT.* Vol. 3. McAfee, 2011.

the Olympic committees of several East Asian nations. Compromises by Shady RAT extended back to 2006. With Beijing hosting the 2008 Olympic Summer Games, strong circumstantial connection between China and Shady RAT could be inferred.

HACKING BACK

Following the McAfee studies, industry reports of cyber campaigns against industry designed to purloin proprietary information, communications, and planning documents became commonplace. China's activities in this area were described as "noisy" as opposed to those of Russia, the other major adversary nation-state heavily engaged in cyber espionage against the United States and its allies.[9] Noisy or not, the sophistication of cyber espionage campaigns aimed at Western public and private institutions increased year after year. Events continued to occur, and sophistication grew. An exemplar of the trend was the compromise of encryption and security firm RSA Security in 2012. The compromise of RSA's security technology rendered an entire layer of computer security useless until its discovery.

That RSA's data protection products were compromised sent shockwaves through the security industry. A division of the EMC Corporation, RSA was built on the namesakes of its creators, Ron Rivest, Adi Shamir, and Leonard Adelman, developers of the encryption algorithm entitled with the first letters of each man's last name. Beyond the algorithm and the company's suite of security products, RSA also built what is the world's largest computer security conference, a trade show with typical attendance in excess of 20,000. That there could be a major breach of RSA's enterprise security was surprising, but even worse, those who got inside RSA were able to collect "information [that] could potentially be used to reduce the effectiveness of a current two-factor authentication implementation as part of a broader attack."[10] The efficacy of RSA's SecureID number generator, a device used to add an additional layer of security for digital authentication for online access, had been compromised. SecureID was widely employed throughout industry in the United States, in the defense sector and in many others as well.[11]

While the compromise to RSA's systems was a significant event, far more worrisome were the breaches that potentially occurred at companies dependent on SecureID tokens for secure access. At the time of the RSA breach, SecureID was nearly ubiquitous among systems administrators and IT executives across industry. The tokens were swiftly replaced. Issuing replacements and instituting other actions to mitigate the hack cost the company $66 million.[12] With the hardware component of the mitigation job completed, RSA launched a campaign to educate its customers on how it had been hacked and what safeguards it would be instituting to protect itself and them. The future of the company depended on it.

RSA Security had been compromised through a highly effective campaign. The attack was delivered via what is perhaps the greatest vulnerability in contemporary business, email.[13] Like most other firms in its field, RSA was highly dependent upon email to conduct its internal and external business.[14] As RSA Security's employees used email extensively, it was the vector targeted by those who compromised it. Emails containing messages and files of likely interest to specifically targeted users were delivered, and once those files were opened, system compromise at RSA Security was possible and occurred.[15] While many have speculated on who perpetrated the RSA hack, most fingers point to Russia, or more likely China.

Rising awareness of Chinese economic and political espionage drew attention from beyond parochial computer and information security circles. A *Bloomberg Businessweek* issue featured the cover headline "Hey China Stop Stealing Our Stuff!" An incident of alleged corporate espionage undertaken within a joint venture between American Semiconductor Corporation (AMSC) and Sinovel Wind Group, a Chinese firm, was detailed. AMSC produced the control system computers for Sinovel's wind turbines and Sinovel was the company's largest customer. Sinovel needed AMSC's control system computing systems to drive its turbines. AMSC saw the relationship as symbiotic, its CEO positing, "We ... saw it as a symbiotic relationship of having China's low manufacturing cost coupled with Western technology ... We would grow as they grew."[16] Burned by the experience, AMSC pulled out of China to focus on other markets. Much as Google had indicated in 2010, the price of doing business there was potentially just too high.

As international business ventures strained under the stress of cyber espionage, the question of how companies could take a more proactive stance on the problem began to assume prominence in the cybersecurity debate. New security firms rose to prominence. They purported to understand not just the malware as the big antivirus firms did, but those actually doing the hacking. If companies were beginning to understand that they were being hacked, what was being compromised and taken, and how it was occurring, these new firms sought to illuminate who was doing the hacking and if possible provide options beyond detecting attacks and mitigating them.

By 2012, several companies were cultivating the concept of a more active defense against cyber attack. Perhaps most aggressive in rhetoric among them was CrowdStrike, which began touting the ability to "hack back" or offer an "active defense" against cyber attacks aimed at corporations.[17] Staffed by former FBI cyber lawyers and investigators as well as former McAfee employee Dmitri Alperovitch, CrowdStrike advocated for bolder actions by victims. The company's president Shawn Henry offered an analogy in what his firm offered. "Not only do we put out the fire, but we also look for the arsonist." While direct actions of "hacking back" in violation of U.S. or international law were disavowed by the company, the possibility that it could make life hard for hackers it identified was not.[18]

Hacking was labeled digital vigilantism by many in the security community; German computer scientist Sandro Gaycken argued that with state capacity to deliver redress for hacking across sovereign boundaries so poor, other actors were needed to provide deterrence or deliver policing.

One of the reasons for using illegal means is that the state just isn't efficient. The prosecutors aren't good enough, partly because they have cheap, ineffective tools to work with. Investigators need more means, and more highly qualified people, to be able to work in a more targeted fashion ... From that perspective, vigilantism could seem justified. It's that way with self-defense: if the state is not there, and I'm attacked, I can hit back.[19]

It was a controversial view. Robert Clark, the Army Cyber Command's chief legal counsel, argued that corporate officials were angry. He summarized their mood with the view, " 'How do I hack back? I want to smack somebody,' " held within corporate circles regarding cyber attacks.[20] A gray area existed in whether security investigators could penetrate the systems of attackers, at least to collect intelligence, but perhaps going further and applying that intelligence to operations designed to disrupt criminal hacking organizations operating in Eastern Europe or Asia.

APT 1

One corporate report on cyber counterintelligence, going beyond the identification not only of malicious software or networks of compromised systems but of hackers—who they were, where they worked, and for whom—radically changed the discussion on active defense and the cybersecurity industry overnight. It came from the company most closely associated with the term "advanced persistent threat," perhaps the one with the best claim to its trademark if there was one, the Washington, D.C.-area cyber intelligence consultancy Mandiant.

Established in 2004, Mandiant's beginnings were in providing services to the U.S. government in cybersecurity. Its work was largely focused in supporting the FBI as its own cyber efforts coalesced, eventually with the creation of its Cyber Division. It was a cybersecurity company focusing on capacity development, not the acquisition of malware samples for antivirus programs. By 2012, with the cybersecurity merger and acquisition a hot sector, information began to circulate that the company's CEO, Kevin Mandia, was in search of a buyer. With a staff in the low hundreds, it was rumored Mandia's price for acquisition was in roughly $450 million.[21]

With Chinese hacking a significant concern, Mandiant's extensive effort in studying the problem had allowed it to amass significant expertise on hackers in the PRC, their methods, and even their identities. The company released the report "APT 1: Exposing One of China's Cyber Espionage Units" on February 18, 2013. In it the company extensively detailed the activities of a cyber element of the Chinese People's Liberation Army, Unit 61938. Based in Shanghai, APT 1's authors knew which building Unit 61938 occupied; a rough estimate of its staff size, somewhere in the hundreds; its linkages to China Telecom; and its attack methodologies.

According to the consultancy, Unit 61938 had likely compromised at least 141 companies in 20 industries, stealing massive quantities of proprietary corporate information since 2006. The average duration of compromise for Unit 61938's targets was a year, with one victim being compromised for almost five years before being detected. APT 1 attacks vacuumed up massive troves of data, often measured in terabytes, via clandestine channels employing RAT software residing on its targets' networks.[22]

The report was a bombshell. While the unit, and its higher-level administrative division of the People's Liberation Army, the General Staff Department's 3rd Department and 2nd Bureau, were not publicly acknowledged echelons of the PLA, Mandiant pursued information about it through the Chinese Internet and found the weakness of many classified cyber organizations, the need to locate and recruit staff. With HR data spilling onto the Internet, Mandiant was able to put together a picture of its staffing requirements and the skills it wanted to retain or cultivate, including English skills as well as those in computer hacking.[23]

Unit 61938's operators often purportedly identified themselves as members of the Comment Crew or Comment Group. Mandiant provided three concrete personas of Unit 61938 operators, one of them through a linkage to Zhang Zhaozong, a retired PLA Navy rear admiral, military academic, and author of articles including "Network Warfare" and "Winning the Information War." Finding Comment Crew members required effort in understanding the underground chat rooms and online forums of the Chinese Web. The public outing of these intelligence operators was significant, but even more interesting to the security was the efficacy of their methods.

While Unit 61938 had been enormously capable in compromising corporate networks and purloining sensitive data from them, Mandiant could rest assured that it was telling the world little new about the method of its success. As one computer scientist opined, "What is remarkable about APT 1 is how effective they [the Chinese] have been with relatively primitive methods."[24] Unit 61938 got superb results employing well-known practices including extensive use of spearphishing email techniques, breaching unpatched or out-of-date systems, and publicly available privilege escalation tools able to subvert system functionality and allow enduring unauthorized remote access to sensitive corporate systems and accounts, including email servers. Although others were doubtlessly engaged in cyber espionage, APT 1 offered a damning case that China was using government resources to steal massive quantities of corporate proprietary data in the United States and its Western allies. Data could easily be gotten out of corporations by cyber means; what the United States was also learning was that critically sensitive data could also be just as easily taken by insiders.

MANNING

While the cyber espionage activities of China and other nation-states were receiving considerable attention in the United States, a second problem arose for the U.S. government and firms it depended upon to perform many of its critical functions, especially in the areas of international affairs and national security. While leaking sensitive or classified information was nothing new in the United States, the advent of widely networked computing made getting sensitive data, copying it, and sharing it with the world far easier. Daniel Ellsberg and his colleague Anthony Russo, both employees of the RAND Corporation, manually photocopied over 4,100 pages of documents that eventually were leaked to the *New York Times* in 1971 and came to be known as the *Pentagon Papers*.[25] Almost 40 years later, the U.S. wars in Iraq and Afghanistan had grown unpopular with Americans as well. By February 2008, 54 percent of Americans polled in Pew survey stated the decision to use military force in Iraq was wrong. (Four years earlier, as the Iraqi insurgency began to grow, support for intervention in Iraq hovered around 55 percent, while almost three quarters of Americans supported intervention in March 2003, the month U.S. and coalition forces invaded.)[26]

Barack Obama ran his presidential campaign through the primaries in 2008 often criticizing the decision to invade Iraq and in particular the vote of his chief rival, Hillary Clinton, in favor of invasion in 2003. Obama criticized the warrantless wiretapping program and offered an agenda that would remove U.S. forces from Iraq in his first term. He also offered a platform emphasizing increased transparency in government, and after his election, John Podesta, director of the transition team, stated it would be "the most open and transparent transition in history."[27]

Transparency and openness were important themes of the time. The George W. Bush presidency was considered obsessively secretive on matters of state and security while at the same time allowing considerable room for political lobbying often in pursuit of lucrative contracts.[28] Beyond the backlash against the war in Iraq and handling of the economy, other forces for openness were at work. One was Wikipedia, a free online encyclopedia written, edited, and moderated by volunteers that was scoffed at and criticized by academics and print encyclopedias, but had all but run its competitors out of business in a few short years after gaining popularity in the mid-2000s. Wikipedia's core message, enunciated by its co-founder Jimmy Wales, that "The radical idea behind Wikipedia is for all of us to imagine a world in which every single person on the planet is given free access to the sum of all human knowledge and that's what we are doing."[29] Wales, a businessman with a finance degree, had stepped forward to be an advocate for free and open content, becoming the "benevolent despot" of the Wikipedia project.[30]

Wales's message cohered with beliefs held by adherents to the free software movement, the concept that "information wants to be free." Another charismatic figure, Julian Assange, combined the message of the open source and free software/content communities with the zealous pursuit of transparent and open government. In 2006, with a set of collaborators, Assange, an Australian, established WikiLeaks, an organization whose objective stands today as "to bring important news and information to the public [through] an innovative, secure and anonymous way for sources to leak information to our journalists."[31] Unlike Wales, Assange's motivations were not free information for everyone, but to provide an avenue not just for whistle blowers to call foul but rather to lift the veil of secrecy from government, potentially all governments, as well as other organizations. Assange, the public face of the organization, claimed its "main purpose is to create an 'uncensorable' version of Wikipedia where people around the world could post leaked documents and other things governments didn't want seen, without fear of the material being suppressed or the source being traced."[32]

WikiLeaks' first major submission to be reported on publicly came in 2007. The leaked document was a 2003 U.S. government manual regarding the operation of the detention center constructed at Guantánamo, Cuba. Controversial in it was a directive that detainees at the facility would not be allowed access to monitors from the International Committee of the Red Cross.[33] Early in 2008, it released a set of videos documenting unrest in Tibet while facing an increasingly stiff set of legal challenges from the U.S. government after WikiLeaks posted allegedly confidential, personally identifiable customer information from a Swiss bank. But efforts to shut down the wikileaks.org domain name were frustrated by its replication in foreign Internet domains.[34] While the United States could ask the operators of the U.S. Top Level Domain (TLD) to shut down the address, it would have a far more difficult time in convincing many or all foreign TLD operators to do the same. Shutting down WikiLeaks became a multilateral, international issue.

More leaks to the site followed. WikiLeaks called for submission of reports produced by the Congressional Research Service (CRS). Unclassified and often publicly available via transparency websites including the Federation of American Scientists Project on Government Secrecy, CRS reports are explicitly meant for readers within the U.S. Congress, its members and staff, not the public.[35] WikiLeaks had thus far received small batches of documents, not massive troves of them. The Defense Department fretted at the operational security risk of WikiLeaks' continuing effort to acquire and publish secret documents about the organization, producing a report on the organization's potential threat to Army operations in 2008. The report was then leaked to WikiLeaks and published by the organization in 2010.[36] But the first piece of WikiLeaks' massive haul of classified and sensitive U.S. government documents came in April 2010 with the release of gun camera video footage taken in Iraq from a U.S. Army attack helicopter showing the killing of civilians including a pair of journalists from the Reuters news service.[37] The video represented the tip of the iceberg.

Two months after the video's release came the news of the arrest of a U.S. Army intelligence specialist, PFC Bradley (later Chelsea) Manning, for leaking it. Manning had boasted to Adrian Lamo, a hacker sympathetic to WikiLeaks, that he was behind the leak of the Iraq video as well as another video of an air strike in Afghanistan. But his third item was far more ominous. He claimed to have given 260,000 diplomatic cables and classified military reporting to WikiLeaks as well.[38]

WikiLeaks had indeed received a massive set of documents, so large that it must have been inclined to distribute the job of reading them. On July 25, 2010, three newspapers—the *New York Times*, the *Guardian*, and *Der Spiegel*—announced that they had received thousands of military incident and intelligence reports, over 92,000 in total, many of them classified.[39] The documents were a window to the Defense and State Departments' picture of its wars in Iraq and Afghanistan. All three papers began producing stories on items contained within the release, but waited to do so until WikiLeaks published the entire set on its website. The Obama administration condemned the act.[40]

Damaging as the release of DoD reports was to the U.S. government, the release of State Department cables overshadowed them. Where Manning had held access to military information regarding operations in the Central Command area of responsibility, his access to cables was of global scope via the SIPRNet DoD classified computer network. On November 29, 2010, the public came to know that what Manning had boasted to Adrian Lamo, his unauthorized copying and passage of more than one quarter million U.S. diplomatic cables to WikiLeaks, was indeed true. Five papers, the three in receipt of the prior release of the military documents as well as Spain's *El Pais* and France's *Le Monde*, received large numbers of diplomatic cables from WikiLeaks on which to report. As one summary assessed, the cables offered "an unprecedented look at back-room bargaining by embassies around the world, brutally candid views of foreign leaders and frank assessments of nuclear and terrorist threats."[41]

While the papers did not take lightly the responsibility for reporting on the massive number of classified cables, the damage to U.S. interests and relationships produced by their release was enormous nonetheless.[42] (Perhaps the only significant upside noted in the press was the high quality of writing by officers of the Foreign Service.)[43] Again, as with the leaked DoD reports, WikiLeaks again released the raw content, the cables themselves, on its website, although only after the chain of custody for the encrypted document archive and the encryption passphrase for it broke down in a series of errors and an ongoing feud between Assange and WikiLeaks' German spokesman, Daniel Domscheit-Berg. The entire archive of some 251,287 cables was made fully available via the WikiLeaks site in September 2011.[44] WikiLeaks' " 'cutting-edge cryptographic technologies' [used] to receive material electronically" had failed to protect the content that it had been given.[45]

No comprehensive review of the WikiLeaks diplomatic cable breach has been made public. However, PFC Manning would eventually stand trial. Consideration of the cable breach's importance on international affairs received great attention. John Kerry, who agreed with the generally damaging sentiment regarding the cable breach in Washington's foreign policy circles, was later graded on his potential abilities as when nominated for secretary of state in 2013. State reporting on his work as an international negotiator during his 27 years on the Senate Foreign Relations Committee, which he chaired from 2009 until his departure from the body, was available in assessing his suitability for the top diplomat slot.[46] WikiLeaks gave the world a strong understanding of the inside baseball of the State Department, but there was evidence of the breach having impact on world events, chief among them the Arab Spring uprisings that sprang up only weeks after the cables began being reported.

In Tunisia, the first of the states to face massive popular uprising against a nondemocratic leader, evidence of the regime's incredible accumulation of wealth was exposed. One reporter postulated, "it was clear that the diplomatic cables had sparked a realisation [sic] with the Tunisian people that if the world knew and arguably empathized, then 'enough was enough.' "[47] The Lebanese *al-Akhbar* newspaper's website was blocked by the Tunisian government after it published reporting of a cable characterizing the opulence and corruption of President Zine al-Abidine Ben Ali and his inner circle of power brokers as well as their increasingly heavy-handed means of coping with dissent.[48] Detailed reporting of corruption at the top quite possibly "stirred things up." As one Tunisian military officer commented in a military-military exchange shortly after the revolution, the regime's excess was known, but that officials from the United States could characterize it as so excessive, itself a very wealthy country, was especially significant. When the call came for the battalion and company commanders of the Tunisian army to quell the uprising, they refused.[49]

OPEN SECRETS

How to remedy the repeated, seemingly chronic loss of sensitive information, from sources inside and outside the U.S. government, grew unabated through the first term of the Obama administration. The head of the NSA intelligence officials decried hacking the greatest transfer of wealth in history, with the theft of intellectual property a significant slice of the total.[50] For the Chinese hackers, the United States held little recourse. Although the APT 1 report identified three hackers ostensibly working within a professional military cyber intelligence organization in the PLA, getting at them was another matter. China's military hackers may have been fairly easy for Mandiant to spot, but not for the U.S. government to stop, prosecute, or neutralize.

Nonetheless, Attorney General Eric Holder produced an indictment by grand jury in the Western District of Pennsylvania of five members of Unit 61398: Wang Dong, Sun Kailiang, Wen Xinyu, Huang Zhenyu, and Gu Chunhui. In the May 19, 2014, indictment, victims of the Chinese hackers included Westinghouse, Solar Wind AG, U.S. Steel, Allegheny Technologies, Alcoa, and a major trade union.[51] Stymied in talks with the Chinese, the United States moved to legal prosecution. The indictments were part of a "strategy by the Obama administration to hold China accountable for ... a growing campaign of commercial cyberspying."[52] One of the indicted was Wang Dong (a.k.a. Ugly Gorilla), who had been previously fingered in the APT 1 report. But unless any of the five traveled to the United States or another state willing to detain and extradite them to it, the chance of moving forward on the case was essentially zero.

With Manning, the U.S. Army had recourse. He was arrested during his tour in Iraq after travel to the United States. The extensive set of materials he had given to WikiLeaks were unknown to the general public until months after his arrest. Manning had boasted to Lamo, but the leaked gun camera footage was only the weakest of hints with regard to exactly how much sensitive and classified material he had copied from the DoD servers receiving State Department cable traffic on a daily basis through the Net Centric Diplomacy (NCD) program. While safeguards on the NCD cables at the DoD were doubtlessly weak, the atmosphere of "need-to-share" trumped traditional biases in conserving information and provision of strong powers of originator consent with regard to sharing of classified material. Indeed, the only public acknowledgment of information security risks in NCD were those regarding controls for personally identifiable information of American citizens prohibited by the Privacy Act.

When asked in a 2011 congressional hearing on WikiLeaks regarding safeguards on the NCD database, Under Secretary for Management Patrick Kennedy stated, "It is the receiving agency's responsibility to secure and make accessible the received information based on agreed upon terms. Recipient agencies are expected to maintain adequate security for their own systems and networks."[53] State's dissemination controls for cables weren't mapped over to the DoD; thus, a single low-level analyst with access to the DoD's SIPRNet secret-level computer network could access all of the NCD database's content. Anyone at DoD with collateral classified secret access could read NCD, and apparently copy it as well.

Punishment for Manning did come. Tried in a military court at Fort Meade, headquarters to the National Security Agency and DoD Cyber Command, Manning admitted guilt to several charges, and was convicted of multiple counts of espionage, theft, and fraud on July 30, 2013. Manning, who had by then chosen to identify himself as female and named himself Chelsea, avoided conviction on the most serious charge, that of aiding the enemy.[54] Less than a month after his conviction he was sentenced to 35 years in prison.

Assange, the recipient of Manning's archive, was also pursued through legal channels. The U.S. government pursued action to deprive WikiLeaks of both its capacity to host its data on the Internet and also to receive financial support. While in Britain, Sweden requested Assange's presence to submit to questioning regarding charges of sexual assault. Released on bond, he eventually chose to seek refuge in the Ecuadorean embassy in June 2012. Those who raised his bond, including members of the British aristocracy, a Nobel Prize–winning biologist, and several others, eventually lost £200,000 they collectively raised in bail.[55] WikiLeaks remains in operation, but has not garnered the same level of attention since receiving the Manning archive.

The WikiLeaks episode and foreign cyber espionage activities show an important weakness in U.S. efforts to protect information. U.S. government agencies suffer from a serious insider threat problem, in that trusted public servants have leaked and continue to leak large quantities of sensitive information. At the same time the U.S. government and U.S. firms continue to be routinely probed and compromised by foreign states and nonstate actors determined to purloin data that are useful to political and economic objectives.

It remains unclear that any significant improvement is being achieved in warding off foreign intelligence services cyber espionage activities or in convincing disgruntled or disheartened insiders from making visible what they believe is necessary to receive public attention. Manning, although convicted on espionage charges, is not truly a spy. He did not take his documents to Moscow or Beijing. Nonetheless, both these countries have built impressive cyber espionage arms capable of stealing and keeping secret what they want while making public what is useful to put in the public sphere, such as the telephone conversation between Assistant Secretary of State Victoria Nuland and U.S. Ambassador to Ukraine Geoffrey Pyatt.[56] Russia, at least, has shown that it can steal information and it can also make good use of it for propaganda purposes when necessary as well. This is something the U.S. foreign policy establishment appears unwilling to do thus far.

OPM

For the billions spent and thousands of employees and contractors it has thrown against the problem, the U.S. government seems no better to cope with the cybersecurity issues it faced in 2015 than it did in 2005. No development is more emblematic of this truth than the breach of employee records stored at the Office of Personnel Management (OPM) that came to light in June 2015. The OPM breach, in which the employee records and job applicants of 21.5 million Americans were likely delivered to a foreign power, represents a catastrophic development for the government and its employees.

As the centralized human resources agency for the U.S. government, OPM holds several important roles in announcing federal jobs, managing pension benefits, overseeing training, and, most importantly, conducting the background clearance investigations for millions of federal employees and government contractors. OPM began as the Civil Service Commission, an organization tasked with professionalizing the government workforce following the assassination of President James Garfield by a job seeker on July 2, 1881. Upon establishment in 1883, the commission was run by no less capable an individual than Theodore Roosevelt. It would eventually be reorganized as the Office of Personnel Management in 1978 and its mandate grew over time to cover employees beyond those in the Civil Service alone.

By 2005, the pressing issue for OPM was clearing of employees, both government hires and contractors, to replace retirees and staff up federal agencies with cleared workers engaged in counter-terrorism, homeland security, and intelligence activities. (The CIA, however, continued to maintain its own, independent personnel system holding its records and clearing staff internally.) OPM's major issue was in pulling down the backlog of employees requiring extensive background investigations to perform duties requiring secret- or top secret-level security clearances regarding access to classified information.

The starting point for such investigations is the federal Standard Form 86 (SF-86). It is a 127-page document, filled with demographic information, job history, record of acquaintances and family ties, biographical data, and, perhaps most importantly, derogatory information that the candidate provides about himself or herself. The SF-86 is the document employed by OPM investigators in their reporting on job candidates' worthiness to carry a security clearance. These investigators then interview a dozen or more associates of the clearance candidate, as well as neighbors and other acquaintances. In tandem, an employee's SF-86 and investigation report represent a comprehensive view of the person as well as any perceived weaknesses or vulnerabilities that could factor into the final decision to clear the candidate. It is an intimate view of the individual that few other employers could hope or want to hold.

Through the last decade, OPM drove down its backlog of investigations, migrated contract investigation positions to government billets, and pushed to centralize employee background information. In 2004, clearance investigations for the DoD were moved to OPM, in an attempt to streamline the process. While investigations typically required 140 or more days to complete in FY 2005, the agency had pushed that figure down to less than 40 days in FY 2012, a tremendous improvement. But DoD officials questioned the quality of investigations undertaken by OPM on its abbreviated schedule as well as gaps in employee background information reported to it.[57]

In addition to carrying out the preponderance of clearances, OPM also began work to centralize its database infrastructure. In May 2014, the agency announced it was working at "streamlining a database with records on feds and contractors with access to security clearance investigative records, with the apparent goal of putting an additional layer of security over the actual contents of government background investigations."[58] OPM intended to keep "security background files on a protected local network or in a locked storage facility."[59] The consolidation of this data represented a potentially enormous single target for data theft by any party interested in knowing the makeup of the U.S. government–cleared workforce, including each and every person composing it.

Taken were the contents from millions of submissions to the Electronic Questionnaires for Investigations Processing (e-QIP) database. Up until 2003, prospective federal employees entering cleared positions submitted their SF-86 on paper.[60] The e-QIP system allowed job seekers as well as serving employees recertifying their clearances to access it conveniently and easily via the Internet. (e-QIP is currently "accessible only for limited user testing. The application will remain inaccessible to most users until testing is complete.")[61] Yes, e-QIP employed Transport Layer Security encryption between the user's browser and the Web server, but how those contents were protected once inside OPM is another matter. It appears that even the most basic practices of data encryption and obfuscation had failed to be instituted. Social Security numbers of every individual were stored in unencrypted plaintext, for instance.[62]

The defenses for such a repository should, no doubt, have been formidable. Unfortunately, they were not. OPM's employee records were stored in a manner that appears to violate everything from NIST controls and guidelines to federal contracting law. While details continue to emerge regarding the OPM breach, testimony by agency leadership and public acknowledgments indicate that there was a massive compromise of the OPM's systems, likely by the agents of a foreign power. A single word appears repeatedly in appraisals of the OPM breach: catastrophic. J. David Cox, president of the American Federation of Government Employees (AFGE), called the event an "abysmal failure," and former NSA counsel Joel Brenner declared it "a gold mine for a foreign intelligence service."[63] Another AFGE official acknowledged, " 'We've been told that they got the whole personnel data central file.' "[64]

How the breach at OPM was discovered remains a point of controversy. While the *New York Times* reported that DHS's EINSTEIN network security platform found it, this has been debated. CyTech Services, a security company based in northern Virginia, claimed the following in a press release about the demonstration of its CyFIR incident response software:

Using our endpoint vulnerability assessment methodology, CyFIR quickly identified a set of unknown processes running on a limited set of endpoints. This information was immediately provided to the OPM security staff and was ultimately revealed to be malware. CyTech is unaware if the OPM security staff had previously identified these processes. CyTech Services remained on site to assist with the breach response, provided immediate assistance, and performed incident response services supporting OPM until May 1, 2015. During this time, CyTech provided on-site support at OPM to the OPM security personnel as well as representatives of the FBI and US-CERT.[65]

An OPM spokesman refuted CyTech's claim, declaring "that CyTech was somehow responsible for the discovery of the intrusion into OPM's network during a product demonstration is inaccurate."[66]

Such a product demonstration could have detected the breach, as security products and tools often win sales in such real-world demonstrations. Such demonstrations often do locate indicators of compromise, often on real working systems. Indeed, detection of vulnerabilities or breaches by such products is considered the surest path to getting customer attention.[67] It is important to note that many security products are driven by databases of known compromises, vulnerabilities, or malware and that if the indicator is not in the database, then no alarm may sound. The same goes for intrusion detection tools, which are only as effective as the rules they adhere to in analyzing network traffic or computer activity. More often than not, breaches are found when disruptions in ordinary systems occur or analysts and administrators observe unusual behavior not detected by security services or tools. CyFIR is a forensics tool, used to find indications on systems after they have been compromised. Knowing exactly what found the OPM breach may be a subject of some dispute; its impact is not.

Getting to the bottom of how the OPM breach occurred is complicated by various and sometimes conflicting reports. What rendered OPM vulnerable in some part has to do with how the federal government conducts major IT projects. Much as the U.S. government buys all manner of hardware from firms in the private sector, from automobiles to military aircraft, the same goes for IT hardware and even IT services. As mentioned earlier, the government buys commercial, off-the-shelf (COTS) IT products, such as PCs, mobile phones, and servers, to perform business functions, just as they are in the private sector. These devices are largely run on unclassified networks and are connected to the Internet by commercial ISPs in a manner similar to private firms and other organizations.

In addition, the government contracts companies to build the pieces of functionality desired to deliver business functions, like the operation of large databases, to private firms. Those firms are hired to collect project requirements and deliver the desired functionality to the customer agency. Contractors often work shoulder to shoulder with agency personnel and have similar levels of access to networks and other computing resources as federal employees. They carry contractor credentials (both physical and digital) that grant them access to buildings and systems so that they may produce the deliverables dictated under the terms of the project. This allows agencies to dynamically supplement their workforce with IT workers when they are needed rather than maintaining permanent development staff in-house. Just as in the corporate sector, the work is outsourced.

So while OPM was centralizing its personnel database, it did so with the support of IT services firms who translated OPM requirements into integrated systems of software and hardware to deliver the desired functionality. One of the firms contracted to provide IT integration services to OPM was KeyPoint Government Solutions, a spinoff of Kroll, Inc., a firm expert in corporate investigations and due diligence. KeyPoint was the outgrowth of Kroll's government background investigation business, which grew enormously as it provided background checks for the Transportation Security Administration and other DHS components.[68] "When the OPM breach was discovered in April [2015], investigators found that KeyPoint security credentials were used to breach the OPM system."[69] Former OPM director Katherine Archuleta stated in congressional testimony, "I want to be very clear that while the adversary compromised a KeyPoint user credential to gain access to OPM's network, we don't have any evidence that would suggest that KeyPoint as a company was responsible or directly involved in the intrusion[.]"[70] Archuleta should have been concerned about KeyPoint, as the company was breached in 2014 and the records of some 48,000 federal employees were compromised.[71]

Entering with valid KeyPoint credentials, the hackers who purloined OPM's repository of personnel records found an agency sorely deficient in its efforts to protect its critically important store of records. An OPM internal audit report regarding FISMA compliance enumerated these deficiencies, and likely also provided valuable intelligence to those who breached its systems. The audit report exposed a set of gross lapses in information security practice at the agency. The audit found, "Eleven major OPM information systems are operating without a valid Authorization." These systems did not achieve the baseline level of security required of federal civilian information systems mandated under FISMA. OPM did not maintain "a comprehensive inventory of servers, databases, and network devices," meaning that it did not know what machines resided within its facilities and did not utilize the agency network, or even the full composition of the network. Multifactor authentication had yet to be deployed in accordance with an Office of Management and Budget requirement. And finally, at the time of the audit, "Several information security agreements between OPM and contractor operated information systems [had] expired."[72]

All of these weaknesses meant that OPM, despite holding the central repository for every federal employee from facilities managers to intelligence officers, was an extraordinarily easy target. It did not know the IT resources it had, it did not meet minimum standards in protecting them, and it was operating at a reduced capacity to detect attempts to compromise its systems. *OPM was grossly negligent in its own efforts to secure its critically important repository of employee data.*

Furthermore, information security assets held by other government agencies failed to detect the breach. DHS's EINSTEIN system may (or may not) have detected the breach, but it certainly didn't prevent it from happening. While EINSTEIN is able to monitor traffic at the trusted Internet gateways employed by the U.S. government, it delivers an incomplete solution. But EINSTEIN is not adapting to the evolving capabilities of those attempting to gain access to government systems. "Put simply, as new capabilities for Einstein are being rolled out, they're not keeping pace with the types of threats now facing federal agencies."[73] Once again, we observe another event that demonstrates how the party on the offense is able to defeat the defenses emplaced to protect digital information of great value.

And once again, attribution is leveled at China. Although Admiral Mike Rogers, the head of U.S. Cyber Command, declined to identify the perpetrator, China is again identified as the most likely culpable party.[74] The OPM breach is yet another likely success for Unit 61398 or the PLA or another unit. OPM's breach shared characteristics with those of Anthem and Premera Blue Cross, two of the nation's largest health insurance providers, two incidents linked to China.[75] As the OPM breach news broke, Ellen Nakashima of the *Washington Post* asserted that "Hackers working for the Chinese state breached the computer system of the Office of Personnel Management." She went on to assert that "It was the second major intrusion of the same agency by China in less than a year and the second significant foreign breach into U.S. government networks in recent months."[76]

But U.S. government response was curious. Reports emerged that President Obama was mulling over sanctions against those who perpetrated the OPM breach. Sanctions "could be used by the government to target hackers and their associates."[77] But the administration took the unusual step to not publicly level blame on China as it had done before, or as it did with North Korea regarding Sony after the 2014 breach at the entertainment company was publicly attributed to Pyongyang with sanctions following. While sanctions were still under consideration, a number of potential issues were raised as standing in the way of publicly blaming China on the OPM breach. Sources stated the U.S. response was tempered by a desire not to disclose sources and methods in attribution of the attack and the pursuit of a criminal investigation on the matter. Former NSA director Michael Hayden offered, " 'I don't blame the Chinese for this at all. If I [as head of the NSA] could have done it, I would have done it in a heartbeat. And I would have not been required to call downtown, either.' "[78] If responsible, the Chinese weren't doing anything the NSA wouldn't have tried or hadn't already accomplished.

OPM's breach is yet another security failure for major U.S. government computer system, employed to store millions of sensitive records. The compromise of OPM contractors USIS and KeyPoint should have set off alarms inside OPM. They did not. Basic security principles were overlooked and best practices ignored. Although OPM director Katherine Archuleta would eventually resign because of the breach, here remarks to Congress did little to placate members of the government oversight committee. Archuleta asserted the following:

But for the fact that OPM implemented new, more stringent security tools in its environment, we would have never known that malicious activity had previously existed on the network, and would not have been able to share that information for the protection of the rest of the Federal Government.[79]

In response, Jason Chaffetz, the chair of the House committee, decried "negligence" in senior management, and calling for them to be sacked. The Utah legislator did little to contain his disgust on the state of affairs in OPM's IT, fuming, " 'They're still operating on a COBOL operating system, for gosh sakes.' "[80] When it was hacked, OPM was transmitting and storing critically important data on systems that were artifacts of pre-Internet computing. One can only hope such practices will change.

CHAPTER 10

Snowden

No single name has expanded the discussion and heightened awareness on the issues of cybersecurity and online privacy than Edward Snowden. Nothing made this point clearer to the author than a short taxicab ride discussion during a trip to the University of Toronto's Munk School for a Connaught Institute research seminar in July 2013. On the cab ride, the driver, a gregarious native of the city possessing a strong Ontario accent, asked what the event would cover. I explained regarding Internet surveillance, cybersecurity, and various other computing and society topics. His response of acknowledgment said it all. "You mean the Snowden business, eh?"

Considered here are the facts we uniformly know about what Snowden took and gave to journalistic outlets, primarily the *Guardian* newspaper and documentary filmmaker Laura Poitras. Beyond that, there are manifold issues to consider. Initial outcry on what Snowden leaked emphasized the privacy and civil liberties rights of U.S. citizens. In addition, there was the issue of international fallout and relations between the United States and its allies. Also, there was the issue of relations between the U.S. government and the technology industry centered in Silicon Valley as well as the scientific community in cryptography. Finally, one must consider the activities and motivations of the Chinese and Russian governments in the conduct of the Snowden affair.

HNL–HKG–SVO

Edward Snowden, a fairly low-level contract employee of the National Security Agency, has become an iconic figure in the battle for cyberspace. Setting aside all discussion of Snowden the person, and why he shared a massive trove of classified Department of Defense information with several journalists, the objective facts of his actions need review. How things unfolded between Honolulu, Hong Kong, and eventually Moscow is a narrative unto itself. The psychology of Snowden and his motivations are worthy of much deeper independent study. That said, these are the facts of a 35-day journey from the most secretive agency of the U.S. Intelligence Community to his asylum in Vladimir Putin's Russia.

On May 20, 2013, Snowden boarded a flight from Honolulu to Hong Kong and brought with him a considerable archive of digital documents produced by or for the NSA, its British counterpart GCHQ, and other Western signals intelligence agencies. One week later, filmmaker Laura Poitras along with *Guardian* journalist Ewan MacAskill and blogger and columnist Glenn Greenwald met Snowden at the Mira Hotel in Kowloon. When the four met, Snowden passed a large set of classified data to Poitras and the reporters. On June 5, the *Guardian* published the first exclusive story generated from the archive.[1] Four days later, on June 9, the release of a video of Snowden shot by Poitras made his identity public.[2] The following day, he checked out of his hotel and separated from Poitras, Greenwald, and MacAskill in the custody of Hong Kong attorney Jonathan Man.

Nearly two weeks after departing the Mira Hotel with civil rights lawyer Man, Snowden boarded a flight to Moscow, operated by Russian flag carrier Aeroflot, arriving at Sheremetyevo Airport on June 23.[3] At the Moscow airport, he remained in a transit facility, his U.S. passport canceled by the State Department, until August 1, when the Russian government issued him a temporary entry document.[4] He has remained in Russia since. Those are the facts. What he did and why he did it remain the subject of considerable debate. But his actions in leaking a massive quantity of U.S. and allied signals intelligence information had a seismic impact in the geopolitics of cyberspace.

THE LEAK

In a media atmosphere where a single classified U.S. government document had the potential to produce a significant news story, the Snowden archive represented a journalistic treasure trove. After Snowden's flight, "an NSA investigation . . . established the chronology of the copying of 1.7 million documents that were stolen from the Signals Intelligence Center in Hawaii."[5] PowerPoint briefing slide decks, reports, and memoranda became centerpieces of news stories for the reporters at the *Guardian*. Snowden had told filmmaker Laura Poitras, who documented her meeting with the NSA contractor and the reporters in Hong Kong, that a team of journalists would be required to sort through the massive quantity of information he had taken from U.S. government computer systems.[6] Greenwald and MacAskill had several days to comb through the archive before the *Guardian* ran its first piece.

Greenwald chose to lead with a story regarding the U.S. government's order, signed by a Foreign Intelligence Surveillance Court (FISC) judge, Roger Vinson, requiring Verizon to provide ongoing telephony metadata. It called for the company to produce " 'all call detail records or "telephony metadata" created by Verizon for communications between the United States and abroad' or 'wholly within the United States, including local telephone calls.' "[7] This order shed new light on the allegations made and evidence provided by Mark Klein regarding surveillance undertaken in Room 641A of AT&T's Folsom Street offices in San Francisco. Greenwald's first article reintroduced the warrantless wiretapping activities of the U.S. government purportedly undertaken after the 9/11 attacks and discussion on the nature and employment of telecommunications metadata.

Next came articles from both Greenwald and Barton Gellman of the *Washington Post* on PRISM, an NSA program allegedly providing direct systems access to multiple large Internet companies including Google, Facebook, and Apple. In a slide deck verified as authentic by the *Guardian*, the PRISM program was reputedly designed to "[facilitate] extensive, in-depth surveillance on live communications and stored information," collected, saved, and transmitted by the major U.S. Internet firms.[8] Although such capabilities seemed possible and were even joked about, PRISM represented something altogether new in offering evidence of signals intelligence collection in regard to cloud computing and social media.[9]

Response to PRISM from the Silicon Valley firms identified in the NSA slide deck was emphatic in denying cooperation in the program or even complicity in it. Google was adamant in denying knowledge of PRISM, stating:

First, we have not joined any program that would give the U.S. government—or any other government—direct access to our servers. Indeed, the U.S. government does not have direct access or a "back door" to the information stored in our data centers. We had not heard of a program called PRISM until yesterday.[10]

Other companies were equally caught off guard by the capability touted in the leaked slides. While the large technology firms had complied with subpoenas and national security letters requesting data for criminal investigations or intelligence activities, they made a compelling case that bulk collection of their interactions with users and customers was not something that had been engineered with the U.S. government.[11] Other companies, most notably Research in Motion/BlackBerry, had faced pressure from India and other foreign governments to provide backdoors in encryption.

The question, however, to which degree the U.S. government could enlist the products and platforms of Silicon Valley, with the knowledge of those companies or not, in pursuing its intelligence objectives had sweeping impact on a set of actors, not least the citizenry of the United States, at home and abroad.

DOMESTIC SURVEILLANCE ISSUES

That a massive program of Internet surveillance might be directed at the citizens of the United States came as a shock for those who felt such initiatives might have been abandoned after George W. Bush left the White House. The Snowden documents indicated that President Obama, who criticized online surveillance while a U.S. senator, retained a large and ostensibly intrusive cyber intelligence apparatus that could engage in massive bulk collection activity.

An immediate issue for civil liberties groups regarded whether PRISM violated Section 702 of the Foreign Intelligence Surveillance Act (FISA). Senators Ron Wyden and Mark Udall, sitting on the Intelligence Committee, revealed the existence of a classified opinion from FISC, questioning whether the authorities ostensibly covering the PRISM program were circumventing Section 702 and potentially represented a violation of the "Fourth Amendment's prohibition on unreasonable searches and seizures."[12] Wyden and Udall had asked NSA Director Keith Alexander for clarification of his remarks regarding the scope of NSA's collection, alluding to inconsistencies between classified and unclassified testimony.[13] For the Electronic Frontier Foundation and ACLU, the Snowden archive was an impetus to intensify their public and legal campaigns against potential digital surveillance on U.S. citizens.

Uproar on the potential trampling of civil liberties through NSA collection programs emanated from voices across the American political spectrum. Representative John Sensenbrenner, the sponsor for the Patriot Act, the emergency legislation hurriedly passed in 2001 following the 9/11 attacks, opined, "I'm sure somebody can come up with a great computer program that says: 'We can do X, Y, and Z', but that doesn't mean that it's right." Director of National Intelligence James Clapper's March 2013 testimony to the Senate Intelligence Committee was particularly damning in light of the Snowden documents. When asked if the NSA collected data on millions or hundreds of millions of Americans, the DNI replied, "No, sir ... Not wittingly. There are cases where they could, inadvertently perhaps, collect – but not wittingly."[14]

Massive scrutiny was applied to how the Patriot Act's provisions were applied in a classified legal process, and the debate there would continue for months. The breach represented further damage to public trust of the American presidency and federal government. Bill Keller of the *New York Times* reminded readers that more than a year passed between the paper's receipt of significant information on warrantless wiretapping activities and the first story it published on it. The delay he attributed to a declining trust in government emanating from mishandling of the Iraq invasion and the privatization of military operations there. "One major casualty of Iraq, we are reminded, was faith in those who govern us," Keller argued.[15] With public trust of the signals intelligence enterprise in question, the efficacy of the NSA's intelligence collection in foiling terror attacks was debated. While points were made claiming either the considerable utility or the marginal uselessness of the NSA in foiling terror plots, then-director Alexander made clear his position as head of the agency in a June 18, 2013, congressional hearing. Summarizing his remarks he stated, "I would much rather today be here to debate this point than try to explain why we failed to prevent another 9/11."[16] Whatever damage the NSA might be doing to ideals of privacy or civil liberties in the United States appeared an acceptable cost to the agency's chief executive.

INTERNATIONAL FALLOUT

While Americans considered the erosion of their privacy, international dialogue on cybersecurity and Internet Freedom was thrown a massive curveball by the series of revelations published in the *Guardian*.[17] Documents emerged describing the Five Eyes intelligence sharing relationship between the signals intelligence services of the United States, United Kingdom, Australia, Canada, and New Zealand. What came to light was not only the considerable intelligence effort expended applied to monitoring terror groups and their adherents, but also significant activity directed at traditional allies in NATO and elsewhere around the world.

First of these activities to be published on was that of collection undertaken during the 2009 G20 summit meetings in London in which the main agenda item was international reaction to the 2008 global financial crisis. Conducted on Britain's home turf, GCHQ gained access to minister-level delegates' mobile devices. The collection provided, "For the first time, analysts had a live picture of who was talking to who that updated constantly and automatically."[18] While the NSA attempted to get inside the communications of Russia's Medvedev, activity was also undertaken to monitor the South African and Turkish delegations. Particularly effective compromise of BlackBerry smartphones was noted and the summary briefing document detailed extensive electronic eavesdropping aimed at Turkish government officials.[19] Such espionage aimed at the leadership of a NATO ally came as a surprise, but not to those aware of intelligence policy and practices.

Five Eyes espionage was aimed at targets in the governments of other allies. Another Snowden document touted the NSA's capacity to tap the cell phones of some 35 significant world leaders. Reporters from Der Spiegel approached the German government with evidence of surveillance aimed at its top leadership, including Chancellor Angela Merkel. Given the raw information, Germany's Federal Intelligence Service, the BND, confirmed that Merkel's personal phone had been targeted. Merkel summoned the U.S. ambassador to Berlin to verify the action. In a call from President Obama's national security advisor, Susan Rice to Christoph Heusgen, Merkel's foreign policy advisor, the American could not deny previous surveillance of the chancellor's phone, asserting only that "the possibility the chancellor's phone was under surveillance could only be ruled out currently and in the future."[20] A German investigation on the tapping of Merkel's phone was closed in June 2015 for lack of evidence.[21]

Other leaders were also monitored, including the presidents of Brazil and Mexico. Merkel, who grew up under East Germany's Stasi surveillance, made clear her disdain for the activity.[22] Also perturbed was Dilma Rousseff, Luiz Inácio Lula da Silva's successor. Rousseff characterized the NSA's activities as " 'a breach of international law and an affront' " to her country.[23] She then called off a state visit to Washington after the extent of signals collection directed against top officials of the Brazilian government was reported. The extensive collection undertaken by the NSA and its Five Eyes sister services were perceived by the Brazilians to undercut the firm U.S. position that its signals intelligence operations were not undertaken in support of economic goals.

More evidence of spying against foreign leadership targets appeared including documents shared with the Australian Broadcasting Corporation and the *Guardian*'s Australian paper regarding espionage directed against Indonesian president Susilo Bambang Yudhoyono in 2009. Documents emerged detailing how the NSA's Australian counterpart, the Australian Signals Directorate (ASD), had collected communications between Indonesian government officials and attorneys of a major U.S. law firm, Mayer Brown, who had been retained to assist with the negotiation of international trade talks. While not apparently aimed at narrow collection of intellectual property or corporate proprietary information of a foreign firm, it blurred the line NSA drew on economic espionage, and worse, provided confirmation that Five Eyes partners shared intelligence on each other's nationals.[24] Such activity was deemed legal by the U.S. Supreme Court in a decision regarding a 2008 amendment to the FISA law in which the majority argued that "journalists, lawyers and human rights advocates who challenged the constitutionality of the law could not show they had been harmed by it and so lacked standing to sue."[25]

According to reporting generated from the Snowden archive, the ASD was not alone among the Five Eyes in performing signals intelligence against economic targets. Communications Security Establishment Canada (CSEC) was identified as targeting the Brazilian Ministry of Mines and Energy, the government agency responsible for development of the country's oil resources.[26] That Canada, itself a significant exporter of oil, would target Brazil's energy ministry as it ramped up a potentially massive offshore oil project in the pre-salt area of the continental shelf was an interesting development.

Confirmation of the NSA revelations' impact on U.S. relations with friendly nations was strongly indicated when Barack Obama returned to Berlin in 2013. While 200,000 Germans had greeted the American presidential candidate in his speech at the Brandenburg Gate in 2008, he was received much less enthusiastically upon return, in large part because of the NSA issue. There was undoubtedly significant damage done to the international relations of the United States because of Snowden's actions in leaking the NSA documents.

Particularly harmed was the U.S. position as a steward of cyberspace and the party responsible for Internet governance oversight through ICANN and its status with the U.S. Department of Commerce. Dilma Rousseff convened the April 2014 NETmundial conference largely as a referendum on the continued U.S. role in overseeing ICANN. The conference's nonbinding summary document included a declaration on surveillance not seen at major Internet Governance Forum conference before:

Mass and arbitrary surveillance undermines trust in the Internet and trust in the Internet governance ecosystem. Collection and processing of personal data by state and non-state actors should be conducted in accordance with international human rights law.[27]

More pressure came from the ITU on the surveillance issue, with the World Congress on Information Technology meetings increasingly employed to question the U.S. role in Internet governance. Even the editor of the *Communications of the Association of Computing Machinery*, computing's professional group, stated, "we can no longer trust the U.S. government to be the 'Internet hegemon.' "[28]

Faced with this pressure, the U.S. government chose to phase out its contract with ICANN. The contractual relationship between ICANN and the Commerce Department slated to be dismantled remains without a successor arrangement determined at the time of writing.[29] ICANN's CEO hinted at moving the organization's offices from Marina del Rey, California, to Geneva, ostensibly putting it on a similar footing to the ITU and other UN-umbrella international organizations.[30] The Snowden effect has been to poison the image of the United States as a reliable government to entrust with managing the multi-stakeholder process of Internet governance. Many of the world's leaders and many in technology as well likely felt how Hillary Clinton did. She characterized not only national but also global opinion in characterizing that "People felt betrayed. 'You didn't tell us you were doing this.' "[31]

BAD CRYPTO AND TAILORED ACCESS

A much smaller constituency offended by NSA activity was the mathematical and computational community involved in cryptographic research. That the NSA would work to break encryption systems and algorithms should come as absolutely no surprise. With the establishment of the NSA in 1947, the United States made a long-term postwar commitment to code breaking as well as communications security roles.[32]

In parallel, scholarly work in encryption continued, and by the 1970s several breakthroughs occurred in the field, enabling the dissemination of cryptographic keys to be undertaken by computational function rather than physical distribution of matching keys between encrypting and decrypting parties. The Diffie-Hellman key exchange, which enabled the exchange of cryptographic keys over an open channel, opened the door to the encryption now employed in Web browsers to pass credit card data and other sensitive information over countless sessions each day. Fearing a significant loss in signals intelligence capability, the U.S. government put up a vigorous effort to control the widespread dissemination of encryption processes and technologies during the "Crypto Wars" of the 1990s.[33] A 1999 appellate court decision deemed "that restrictions on cryptography were illegal, because crypto algorithms were a form of speech and thus covered by the First Amendment."[34]

Although the NSA and FBI had argued vigorously that the distribution of encryption technologies should be vigorously controlled, the court decision essentially silenced them. With the wars at an end, those outside the NSA were left to wonder what capabilities it might be developing to break or subvert the widely adopted encryption technologies distributed across the Internet and billions of computers. The Snowden archive provided answers in a twofold approach, by ostensibly incorporating flawed cryptographic techniques into government-promulgated standards and developing process and techniques for Tailored Access Operations (TAO) in which the security of individual computers could be compromised, thus defeating the encryption undertaken on the device itself.

Once again a Snowden-leaked NSA memo provided declaration that the agency was "winning its long-running secret war on encryption, using supercomputers, technical trickery, court orders and behind-the-scenes persuasion."[35] Many of the techniques for compromise had been matters of conjecture for a decade or more. One item particularly upset the academic and nongovernment cryptographic community.

Documents in the archive suggested that "NSA [had] control and influence over the setting of encryption standards," found in commercial applications and elsewhere. Following the release of Snowden documents on the potential subversion of cryptographic algorithms and processes, the National Institute of Standards and Technology released supplemental bulletin seeking review and comment on a random number generation algorithm. Although no wrongdoing by the NSA or any other U.S. agency was mentioned, the document stated that "recent community commentary has called into question the trustworthiness of these default elliptic curve points."[36]

The documents also suggested that NSA worked with security vendors to subvert encryption technologies. Bruce Schneier, a cryptographer with prior experience in the U.S. government, summed up the activity.

Basically, the NSA asks companies to subtly change their products in undetectable ways: making the random number generator less random, leaking the key somehow, adding a common exponent to a public-key exchange protocol, and so on.[37]

The alleged capabilities did not add up to breakthroughs in cracking well-known encryption algorithms, but rather a watering down the implementation of those algorithms sufficiently to give the NSA a leg up in defeating encryption implementations.

But in defeating encryption, there was another option, the services of the NSA's Office of Tailored Access Operations. The TAO program covered activities where systems security was compromised on an individual or organization's computer or device. Leaked documents again showed operations under way were designed compromise the integrity of computers either in their path to delivery or already in the hands of targeted entities. As one document reviewed by Der Spiegel touted, TAO offered "some of the most significant intelligence our country has ever seen" and "access to our very hardest targets."[38] Once again the existence of such an organization shouldn't have come as a surprise, but when its existence became public knowledge, there was concern nonetheless.

Security experts pondered to what degree the NSA was aware of unknown security vulnerabilities in widely distributed computer software and hardware. Menacing as cyber espionage appeared to targeted individuals and countries, information on TAO also indicated how the office's activities were a form of reconnaissance for acts of cyber conflict. One briefing deck described TAO activities stretching across "servers, workstations, firewalls, routers, handsets, phone switches, SCADA systems, etc."[39] The last item, those computers running pieces of infrastructure—power plants, water systems, and electrical grids—offered an idea of how the Department of Defense was developing the targeting capability and tactics for engaging in offensive cyber operations.

News of the considerable effort to subvert cryptographic systems of foreign powers and possibly U.S. tech companies was greeted with hostility in Silicon Valley. One slide included a description of how to disable SSL encryption on Google Front End servers that bridged the company's massive internal computing cloud with the open Internet. In a diagram describing the MUSCULAR program undertaken by the NSA and GCHQ, the presence of clear text in traffic between Google data centers was noted. Ostensibly, GCHQ, as a second (i.e., non-American) party could collect on the streams of data passed in the clear between the Google's data centers as well as Yahoo.[40] MUSCULAR appeared to be aimed at monitoring the cloud infrastructure of a company providing email services for half a billion accounts.[41]

Google responded by emplacing encryption between its data centers.[42] It continued to ramp up security practices and capabilities. A year after the first Snowden stories, Google's CEO touted, "If you have important information, the safest place to keep it is in Google. And I can assure you that the safest place to not keep it is anywhere else."[43] The company's effort began paying off. In April 2014, a Google security analyst found the Heartbleed bug in the nearly ubiquitous OpenSSL encryption libraries employed to encrypt sessions between servers and Web browsers.[44] The bug in OpenSSL, which permitted an attacker knowledgeable of it to fetch data from servers with complete impunity, was a catastrophic weakness in the Internet ecosystem.

In the wake of Heartbleed's discovery, questions were raised as to the U.S. government's knowledge or use of it in compromising systems. Reports citing anonymous government sources quickly emerged that the NSA knew about it for two years. A statement from the ODNI refuted those claims, asserting that neither the NSA nor any other agency was "aware of the so-called Heartbleed vulnerability before 2014."[45] Nonetheless, *Heartbleed raised a fundamental question of how the NSA as well as those to whom it reports determines the need to stockpile security vulnerabilities for intelligence purposes versus sharing such information with technology firms and the public.* This issue remains without satisfactory resolution even in the post-Snowden review undertaken by a commission of experts convened by the Obama administration.

A BLACK BAG OPERATION?

One other major element of the Snowden affair requires consideration before summation of the government response to it. Interesting was the timing of Snowden's leak, as Glenn Greenwald's first story ran in the *Guardian* just days before the first major international summit between Barack Obama and Xi Jinping in California. As mentioned before, the cybersecurity issue stood high on Obama's agenda for the summit, but the leaked NSA documents made whatever talking points prepared for the meeting irrelevant. Because the timing of the Snowden leak was so opportune for China, it is worth considering whether Edward Snowden was in any way handled, wittingly or not, by operatives of a foreign intelligence service.

A former member of Obama's cabinet offered that "there are only three possible explanations for the Snowden heist: 1) It was a Russian espionage operation; 2) It was a Chinese espionage operation, or 3) It was a joint Sino-Russian operation."[46] Former U.S. Naval War College professor and NSA employee John Schindler emphatically expressed his belief that Snowden's actions were not undertaken as activism for a transparency campaign, but rather a foreign intelligence operation. A former NSA counterintelligence officer—a spycatcher—Schindler holds a high degree of credibility in understanding how foreign intelligence services target U.S. sources.

The question is at what point Snowden may have been contacted by officers of a foreign intelligence service and by which one. Schindler has doggedly pursued answers to this question. He offers evidence that Snowden celebrated his 30th birthday in the Russian Consulate to Hong Kong and that it is likely that he was in contact with controllers from Moscow's intelligence service before taking the position at Booz Allen Hamilton that provided his extensive access to the massive trove of data he took with him.

All roads here lead to Wikileaks. We know that Snowden in late 2012 reached out to Glenn Greenwald and other members of the spy-ring – all of whom can be considered cut-outs for Wikileaks when not paid-up members – that stands behind the massive leaks. After making this contact, Ed[ward Snowden] took a contractor job with Booz Allen Hamilton to increase his access to NSA secrets. I've been stating for a while now that Wikileaks is functionally an extension of Russian intelligence; it's become a minor meme as a few journalists have decided that such a scandalous viewpoint is worth considering.[47]

While the journalist making the allegations of Russian ties to WikiLeaks, Joshua Foust, is a freelancer, he previously worked as a U.S. government intelligence analyst and has worked as a fellow of the Foreign Policy Research Institute, a right-of-center think tank. He argues that short on cash after the U.S. government leaned on banks and credit card companies to cease allowing donation transactions with WikiLeaks, the organization came under some degree of influence from Russia.[48] James Ball, an editor at the *Guardian*, highlighted the connection between Assange and Israel Shamir, who reputedly has aided the Belarusian government and had a role in the falling-out between Assange and Daniel Domscheit-Berg, WikiLeaks' former spokesperson.[49]

Along with WikiLeaks' inconsistencies and internal issues, another chink in the Snowden as transparency activist narrative came from his correspondence with Barton Gellman. He was under time pressure. "Snowden asked for a guarantee that The Washington Post would publish — within 72 hours — the full text of a PowerPoint presentation describing PRISM." In addition, "He also asked that The Post publish online a cryptographic key that he could use to prove to a foreign embassy that he was the document's source."[50] Which foreign embassy needed confirmation? That question remains unanswered.

Finally, not to be lost in the shuffle in conjecture on whether or not Snowden was indeed "handled" by the intelligence services of Russia or China is the other Hawaii espionage case, that of contractor Benjamin Piece Bishop, a retired U.S. Army officer. Bishop was charged with "communicating classified national defense information to a person not entitled to receive such information" in March 2013.[51] Passing classified documents to a Chinese woman half his age to whom he was romantically linked, Bishop plead guilty to the charge and was sentenced to seven years in prison the following year.[52]

Was Snowden's flight to Hong Kong and on to Moscow an espionage operation? To counterintelligence practitioners, it does look like it. That said, NSA whistleblowers Bill Binney and Thomas Drake vehemently disagreed with their agency and had their lives turned upside down for their acts of dissent.[53] The author sees the operation thesis as an interesting one, but does not hold sufficient evidence to declare it an undeniable fact.

RESPONSE AND CLOSURE

Public outcry on the Snowden affair led to the President's Review Group on Intelligence and Communications Technologies, a body of former intelligence and national security officials and national security lawyers. Their report, released in December 2013, offered suggestions for reform of digital surveillance undertaken by the U.S. government, on both U.S. persons and foreign nationals.[54] Also relevant in the discussion of intelligence reform was the Privacy and Civil Liberties Oversight Board (PCLOB), an independent agency of the executive branch established in 2004 to provide advice on privacy and civil liberties issues.

Ultimately, Obama delivered reform via executive order with Presidential Policy Directive 28 (PDD-28)—Signals Intelligence Activities. The order identified principles for the collection of signals intelligence, drew limitations on bulk collection, refined the process for signals intelligence collection, and established safeguards for personal information as well as instituting a reporting requirement. The first anniversary of PPD-28 brought with it a report (delivered via the Tumblr blogging platform).[55] In addition, agencies of the IC have developed their own policies for the protection of personal information, for those who fall under the category of U.S. person as well as those who don't.[56] The NSA emplaced new safeguards and made public its policy on them in January 2015.[57] Also, adopting behavior found in the firms that are the largest collectors of individual data, the IC issued a Transparency Report for 2013. It covered "U.S. Government surveillance programs while protecting sensitive classified intelligence and national security information" and detailed specific numbers of FISA orders, individuals targeted under Section 702 of the FISA law, National Security Letters, and the number of pen register/trap and trace instances.[58]

But the signals intelligence enterprise remains very much intact. Attempts to substitute new software for the bulk collection of metadata remains stymied by technological limitations according to a report by the National Academies.[59] Throwing open the signals intelligence enterprise to a degree by which it satisfies critics has not happened. According to Schindler, "The bottom line is that President Obama's reforms contain *no significant changes* to how NSA does business as the leading foreign intelligence agency in the United States and the free world."[60]

After Room 641A became an item of public knowledge, the weak state of public debate or even private discussion between the U.S. government and privacy rights advocates was apparent. The NSA had tapped the Web and was going to continue doing so. Before Snowden, this was the case.

[T]here exists a disconnect between [intelligence agencies and their advocates and those arguing for civil liberties, in] a debate without discussion. Until these groups, the intelligence agencies, privacy advocates, and telecom companies, are able to get back around the table to bargain as they did in the period between the Church Commission and September 11 there will be little accord among them. Desperately needed is this type of interplay on the emergent phenomena surrounding *webtapping*. Today policy–makers rarely hear more than monologues distorted by incomplete technical knowledge of the topic.[61]

There have been changes, but what still remains a point of concern is that the congressional figures responsible for oversight and even the officials of the executive branch employing cyber-enabled signals intelligence do not well understand the methods employed and how they impact the speech undertaken by U.S. citizens.

As Edward Snowden sat in his Hong Kong hotel room in 2013, President Obama gave a speech on the issue of leaking and the necessity of a vigorously investigative Fourth Estate in a healthy democracy.

As Commander-in-Chief, I believe we must keep information secret that protects our operations and our people in the field. To do so, we must enforce consequences for those who break the law and breach their commitment to protect classified information. But a free press is also essential for our democracy. That's who we are. And I'm troubled by the possibility that leak investigations may chill the investigative journalism that holds government accountable.

Greenwald's reporting two weeks later stood as a test of the president's words. It is a situation that has yet to reach some state of balance.

The eventual fate of the NSA leakers remains unclear. Although Greenwald's partner was detained in Britain while reportedly carrying an archive of documents, he was eventually released. Poitras remains in Germany, as does Jacob Appelbaum, who has held custody of Snowden documents. Both fear detention upon arrival on U.S. soil. Also remaining outside the United States and holding an extended residency permit, as of October 2015, Edward Snowden remains a free man in Russia.

CHAPTER 11

Cybercrime and Punishment

Rare is the day that a news headline does not appear regarding a massive data breach at a major retailer or some massive credit card scam. Determining what constitutes crime in cyberspace, adding up the size of the cybercrime problem, and determining how that crime may be managed are important issues for the forces of law enforcement around the globe. Cybercrime is both a domestic and an international issue, in which actors may use a small set of tools, for starters an Internet-connected personal computer, to achieve spectacular results.

Cybercrime is perhaps the best area for improvement in the cybersecurity arena, in regard to national and international policymaking. This is because there is much agreement that the impact of criminal activity in cyberspace, whether online fraud or the transmission of pedophilia-related imagery, is negative. In cybercrime, we hold an international treaty, the Budapest Convention, which provides a framework for international cooperation in investigating cybercrimes, apprehending the perpetrators, bringing them to trial. Yes, there are safe havens for online criminals, particularly Russia and the countries of the former Soviet bloc; the common values shared by police agencies around the world provide a vehicle for taming the problem.

ROBBING THE BANK

"Why did I rob banks? Because I enjoyed it. I loved it. I was more alive when I was inside a bank, robbing it, than at any other time in my life. I enjoyed everything about it so much that one or two weeks later I'd be out looking for the next job. But to me the money was the chips, that's all."[1] Willie Sutton, a professional bank robber who is estimated to have stolen $2 million across a lifetime and escaped prison three times, said these words. He was also incorrectly quoted that he robbed banks

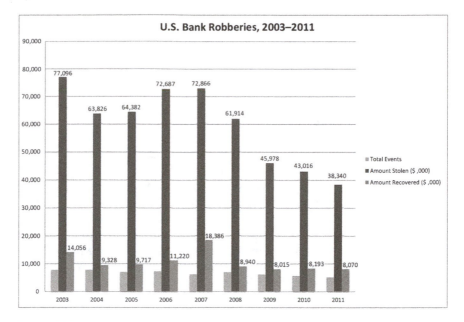

Figure 11.1

"because that's where the money is." Today, cyberspace is where the money is. It is increasingly held in digital form and passed across the links of cyberspace. The criminals who steal in cyberspace are increasingly sophisticated, hard to detect, and even harder to catch. Crime has become a digital enterprise and business in it is booming.

Emphasized here is the international dimension of cybercrime, because it is possible today to rob a bank, retailer, or other organization from a great distance. In the United States today, robbing banks—actually walking into a bank branch and demanding money—is getting harder and the spoils of that activity are shrinking. Bank robbery statistics collected by the U.S. Federal Bureau of Investigation (FBI) over the last decade bear that argument out. In 2003, there were some 7,644 robberies, burglaries, and larcenies at U.S. banks, savings and loans, credit unions, and armored car companies, and a total of $77,096,415 was stolen. By 2011, the last year in which full statistics are available from the FBI, the number of incidents fell to 5,014, with some $38,343,501 taken (Figure 11.1).

Robbing banks is not incredibly lucrative, with the average take often in the neighborhood of $1,000, while the potential for incarceration is quite high, a 60 percent clearance rate to conviction.[2] With nearly a century of experience in investigating bank robberies in the United States, the FBI has produced an exact measurement of the problem.

But cybercrime, which essentially boils down to theft and robbery by computer, is different. Quantities are hard to know. It's even difficult to know if a theft has occurred at all. This is the new frontier for law enforcement agencies and it has become an area of emphasis for the FBI. At the 2012 RSA computer security conference, then-FBI director Robert Muller opined, "Terrorism does remain the FBI's top priority, but in the not too-distant-future we anticipate that the cyberthreat will pose the greatest threat to our country."[3] He spoke, no doubt, of the many areas of FBI responsibility where computing, the Internet, and cyberspace are radically recasting how his agency and other organs of law enforcement investigate cases and produce evidence able to generate successful prosecutions, in areas including fraud, counterintelligence, digital piracy, and theft.

Robbing banks by digital means is thus but one concern, and to better understand how law enforcement has evolved in cyberspace recently in a very short span of time, we must consider the larger economics of what has value in the digital domain, what may be stolen, and how to measure that theft.

SIZING THE THEFT: ASSIGNING VALUE TO INFORMATION

Placing bounds on what exactly constitutes cybercrime, or even theft via cyberspace, is difficult. Measuring loss goes far beyond the missing loot from bank robberies, which can be measured down to the penny. All manner of cyber incidents can be considered part of the cybercrime issue. Piracy of music or video content via peer-to-peer software qualifies, as does theft of corporate plans or intellectual property. Transmission and storage of child pornography is a cybercrime offense, so is the subversion of a computer system for employment as a remote spam email machine. Fraudulent email campaigns offering offshore riches are yet another cybercrime item. Perhaps most visibly growing is the problem of massive data breaches, where unauthorized parties steal large quantities of information useful for perpetrating identity theft or credit card fraud.

Data breaches are hardly a new problem in cybersecurity, but their impact continues to grow. In December 2013, Target, the United States' second largest discount retail firm, was reported to have been the victim of a data breach. Brian Krebs, an independent security expert and blogger, broke the news regarding the Target breach.[4] At least 40 million credit and debit card numbers were taken from the company. The perpetrators collected customer data as well as credit and debit card information as it was passed from retail point-of-sale terminals to centralized storage facilities within a corporate data center. Estimates on the cost of replacing compromised credit and debit cards resulting from the breach reached

$200 million, according to the Consumer Bankers Association and Credit Union National Association.[5]

Beyond the cost of issuing credit cards, which were borne by the banks, there were broader costs to Target. In the immediate wake of the data breach report surfacing, the change in value of the company's stock was negligible. But over the holiday shopping season and into the New Year, Target's stock fell considerably, from $66.89 on November 15, 2013, to $56.06 on February 14, 2014, some 16 percent of its value. Competitor Wal-Mart's stock value also fell during the same period, but only by four percent.[6] In addition to the decline in stock price, Target stated the breach resulted in $61 million in expenses, offset by $44 million in insurance.[7] Company officials stated earnings were dented by a 6.6 percent decrease in sales in the fourth quarter of 2013.[8] The company's chief information officer resigned, followed later by CEO Greg Steinhafel.[9] Target was damaged by its breach and Wall Street seems to have noticed, but how it will measure the impact of incidents like the Target breach or the more recent cyber attack against Sony requires investigation on the economics of digital information.

PRICING INFORMATION

In microeconomics, production is the sum of two factors, capital (K) and labor (L). Divergence of opinion regarding Information and Computing Technologies' (ICT) role in economic activity exists, however. A central concern in the debate revolves around the ability to quantitatively predict economic growth. Dale Jorgenson argued that declining prices of ICT coupled with its widespread adoption across the span of the U.S. economy produced significant productivity growth.[10] After the dot-com collapse in 2000–2001, many found it easy to mark ICT's role in economic activity as hyperbolic—however, research after that decline indicated that ICT can indeed contribute to strong growth.[11]

But how is information's value assessed? Stigler contributed to the discourse on this topic with an explanation of economics' failure to address this question. He offered:

One should hardly have to tell academicians that information is a valuable resource: knowledge *is* power. And yet it occupies a slum dwelling in the town on economics. Mostly it is ignored: the best technology is assumed to be known; the relationship of commodities to consumer preferences is a datum. And one of the information-producing industries, advertising, is treated with a hostility that economists normally reserve for tariffs or monopolists.[12]

Some 50 years after Stigler's study of advertising, one of the world's largest technology companies, Google, is chiefly an advertiser, generating nearly $60 billion in advertising revenue in 2014, its largest single area of revenue.[13] In the interim, scholarship has addressed advertising,[14] but the issue of information valuation has collided with the theft of digital products. A clear case of digital theft exists in the music industry. According to the Recording Industry Association of America (RIAA), since 1999, music sales in the United States fell by 47 percent, from $14.6 billion to $7.7 billion.[15] The Business Software Alliance and Motion Picture Association of America, trade associations representing the software and film industries, respectively, offer further statistics regarding lost or declining revenue due to unauthorized reproduction of digital content, an activity labeled as piracy.

What has attracted more attention recently is activity that may be labeled economic espionage or even state-supported economic espionage. The theft of output from research and development efforts in U.S. firms by foreign entities has been labeled the "greatest transfer of wealth in history" by General Keith Alexander, the then-director of the National Security Agency and the Department of Defense's Cyber Command.[16] Measurement in aggregate of the theft on corporate R&D is difficult for a variety of reasons. Unlike bank robberies, or even online fraud, it is difficult to quantify the loss produced by theft of intellectual property borne of research and development activity. Firms are not necessarily compelled to report it, nor are they often in a position to even detect such theft. Indeed, U.S. firms may often only learn about such a theft after being tipped off by government.

The size of the IP theft issue has been pegged by a "rough guess" from CSIS's James Lewis and Stewart Baker of $100 billion per year, in a report drafted for McAfee, the computer security branch of microprocessor manufacturer Intel. Lewis and Baker base their admittedly "crude extrapolation" on the basis of estimates including studies of overall intellectual property theft in Germany ($24 billion per year) and Britain ($27 billion per year).[17]

Economic espionage designed to purloin IP is another facet of the cybercrime problem, and perhaps even more difficult to measure than forms of fraud and piracy. Beyond these issues of theft exists the additional problem of costs associated with response and remedy of cyber incidents, as well as the spending necessary to prevent future incidents. Another source of data regarding the cost of cybercrime comes from the FBI, which established the Internet Crime Complaint Center (IC3) in 2000.

If accurate statistics are to be found on cybercrime in the United States, IC3's are likely the best available. Working in conjunction with the National White Collar Crime Center as well as the Bureau of Justice Assistance, IC3 has been collecting complaints and producing annual reporting regarding them since its inception. The reports capture a variety of demographic and geographic data as well as estimates of loss tied to the cybercrime event. Additionally, IC3's position as the public face of the Department of Justice

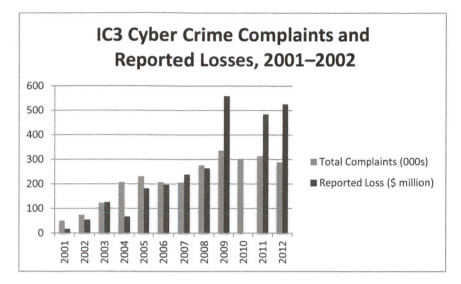

Figure 11.2

on cybercrime issues permits it to generate descriptive elements regarding new forms of fraud and crime enabled by information technologies.

Since 2001, the IC3 trends on complaints and losses went through considerable growth and then reached a relative plateau after 2009 (no loss figure was reported for 2010; Figure 11.2).

Reporting of cybercrime incidents in the United States is complicated. While the purported victim is present in a clearly understood jurisdiction, the perpetrators of the alleged crime may not be in the same city, state, or even country. Although local and state police departments and other agencies may have cybercrime offices, the capacity to investigate such cases requires technology and skills in proper collection of digital evidence and forensic analysis. Cases of computer fraud shift to federal law enforcement and prosecution, but in this restrictive category, the number of cases was quite small, just 120, and the rate of successful prosecution quite high, with 154 of 168 defendants being found guilty at trial or admitting guilt.[18]

As we will consider below, how law is applied effectively to police cyberspace remains a challenge, with statute seemingly always behind the unrelenting pace of technological advance. Add to that the problem of harmonizing national and international law, the matter of arrest, trial, and conviction becomes massively complex.

WHICH LEGAL REGIME?

Cybercrime law in the United States largely descends from computer crime law drafted as white-collar crime aimed at or within the financial sector. The 1986 Computer Fraud and Abuse Act (CFAA, 18 U.S.C. §1030) established the concept of a protected computer, which is a computer

A. exclusively for the use of a financial institution or the United States Government, or, in the case of a computer not exclusively for such use, used by or for a financial institution or the United States Government and the conduct constituting the offense affects that use by or for the financial institution or the Government; or
B. which is used in or affecting interstate or foreign commerce or communication, including a computer located outside the United States that is used in a manner that affects interstate or foreign commerce or communication of the United States[.][19]

As society has deployed firewalls, antivirus software, and other technical security apparatus, the law on protected computers has grown to cover most computers in the United States, and many outside it. In addition, wrongdoing with regard to computing in the United States has evolved as computer crime has become cybercrime—the computers have been interconnected to the global network of Internet Protocol devices.

As amended, legal scholar Orin Kerr has characterized the CFAA as "ever-expanding." Kerr states of the cumulative development of U.S. cybercrime statute, "Faced with the uncertainty of the new world of computer crimes, Congress has opted for very broad and unclear prohibitions."[20] Revised several times since the 1980s, U.S. federal cybercrime law was extensively overhauled via the Uniting and Strengthening America by Providing Appropriate Tools Required to Intercept and Obstruct Terrorism Act of 2001, a.k.a. the Patriot Act.

Thus, the cases prosecuted are very broad indeed. Robert Tappan Morris, creator of the 1989 "Morris worm," which crippled the then-nascent Internet, was prosecuted for violating the CFAA. In addition to changes as a result of the Patriot Act, computer security law was again amended in 2002 and in 2008 through the Identity Theft and Restitution Act.

Recent cases predicated on violations of the CFAA have included those against Bradley (Chelsea) Manning for his disclosure of classified information to the WikiLeaks organization as well as Thomas Drake, an NSA whistleblower. These are the sort of national security–oriented violations for which the CFAA was designed; however, a number of additional cases demonstrate how its breadth can produce applicability to a variety of other potential offenses. In *United States v. Drew*, federal prosecutors argued that Lori Drew violated the statute in her aggressive cyber bullying that would lead to the suicide of 13-year-old Megan Meier.[21] One of the most controversial recent cases for cyber theft was against Aaron Swartz, for his use of MIT's computer network to copy scholarly works from the JSTOR archive. The case was dismissed in 2013 after Swartz's suicide.

THE INTERNATIONAL DIMENSION

With cybercrime a rapidly growing but vague area of legal activity in the United States, a major issue is extension of U.S. law to other countries. International convention on cybercrime does exist, however, in the form of the Council of Europe's Convention on Cybercrime. An international treaty ratified by the members of the European Union as well as the United States and a small, but growing number of other countries, the Cybercrime Convention, also known as the Budapest Convention, is a piece of transnational law designed to developed the international capacity for investigating cybercrimes and enforcing laws across geographic boundaries.

The convention defined four forms of computer-related crimes: fraud and forgery, child pornography, copyright infringement, and other forms of security breach and intercept. In addition, it lays out "domestic procedures for detecting, investigating, and prosecuting computer crimes, and collecting electronic evidence of any criminal offense" as well as facilitating international cooperation.[22] But it must harmonize law over a rapidly evolving set of technologies and human interactions based upon them, thus being fairly categorized at the time of enactment as a good start. Hopkins considered the legal problems faced a decade ago and they seem as relevant today.

Computer crimes are difficult to solve due to the absence of geographical borders and the inherent ability to swiftly transfer and manipulate information instantly. Nevertheless, technological advances will continue to challenge law enforcement officials. As long as signatories are permitted to codify cyber criminal laws domestically and countries remain unsubscribed to the Convention, authorities may be unable to obtain sufficient evidence to prosecute crimes. We must reach a global consensus to harmonize not only the crimes themselves but also the investigative and prosecutorial procedures that will enable law enforcement to prevent and convict cybercrimes. Success will hinge upon the cooperation of all countries, both parties to the Convention and those that are not.[23]

With this consideration of the international law a decade ago still very relevant today, we shift focus to the problem of law enforcement, an issue grabbing more attention and resources of police agencies and prosecutorial bodies.

CATCHING THE CYBER CRIMINALS

Cybercrime enforcement has become a priority for the United States, and its lead federal law enforcement agency for the area, the FBI. The FBI's Fiscal Year (FY) 2014 budget request totals $8.3 billion paying for a staff of roughly 70,000. FBI's Cyber Division has risen in prominence with some 756 special agents, and an even larger number of analytic and support staff is funded. Furthermore, the FBI has requested an additional $82 million be dedicated to a "next generation" cyber program.[24] While it is very good at catching bank robbers, the FBI remains deeply challenged in catching cyber criminals who may perpetrate their crimes from almost anywhere on the planet.

Cybersecurity efforts cut across a variety of law enforcement areas, and with so much criminal activity undertaken in digital form, cyber law enforcement will likely continue to grow. The FBI's employment of a "ten most wanted" list of at-large criminals sets the agenda for the agency, and in response to its cyber portfolio the FBI now has a cyber most-wanted list as well. While murderers and violent criminals dominate the general FBI most-wanted list and Islamic terrorists the terrorism one, the FBI's cyber most-wanted list is predominantly filled with Eastern Europeans. Charges against them include fraud, wire fraud, unauthorized access to a protected computer, identity theft, bank fraud, computer fraud, engaging in surreptitious interception, and various related conspiracy charges. Standouts included Shaileshkumar Jain and Bjorn Sundin, who duped people in some 60 countries to buy over 1 million downloads of false antivirus software.[25] Alexey Belan, a Latvian-born Russian citizen, holds the highest reward for evidence leading to capture, $100,000, for his alleged theft of databases belonging to three e-commerce companies in Nevada and California.[26]

How the FBI and other law enforcement entities have fared in actually catching cyber criminals is difficult to measure. There have been sensational cases, however. Kevin Mitnick's two-year period in the 1990s as a fugitive inside the United States drew much attention. (Mitnick was caught, convicted of computer fraud, and served 46 months in federal prison. He is now a cybersecurity consultant.)

An enormously effective robber of banks, albeit by breaching the credit and debit card databases of major retailers, was Albert Gonzalez. A New York Police Department plainclothes detective arrested Gonzalez in July 2003 after he was caught in the act of withdrawing large quantities of cash via an automatic teller machine.[27] Soon after, he was employed as a consultant to the U.S. Secret Service. While working there, Gonzalez adapted to continuing technological innovation in the retail and financial sector and moved from withdrawing cash from ATMs to pulling large quantities of customer credit card data and then selling those data to the illicit market for it.

Gonzalez became expert in "war driving," a variation on the technique of "war dialing," the process of instructing computers to dial in search of telephone modems. Trolling around the strip malls of greater Miami, Gonzalez searched for wireless networks of retail firms and often found transaction data passing from point-of-sale cash register terminals to in-store database computers. In his war driving, he merely eavesdropped upon the network, capturing recently acquired credit card numbers, bundled them up and sold them to the network of buyers for such information, based largely in Eastern Europe. Caught again, Gonzalez eventually accepted a plea bargain, and was named as a co-conspirator in what was called the largest cybercrime case in history (at the time), after two Russian nationals, Vladimir Drinkman and Dmitry Smilianets, were arrested in the Netherlands in June 2012 for electronic theft of credit card data.[28]

Gonzalez's ties to international cybercrime represent a useful notional case study of how law enforcement agencies will confront the issue. *Cyber-enabled thievery across international boundaries remains lucrative, and because attribution is difficult, the capacity of local police agencies to apprehend the alleged remains weak.* Journalist Joseph Menn chronicled the efforts of investigators from the United States and UK in working with Russian counterparts in pursuing members of the now-defunct Russian Business Network (RBN).[29] The RBN was emblematic of the Eastern European cyber-hacker gang organization, operating under the guise of a quasi-legitimate business. In fact, it was a sophisticated cybercrime network as lucrative as many narcotics trafficking or organized crime operations.

How law enforcement agencies in which individuals and organizations are cybercrime targets may challenge organizations is a defining law enforcement challenge for the coming decade or more. That Russia's relations with the West have grown ever more chilly, considering the country's recent occupation of the Crimea and resulting exclusion from the G-8 international dialogue as a new low point, it is unlikely that Moscow's willingness to cooperate on cybercrime issues will return to the level that existed when Menn went to Russia. There are areas of the world in which rule of law can be extended to cyberspace, but there are those that cannot as well.

There have been other successes. One example is in the work of its rapid-response Cyber Action Teams in aiding the governments of Turkey and Morocco in their joint investigation of the Zotob worm, a piece of malware that disrupted computers running the Microsoft Windows 2000 operating system.[30] With U.S. assistance, perpetrators in both countries were located and arrested.[31] This illustrates how the bureaucratic institutions of the state are adapting to the issues created by the global cyber infrastructure. The FBI has developed a cadre of cyber agents who must understand international and domestic law, as well as how IT may be abused or employed to violate those laws. Agents who successfully collect evidence are able to work with prosecutors to successfully take the cases to trial, enhance their careers, and rise in the organization.

This demonstrates that pre-Internet bureaucratic edifices may exert their influence and have a measurable impact.

ANOTHER UNRESOLVED AND GROWING PROBLEM

With practical approaches to remedy of cybercrime undercut by cleavages in the international system, the cybercrime problem will no doubt persist. Global society's dependence on IT continues to grow, and theft in cyberspace, whether fraudulent financial transactions, purloined intellectual property, or any number of other issues is relatively easy to accomplish and hard to prosecute, will also likely rise.

David Wall provides categories for us to think about cybercrime. He sees a cybercrime past of computer crime, of the sort we can understand as the white-collar crime in which fractions of pennies could be shaved off transactions—a technique known as "salami slicing." Then, we saw crime committed in networks, such as stealing information via digital theft. Today, we live in a time where cybercrime is automated by computer and conducted via the Internet.[32]

Thus, the response to cybercrime will need to be automated and broadly constructed. Police agencies will need to constantly evolve and improve if they are to remain relevant in the cyber domain. If they do not, the criminals, who already hold significant entrepreneurial advantage and avail themselves of working in an area that is ripe with opportunity, will grow the gap between wrongdoing and the capacity to manage it.

CHAPTER 12

Virtual Policy in the Real World

Arthur C. Clarke is reputed to have said, "Before you become too entranced with gorgeous gadgets and mesmerizing video displays, let me remind you that information is not knowledge, knowledge is not wisdom, and wisdom is not foresight. Each grows out of the other, and we need them all." Our time is a time of revolutionary transformation in the creation, transmission, storage, and processing of information. But little considered is how the information technologies increasingly embedded in our lives are impacting contemporary politics and society. That cyberspace is so insecure is an enormous issue. We depend on it, but it may not be all that dependable.

So how is the United States managing this? In completing this brief explanation of where the Information Revolution has impacted security and power for the United States, we need to think about where computing is headed and what it means. A few years ago former National Intelligence Council chairman Thomas Fingar indicated the peril of attempting to trend information in a lecture shortly before his retirement from public service. Discussing a 1970s vintage thesis of a colleague at Stanford, which hypothesized that China would rise to become a major petroleum producer, Fingar stated the peril of directing a line "through precisely one data point."[1] Understanding where cyberspace is headed has many data points, of course, but seeing the future is difficult nonetheless.

Certainly in cyberspace individuals can be enormously empowered. Some years ago, the editors of *Time* declared "You" the magazine's Person of the Year in characterizing the participatory Internet of social media.[2] The Internet has been skillfully employed to raise awareness and advocate for change. Consider Jody Williams, who used email to stitch together a massive effort to ban landmines that eventually resulted in the crafting of an international treaty now signed by 133 countries.[3] We have no treaty on cyber weapons, no agreement on use of force in cyberspace, or even a general agreement on how to secure our information technologies.

Through mobile computing, people have willingly become highly intelligent digital sensors. There is much more data produced than ever before, and piecing them together to make sense of the world is the challenge of governments and individuals alike. Dismaying is the reality that the infrastructure of cyberspace, a creation of computer code more than anything else, remains brittle. Almost three decades after the Morris worm, systems can be broken or subverted easily. The United States has continued to build on a weak infrastructure, riddled with bugs. But its IT firms—Google, Facebook, Apple, and Microsoft—exude information power, but for whom?

UNDERSTANDING CYBERSPACE AND STATES

Since the Peace of Westphalia, we have grown accustomed to international politics defined as a system of states. These sovereign states are marked by holding what Max Weber called *Gewaltmonopol des Staates*—the monopoly on violence.[4] National leaders raised armies, managed police forces, and collected intelligence, both internal and external, on threats to the sovereign and his subjects. Of course, at many times, unconventional forces have risen against sovereigns to assert their own political beliefs. The United States was founded out of such a conflict, a revolution, in which a colony broke away from the mother country. Conflicts of asymmetry, what is commonly lumped under the heading of irregular warfare in military doctrine, are common today.[5] Overlain on these conflicts is the cyber component. The Islamic State mobilizes and recruits via social media and its "Hacking Division" assembles target lists of U.S. military personnel and publishes them.[6]

CYBERWAR AND ENDER'S LESSON

As we try to see our cyber future, consulting science fiction is sometimes helpful. Orson Scott Card's *Ender's Game*, published in 1985, provides one way of thinking about our cyber conflicts of tomorrow. Set after planet Earth has defeated an invasion by an alien race dubbed the "Buggers," *Ender's Game* grapples with how humankind can stave off the alien threat once and for all by taking the fight to the enemy. To do so, Earth must develop the best possible military leaders to combat the aliens.

In Card's story, the trainees are extremely young, not even teens. Andrew "Ender" Wiggin, the hero-protagonist is among the youngest.

Ender and his cohort are thrown into a highly competitive regimen of team-based, zero-gravity combat matches, in which rapid processing of game parameters and opponents is fundamental. Decades aren't spent punching tickets or gradually rising through the ranks; there's no time. As the training progresses, these young über-commanders migrate from combat matches to command school, where they enter simulator chambers that we would describe today as virtual reality.

Only when the game ends is the reality made evident to Ender that the preparation and simulation had become, through a virtual platform, actual warfare with a mortal foe that reached its terrible conclusion. Ender's tutor and mentor for the final phase of his service connects the virtual to the real for him:

"Ender, for the past few months you have been the battle commander of our fleets. . . . There were no games, the battles were real, and the only enemy you fought was the Buggers. You won every battle, and today you finally fought them at their home world, where their queen was, all the queens from all their colonies, they all were there and you destroyed them completely. They'll never attack us again. You did it. You."

Real. Not a game. Ender's mind was too tired to cope with it all. They weren't just points of light in the air, they were real ships that he had fought with and real ships he had destroyed. And a real world he had blasted into oblivion.[7]

Card offers us a cautionary note that should be well considered by those who will ask for cyber weapons to be created and those who will employ them. Cyberwar sounds quite unreal, and it may be today, but when we consider that nations continue to advance offensive cyber programs to repeat events such as Stuxnet, the monopoly of capability held by the United States is certain to erode. Indeed, it probably already has eroded.[8]

Naively unaware of the gravity of their experience, Ender and his cohort of adolescent military leaders wage war without knowing its costs, and thus are the sort of risk takers capable of producing decisive leadership through experimentation and innovation. Cyber soldiers who are actively engaged against enemies they do not know, and have only seen and heard via electronic means, are not beyond imagination. Drones and cyber will ostensibly wage tomorrow's war. Indeed even drones that can be hacked via cyber means are a real possibility.[9] Technological development since the 1991 Gulf War has been stunning. Pundits declared the grainy monochrome camera footage of laser-guided missile strikes hallmarks of a Nintendo War. Development in the last 20 years in video games should indicate how far virtual war has progressed. There is what political scientist James Der Derian has identified as the merging of IT, media, and conflict in a hyper-reality.[10]

THE OTHER SIDE OF THE CHESSBOARD: THE WORLD'S CYBER POWERS

There is the rapid shift in geopolitical alignment that covers the span of our text. The rise of cyber geopolitics has occurred across a period in which the United States sent volunteers to fight two major wars while the domestic population coped with an economic crisis of magnitude not seen since the Great Depression. But if there is an undisputed leader in cyber conflict (and intelligence) capability, it is the United States. Nonetheless, there are the other cyber powers.

China's economy has continued to rumble forward, with defense spending rising at an increasing pace as it seeks to assert itself. Huawei, now the world's leading seller of telecommunications hardware, dominates a market sector in which no major U.S. firm competes.[11] China walls itself off from threats, in the form of platforms such as Facebook or Google, content, and ostensibly cyber attacks as well, through strict government control of its portion of the Internet. The hacking chronicled in the APT 1 and other industry reports indicates the degree to which state espionage can support the aims of a government in the business of its state-run or national companies. China is a rising cyber power, but also one on the forefront of walling itself off from what it views as the negative influences of cyberspace, from crime to ideas that threaten the one-party nondemocratic regime managing what is on its way to being the world's largest economy.

China has grown to become the manufacturing hub of the Information Revolution. Some 70 percent of the world's mobile phones are made in China.[12] But although it constructs massive numbers of devices, it is but a part of a global supply chain often dominated by foreign brands. Innovation largely takes place elsewhere, at least for now. As discussed in this book's first chapter, Carr's three pillars of power, military, economic, and information, China is increasingly incorporated into modern cyber-enabled military and a massive technology economy.[13] China's capacity to employ information power remains less clear, as it builds upon a state-controlled information ecosystem that is intolerant of political discourse or even complaints about the weather and related pollution.

Russia too has an information problem, with its oligarchy displeased by "information security" problems produced by open, unfettered access to the Internet. But whereas China's military thinkers have contemplated the use of cyber force, Russia, in at least two cases, Estonia and Georgia, has employed it. The Russians have not perpetrated a "kinetic" hack the likes of Stuxnet that may be attributed to them, but they have demonstrated the capacity to employ cyber espionage techniques. Furthermore, through the country's RT international news organization, Putin's Russia has managed to deploy a sophisticated public diplomacy tool in traditional and new media able to communicate Moscow's view on events.

So while Russia may be economically hamstrung—the national currency all but collapsed in 2015 and low oil prices severely dent the government's budget—it is able to utilize cyber means to intimidate. Neither the possible pipeline cyber attack against Turkey nor the recent German blast furnace failure is conclusively tied to Russia, but Russia's hand in both events would make sense.

Then there is Russia's criminal cyber complex. The former Eastern bloc is a nexus of cybercrime (although Nigeria and other West African states are a haven for more pedestrian fraud schemes involving the Internet). Unwillingness to cooperate with other nations on cybercrime has allowed a multibillion-dollar criminal enterprise to flourish. Russia's hackers are good at what they do. " 'In terms of quality, Russia is the leader.' "[14] That these elite hackers may be tapped by the Putin government to perform tasks for their nation appears an added bonus. And finally, Russia continues to irritate the United States with its hosting of Edward Snowden, from whose archive nothing especially damaging to Russia has emerged.

Cyber power is a factor of cleverness, computer skills, interconnectedness, resources, and motivation. China and Russia clearly are developing it, and have the educational means to develop such talent. Others are trying. There is perhaps no better yardstick for a Western academic to measure the potential cyber power of any state than to observe the number of computer science students flowing from different countries, and to see how many return home. While this is just one data point, it is a marker of capability. In the wake of the Shamoon attack against Aramco, it became obvious that the Saudis would face an uphill battle in developing a domestic cyber capability, as an informal poll of colleagues indicated none of us had ever met one. Lebanese? Sure. Egyptians? Yes. Turks? Indeed. Iranians? Many. But the wealthy states of the Persian Gulf have failed to produce their own IT talent, and choose instead to import it.

There is a rise of the South in cyberspace, however. India continues to develop talent and is in the process of mobilizing it. So too, its longtime nemesis, Pakistan. Interest in computing and information technology continues to grow as a policy issue for other countries of the developing world—Brazil, Indonesia, Kenya, and South Africa, among others. But this large swathe of cyberspace is still developing even as the world's powers build out cyber military forces and attempt to secure their infrastructure. How the rising South's nations will develop their own cyber laws and policies, build out resilient infrastructure, and shape global norms is anyone's guess.[15]

Finally, the United States divides its allies on cybersecurity into two camps: those sharing security agreements, formal or informal, and those in the Five Eyes club that includes the UK, Australia, Canada, and New Zealand. The Snowden documents underscored the sizable gap between how the U.S. perceives its relationships with important NATO allies and the Five Eyes states. While the Five Eyes cooperate closely on signals intelligence in cyberspace, the espionage activities aimed at allied leaders, most painfully the case of targeting German chancellor Angela Merkel, sent a clear message regarding how much America trusts countries it is obligated to defend. As the United States attempts to assert itself in governing cyberspace, promoting international norms, or framing global agreements, it must overcome the fallout of the Snowden affair and disentangle cybersecurity issues from those involving signals intelligence. There are the special cases of France, which openly asserts its justification for conducting economic espionage, and Israel, which may collaborate with the United States, but will go to the lengths it believes necessary to defend itself from the grave threats it faces in a hugely unstable region. Coalition action on cyber issues has been significantly set back by revelation of the extensive nature of signals intelligence activity undertaken by the United States in cyberspace.

AMERICA THE BRITTLE?

Irony abounds that the United States, builder of the Internet and likely the first party to launch a cyber attack aimed at damaging real machinery to achieve its international aims, stands as so vulnerable. America's problem is its attack surface,[16] the interconnected computers of its economy and society, and how they may be subverted, as their vulnerabilities remain largely unmitigated. All the while, the march toward an Internet of Things accelerates. For years, doom saying has dominated arguments on why something should be done about cybersecurity. This is a pragmatic text, one that is aimed at dismissing rhetoric of cyber Pearl Harbor or cyber Katrina, or whatever cyber-prefixed disaster may lurk in the near future. But there have been disasters of sorts. The Manning-WikiLeaks episode demonstrated the potential of how a significant breach of classified information could influence global political events. Worse, the Snowden revelations put U.S. relations in deep jeopardy with critically important allies, while also damaging the relationship between Washington and Silicon Valley. It could be argued that the primitive diagram of how to get at unencrypted internal data traffic at Google, found in a leaked NSA slide, did more to damage the government's relationship with the company than any effort to regulate its business operations.

Google and the other giants of Silicon Valley are doing something about cybersecurity, spurred in part by the Snowden leaks, but also by the discovery of massive security holes such as Heartbleed and the Shellshock bugs found in open source software.[17] But this involves modifying the architecture of the Internet while it is in use. It is a costly activity, and can't be seriously entertained by lean start-ups attempting to raise venture funding by rapidly building out platforms or applications. They cannot expend four years on crafting secure software code as Microsoft did with its release of Windows Vista, it's most significant effort at designing a secure operating system from the ground up.[18] Cybersecurity is expensive to build into software, a luxury for market leaders who can bear the cost.

As a result, the users of software and the Internet undertake security in large part. For large organizations, this is a massive effort as well. JPMorgan Chase now fields a cybersecurity organization of more than 1,000 people, larger than Google's, and led by Gregory Rattray, Condoleezza Rice's chief cyber expert from when she served as the national security advisor.[19] Different industry sectors attempt to collaborate, share intelligence, and learn how to cope with the rising number of cyber attacks that increasingly cut into corporate earnings and claim the jobs of senior staff not demonstrating adequate vigilance. Static defenses such as antivirus software and network firewalls appear inadequate in the face of sophisticated hacker groups often operating at the behest of nation-states or at least tolerated by them.

Government has been of little help thus far, and indeed it seems ill equipped to help itself. The Snowden breach was a massive blow to the NSA, as it exposed so many of the sources and methods the agency had developed to perform its signals intelligence operations in cyberspace over decades. Former CIA director Michael Morrell summed up the incident in a recent post-retirement monograph. " 'You would have thought that of all the government entities on the planet, the one least vulnerable to such grand theft would have been the N.S.A. ... But it turned out that the N.S.A. had left itself vulnerable.' " The NSA's massive reverse indicates a belief in the cybersecurity community that no potential target is beyond risk of compromise.

Nonetheless, a collection of offices spread across the agencies of the federal government, in the FBI, DHS, the Defense Department, and others, work to secure cyberspace. Massive resources have poured into this effort over the last decade, but evidence of success on cyber defense is scant. Instead we are left to read about the compromised systems of the Obama White House. Although no classified communications of the presidential inner circle were successfully eavesdropped upon, the contents of email accounts used for the day-to-day business of the world's most powerful leader were purloined, likely by Russia. Clearly the U.S. government has yet to develop an adequate answer on cybersecurity for its own systems, let alone those of the rest of the nation, despite the countless hours spent on frameworks and policy addresses on the topic.

TOWARD CYBERWAR?

What we can marvel at is the growing capability of offensive capability in cyber military operations. Stuxnet was an incredible exploit of a foreign power's energy infrastructure, the Iranian nuclear enrichment facilities at Natanz. Yes, Stuxnet likely required a human being to deliver the initial payload to the centrifuge farms of the Iranian nuclear program,[20] but it made the stuff of imagination real. It was a crossing of the Rubicon that cannot and will not be reversed. We can talk about norms for cyber conflict and arms control in cyberspace, but the Defense Department's policy document on cyber operations codifies the policy of standing ready to employ cyber tactics and techniques to combat the military enemies of the United States, from nation-states to terror groups.

Can cyber weapons make war less violent and costly? That is doubtful. Consider a Stuxnet-like attack on a major petrochemical facility, one that produces a "cyber Bhopal" event causing thousands of casualties. Such an event would be no less catastrophic than a major bombing raid and would likely be considered employment of a Weapon of Mass Destruction (WMD), possibly provoking a response in kind. That nuclear power plants, oil and gas production facilities, pipelines, industrial plants, and other sites of heavy industry may be the target of kinetic cyber attacks should make us uneasy. While no bombs may fall, damage can be done nonetheless. In demonstrating that kinetic cyber attacks work, Stuxnet opened up a massive area of potential conflict in which states or even non-state actors may conduct operations, at least partially veiled from attribution and thus closed to clear-cut response.

For now, the Department of Defense has chosen to limit its publicly announced doctrine regarding cyber warfare to support its military aims. Ashton Carter stated that the DoD is willing to make use of cyber weapons, if and when they are of utility in more effectively prosecuting a conflict on terms favorable to the United States.

There may be times when the President or the Secretary of Defense may determine that it would be appropriate for the U.S. military to conduct cyber operations to disrupt an adversary's military related networks or infrastructure so that the U.S. military can protect U.S. interests in an area of operations.[21]

Carter has stipulated that the DoD is to "Integrate cyber options into plans," for how it should prosecute conflict.[22] It is preparing for war in cyberspace, but it is also building its defenses and reaching out to develop coalitions as well. Establishing cooperation that works will be critical to averting chaos in and the Balkanization of cyberspace to whatever degree possible.

We should not be so enamored with our cyber weapons, as they provide a utility that does not yet overshadow the application of kinetic force, or the actual occupation of enemy territory. Perhaps the United States could shut off the power in a pair of warring nations to send the example that their conflict is unacceptable, but we should appreciate the potential blowback that may occur from such action too. Cyber weapons will likely recast conflict, delivering not only military outcomes but economic or informational ones as well. That said, we should be leery of prognostication in which cyber armaments stand as a substitute to soldiers and weapons systems.

It is best to close this book with an anecdote on the limits of cognition enabled by technology. At a gathering of military intelligence staff officers in late 2011, a Navy NCO, serving in the U.S. Navy Special Operations Command, issued an important reminder as to the importance of real force and the eyewitness perspective in conflicts undertaken in our cyber age. Following more than a dozen senior intelligence staff officers, who typically offered longwinded presentations that often bordered upon bloviating, he introduced himself, "I'm Master Chief Dave. I'm with DEV-GRU, if you haven't heard of us, Google it."[23]

With the informal confidence abundant in a special operator community hardened by the mistakes and triumphs of more than a decade of chasing down insurgents and terrorists around the globe, Master Chief Dave recalled one of his earliest operations in the War on Terror. Aboard a Chinook helicopter over eastern Afghanistan early in the U.S. intervention following the 9/11 attacks, Dave's unit was ordered to interdict a vehicle, "with a tall man in white robes" among its passengers.[24] They were to set down, stop the vehicle, by force if necessary, and take into custody anyone on the U.S. government's Al Qaeda and Taliban most-wanted list. While he never directly came out with it, the insinuation from the command echelon was clear enough. The tall man might well be Osama bin Laden.

Twenty minutes out from the target, the orders changed. Dave's unit was now only to perform post-strike analysis. Someone higher up the chain of command had opted for an air strike. Targeted by precision munitions, the vehicle was destroyed with clinical efficiency. Master Chief Dave's unit flew in to assess the results. "It turned out the tall white man in robes wasn't all that tall," he recalled. "He only seemed tall because all of the others were women and kids."[25] It would take DEVGRU another decade to reach bin Laden, only after a massive technical and human intelligence operation suggested him to be holed up in Abbottabad. Getting the top target in a decade-long conflict was ultimately left to people willing to recognize bin Laden a few paces away and make the decision to take his life. For all the technology involved in getting bin Laden, he was killed by men who saw him face-to-face.

Cyberspace will transform intelligence, diplomacy, and warfare, but it does not supplant the other human-directed capabilities available to the United States' political leaders. Understanding cyberspace, and effectively engaging in the geopolitics of it, is not an exercise of technological mastery. As was said before, cyberspace is a technically mediated reflection of the human condition. To understand it, we must understand ourselves.

Notes

CHAPTER 1

1. The company pegged the costs of the incident as at least $15 million in the quarter it occurred and a final tally could stand at as much as $100 million. "Sony Says Studio Hack Cost It $15 Million in Fiscal Third Quarter," *Los Angeles Times*, February 4, 2015, available at: http://www.latimes.com/entertainment/envelope/cotown/la-et-ct-sony-hack-cost-20150204-story.html.

2. Tatiana Siegel, "Amy Pascal to Step Down from Top Sony Post," *Hollywood Reporter*, February 2, 2015, available at: http://www.hollywoodreporter.com/news/amy-pascal-step-down-top-755789.

3. Barack Obama, "A New Tool against Cyber Threats," *Medium*, April 1, 2015, available at: https://medium.com/@PresidentObama/a-new-tool-against-cyber-threats-1a30c188bc4.

4. Edward Hallett Carr, *The Twenty Years' Crisis, 1919–1939: An Introduction to the Study of International Relations*, Harper Perennial: New York, 1964.

5. This, of course, is a reference to the Stuxnet cyber attack against the Iranian nuclear enrichment program. Kim Zetter, *Countdown to Zero Day: Stuxnet and the Launch of the World's First Digital Weapon*, Crown: New York, 2014.

6. An April 23, 2013, false tweet from the Associated Press's Twitter account in which the White House was alleged to have been bombed likely triggered a "flash crash" of the New York Stock Exchange, in which automated trading systems drove $136 billion of stock value from the companies listed in the S&P 500. "Markets Sink Briefly on Fake AP Terror Tweet," *CNBC*, available at: http://www.cnbc.com/id/100646197.

7. The Sony breach is mentioned above, but also consider Chelsea Manning's leak of State Department cables to WikiLeaks. Arguments that the Manning-WikiLeaks breach had a catalyzing effect in fomenting the Arab Spring should

be considered. Philip Wiess, "The Evidence That Bradley Manning Helped Start the Arab Spring," *Mondoweiss*, August 6, 2013, available at: http://mondoweiss .net/2013/08/the-evidence-that-bradley-manning-helped-start-the-arab-spring.

8. The GAO weighed in on the possibility of wi-fi-enabled cyber attacks against aircraft in a recent report. "According to cybersecurity experts we interviewed, Internet connectivity in the cabin should be considered a direct link between the aircraft and the outside world, which includes potential malicious actors. FAA officials and cybersecurity and aviation experts we spoke to said that increasingly passengers in the cabin can access the Internet via onboard wireless broadband systems. One cybersecurity expert noted that a virus or malware planted in websites visited by passengers could provide an opportunity for a malicious attacker to access the IP-connected onboard information system through their infected machines." Air Traffic Control, *FAA Needs a More Comprehensive Approach to Address Cybersecurity as Agency Transitions to Next Gen, GAO-15-370,* Government Accountability Office: Washington, D.C., April 14, 2015.

9. Maren Leed, "Offensive Cyber Capabilities at the Operational Level," Center for Strategic International Studies, 2013, available at: http://csis.org/files/publication/130916_Leed_OffensiveCyberCapabilities_Web.pdf.

10. Referenced here is the transfer of a massive archive of diplomatic cables by Chelsea Manning to WikiLeaks. For background on the evolution of the State bureaucracy and the diplomatic cable, see David Nickles, *Under the Wire: How the Telegraph Changed Diplomacy,* Harvard University Press: Cambridge, MA, 2003.

11. Norbert Wiener, *Cybernetics: Or Control and Communication in the Animal and the Machine,* MIT Press: Cambridge, MA, 1948.

12. Turing's contributions to this concept are considered later as well. James Gleick, *The Information: A History, a Theory, a Flood,* Pantheon: New York, 2011, 239.

13. William Gibson, *Neuromancer,* Ace: New York, 1984.

14. And so we may thank Bob Guccione, publisher of *Penthouse* as well as *Omni,* for running Gibson's story. William Gibson, "Burning Chrome," *Omni,* July 1982.

15. While perhaps not properly sourced, the concept is applicable to this work. "Ray Bradbury," *Wikiquote,* available at: http://en.wikiquote.org/wiki/Talk:Ray _Bradbury.

16. Gutenberg's first commercial printing job was, ironically, a run of indulgences for the Catholic Church. "The Gutenberg Press," *Treasures of the McDonald Collection,* Special Collections and Archives Research Center, Oregon State University.

17. Joseph Nye, "Nuclear Lessons for Cyber Security," *Strategic Studies Quarterly,* 19, Winter 2011.

18. Martin Libicki, *Conquest in Cyberspace: National Security and Information Warfare,* Cambridge University Press: Cambridge, MA, 2007.

19. Leonard Kleinrock, "The Internet Trajectory and Technology" (lecture), Rice University, February 5, 2015.

20. See Willis H. Ware, *Security and Privacy in Computer Systems,* RAND: Santa Monica, CA, April 1967; Jerome Saltzer and Michael Schroeder, "The Protection of Information in Computer Systems," *Communications of the ACM,* 17(7), July 1974.

21. Peter G. Neuman, et al., *A Provably Secure Operating System*, Stanford Research Institute: Menlo Park, CA, June 1975.

22. Jeff Atwood, "Given Enough Money, All Bugs Are Shallow," *Coding Horror*, April 3, 2015, available at: http://blog.codinghorror.com/given-enough-money -all-bugs-are-shallow/.

23. Also considered is the relationship between the massive cable release by Manning and the events of the Arab Spring.

24. An exception may be found in Microsoft's Secure Development Lifecycle, which has considerably reduced the number of security-related bugs in the company's operating systems and other major products. There are others. See "Security Development Lifecycle," Microsoft, available at: http://www.microsoft.com/en-us/sdl/.

25. Gus P. Coldebella and Brian M. White, "Foundational Questions Regarding the Federal Role in Cybersecurity," *Journal of National Security Law and Policy*, 4(1): 236, 2010.

26. The annual cost of simply debugging software has risen to more than $300 billion according to an industry study. "Increasing Software Development Productivity with Reversible Debugging," *Undo Software*, 2014, available at: http://undo-software.com/wp-content/uploads/2014/10/Increasing-software -development-productivity-with-reversible-debugging.pdf.

27. The American Chamber of Commerce stands firmly against cybersecurity regulation. See John Thune, "Cybersecurity Legislation: A Way Forward," *Free Enterprise* (blog), September 13, 2013, available at: http://archive.freeenterprise .com/homeland-security/cybersecurity-legislation-way-forward.

28. But explored in Nir Kshetri, *Cybercrime and Cybersecurity in the Global South*, Palgrave: London, 2013.

29. These regimes also receive help from Western companies. See Aida Aki, "Iran Plans Its Own Sanitized Internet with Chinese Help," *Voice of America*, July 31, 2013, available at: http://www.voanews.com/content/iran-plans-its -own-sanitized-internet-with-chinese-help/1713638.html; Morgan Marquis-Boire, et al., *Planet Blue Coat: Mapping Global Censorship and Surveillance Tools*, Citizen Lab: Toronto, January 15, 2013.

30. Herbert Lin, "Laying an Intellectual Foundation for Cyberdeterrence: Some Initial Steps," in Jörg Krüger, Bertram Nickolay, and Sandro Gaycken, eds., *The Secure Information Society*, Springer: New York, 2013.

CHAPTER 2

1. Sophie Curtis, "Quarter of the World Will Be Using Smartphones in 2016," *Telegraph*, December 11, 2014, available at: http://www.telegraph.co.uk/ technology/mobile-phones/11287659/Quarter-of-the-world-will-be-using -smartphones-in-2016.html.

2. Superbowl-Ads.com, available at: http://superbowl-ads.com/article_archive/.

3. LifeMinders ad has been called the worst TV ad in Super Bowl history. Aaron Barr, "Fallon Quits Lifeminders.com Amid Bowl Fumble," *AdWeek*, January 31, 2000, available at: http://www.adweek.com/news/advertising/fallon-quits -lifeminderscom-amid-bowl-fumble-37382.

4. Dashiell Bennett, "8 Dot-Coms That Spent Millions on Super Bowl Ads and No Longer Exist," *Business Insider*, February 2, 2011.

5. Roger Lowenstein, *Origins of the Crash: The Great Bubble and Its Undoing*, Penguin: New York, 2004.

6. Linda Rosencrance, "Teen Hacker 'Mafiaboy' Sentenced," *Computerworld*, September 13, 2001, available at: http://www.computerworld.com/article/2583318/security0/teen-hacker—mafiaboy—sentenced.html.

7. Erik Brynjolfsson, "The Productivity Paradox of Information Technology," *Communications of the ACM*, 36(12): 66–77, 1993.

8. Nicholas Carr, "IT Doesn't Matter," *Harvard Business Review*, May 2003.

9. Daniel Yergin and Joseph Stanislaw, *The Commanding Heights: The Battle for the World Economy*, Free Press: New York, 1998.

10. Michael Lewis, *The New New Thing: A Silicon Valley Story*, W.W. Norton: New York, 2000, 14.

11. There is also a gap between the technical activity in computer security and policy related to it.

12. William Aspray, ed., *Computing before Computers*, Iowa State University Press: Ames, IA, 1990.

13. David Kahn, *The Codebreakers: The Comprehensive History of Secret Communication from Ancient Times to the Internet*, Scribner: New York, 1996.

14. Thomas Haigh, "Los Alamos Bets on ENIAC: Nuclear Monte Carlo Simulations, 1947–1948," *IEEE Annals of the History of Computing*, 36(3): 42–63, July–September 2014.

15. Arthur W. Burks, Herman H. Goldstine and John von Neumann, "Preliminary Discussions of the Logical Design of an Electronic Computing Instrument," in Abraham H. Taub, ed., *Collected Works of John von Neuman*, MacMillan: New York, 1947.

16. Ibid.

17. Alan Turing, "Intelligent Machinery, a Heretical Theory," in Koichi Furukawa, Donald Michie, and Stephen Muggleton, eds., *Machine Intelligence 15*, Oxford University Press: Oxford, UK, 1999.

18. Turing, "Intelligent Machinery, a Heretical Theory."

19. John Markoff, "Computer Wins on 'Jeopardy!': Trivial, It's Not," *New York Times*, February 16, 2011.

20. Erik Brynjolfsson and Andrew McAfee, *Race against the Machine: How the Digital Revolution Is Accelerating Innovation, Driving Productivity, and Irreversibly Transforming Employment and the Economy*, Digital Frontier Press: Cambridge, MA, 2012.

21. Bitcoin is a peer-to-peer electronic cash system, in which computer processing cycles produce a cryptographic product that is uniquely identifiable and thus able to prevent double-spending in the way that peer-to-peer systems can be employed to create an unrestricted number of copies of other file types, such as music or video files. Satoshi Nakamoto, "Bitcoin: A Peer-to-Peer Electronic Cash System," bitcoin.org, available at: https://bitcoin.org/en/bitcoin-paper.

22. Shawn Mankad and George Michailidis, "Discovering the Ecosystem of an Electronic Financial Market with a Dynamic Machine-Learning Method," *Algorithmic Finance*, 2(2): 151–165, 2013.

23. Sameer Soleja, communication with the author, August 7, 2014.

24. Geoffrey Rogow, "Rise of the (Market) Machines," *MarketBeat*, June 19, 2009, http://blogs.wsj.com/marketbeat/2009/06/19/rise-of-the-market-machines/.

25. Austin, Atlanta, Dallas, and Seattle also can claim to have significant portions of their regional economies dedicated to computing or IT innovation.

26. Irving Wladawsky-Berger, "Innovation Hubs in the Global Digital Economy," April 2, 2014, available at: http://blog.irvingwb.com/blog/2014/04/innovation-hubs-in-the-global-digital-economy.html.

27. Paul Ceruzzi, *A History of Modern Computing*, MIT Press: Cambridge, MA, 2003.

28. "About: The SAGE Air Defense System," Lincoln Laboratory, available at: https://www.ll.mit.edu/about/History/SAGEairdefensesystem.html.

29. "Expedia, Inc. Acquires the Travelocity Brand and Other Associated Assets from Sabre Corporation," Sabre, January 23, 2015, available at: http://www.sabre.com/newsroom/sabre-and-expedia-announce-expedias-acquisition-of-travelocity/#sthash.zFEXvv46.dpuf.

30. Gordon Moore, "Cramming More Components onto Integrated Circuits," *Electronics*, 38(8), April 19, 1965, 4.

31. Ibid.

32. Dean Evans, "Moore's Law: How Long Will It Last?" techradar, February 22, 2014, available at: http://www.techradar.com/us/news/computing/moore-s-law-how-long-will-it-last—1226772.

33. As of the time of this book's drafting, the most powerful microprocessor was IBM's zEC12, composed of 2.75 transistors at the 32-nm scale running at a clock speed of 5.5 GHz. "IBM zEnterprise System Technical Introduction," IBM, available at: http://www.redbooks.ibm.com/redbooks/pdfs/sg248050.pdf.

34. Manuel Castells, *The Rise of the Network Society, The Information Age: Economy, Society and Culture Vol. I*, Oxford University Press: Cambridge, MA, 1996.

35. J. C. R. Licklider and Welden Clark, "On-line Man-Computer Communication," *AIEE-IRE '62 (Spring) Proceedings of the May 1–3, 1962, Spring Joint Computer Conference*, 113–128.

36. Leonard Kleinrock, "The Internet Trajectory and Technology," The 2015 Gene Brice Colloquium, Rice University, February 5, 2015.

37. Robert Frankston, "The Computer Utility as a Marketplace for Computer Services," master's thesis, MIT, 1974, available at: http://www.frankston.com/public/?name=TR128.

38. Vinton Cerf and Robert Kahn, "A Protocol for Packet Network Intercommunication," *IEEE Transactions on Communications*, 22(5): 637–648, May 1974.

39. Abhay Bhushan, Ken Pogran, Ray Tomlinson and Jim White, "RFC 561 – Standardizing Network Mail Headers," September 5, 1973, available at: https://tools.ietf.org/html/rfc561.

40. Barry Lerner et al., "Brief History of the Internet," Internet Society, available at: http://www.internetsociety.org/internet/what-internet/history-internet/brief-history-internet.

41. The Department of Defense maintains three significant, widely distributed TCP/IP computer networks for unclassified data, data classified up to the secret level of classification, and top secret classified information.

42. Peter W. Singer and Allan Friedman, *Cybersecurity and Cyberwar: What Everyone Needs to Know*, Oxford University Press: Cambridge, MA, 2014.

43. Slava Gerovitch, "InterNyet: Why the Soviet Union Did Not Build a Nationwide Computer Network," *History and Technology*, 24(4): 335–350, December 2008.

44. Hugh Schofield, "Minitel: The Rise and Fall of the France-Wide Web," *BBC*, June 27, 2012, available at: http://www.bbc.com/news/magazine-18610692.

45. See Erik Brynjolfsson and Brian Kahin, *Understanding the Digital Economy*, MIT Press: Cambridge, MA, 2000; Hal Varian, Joseph Farrell and Carl Shapiro, *The Economics of Information Technology*, Cambridge University Press: Cambridge, UK, 2004.

46. Milton Mueller, "ICANN and Internet Regulation," *Communications of the ACM*, 42(6), June 1999.

47. Paul Twomey, *Securing the Cyber Commons: A Global Dialogue* (conference), March 27–28, 2011, University of Toronto, Toronto, Canada, available at: http://www.cyberdialogue.ca/previous-dialogues/2011-about/.

48. Vinton Cerf, "I Remember IANA," IETF, October 17, 1998, http://tools.ietf.org/html/rfc2468.

49. "Microsoft and Apple Affirm Commitment to Build Next Generation Software for Macintosh," Microsoft, August 6, 1997, available at: http://news.microsoft.com/1997/08/06/microsoft-and-apple-affirm-commitment-to-build-next-generation-software-for-macintosh/.

50. "iTunes Store Top Music Retailer in the US," Apple, April 3, 2008, available at: https://www.apple.com/pr/library/2008/04/03iTunes-Store-Top-Music-Retailer-in-the-US.html.

51. Today downloading music is incredibly easy, and often doesn't involve buying it.

52. Amazon's "one-click" Web purchasing is another example and a concept the company felt worthy of patent protection. Tim O'Reilly, "My Conversation with Jeff Bezos," March 2, 2000, available at: http://archive.oreilly.com/pub/a/oreilly/ask_tim/2000/bezos_0300.html.

53. "Ten Things We Know to Be True," Google, available at: https://www.google.com/intl/en/about/company/philosophy/.

54. "2015 Financial Tables," Google, available at: https://investor.google.com/financial/tables.html. Google's revenues possibly represent as much as 10 percent of global advertising spending. See Ingrid Lunden, "Internet Ad Spend to Reach $121B in 2014, 23% of $537B Total Ad Spend, Ad Tech Boosts Display," TechCrunch, April 7, 2014, available at: http://techcrunch.com/2014/04/07/internet-ad-spend-to-reach-121b-in-2014-23-of-537b-total-ad-spend-ad-tech-gives-display-a-boost-over-search/.

55. Ryan Singel, "Analysis: Google's Ad Targeting Turns Algorithms on You," *Wired*, March 11, 2009, available at: http://www.wired.com/2009/03/google-ad-annou/.

56. Adrian Covert, "Gmail at 10: How Google Dominated E-mail," *CNN Money*, available at: http://money.cnn.com/2014/04/01/technology/gmail/.

57. One can also largely block advertising in Gmail, with information regarding how to do so provided by Google, see: "Remove Unwanted Ads," Google, available at: https://support.google.com/ads/answer/2662850?hl=en.

58. There is an important caveat here on software. Commodity software such as Microsoft Office or Adobe Photoshop is sold on a licensed copy model, which is often subverted by unauthorized reproduction of the software or subversion of the licensing scheme. Also lucrative is enterprise software, such as Oracle or SAP, which is used to input, process, and manage organizational data, often through a Web interface. Another business model in software is open source software with managed support in which organizations pay an outside firm to oversee their deployment and operation of "free" software. Red Hat, a specialist in Linux operating system operations, is an exemplar in this space.

59. Facebook's last ad revenue figure from 2014 was $3.59 billion in the fourth quarter of 2014. Tim Peterson, "Facebook's Mobile Revenue Climbs to $2.5 Billion as Ad Prices Soar," AdvertisingAge, January 28, 2015, available at: http://adage.com/article/digital/facebook-s-mobile-revenue-hits-2-5-billion-prices-soar/296869/.

60. "Stats," *Facebook*, available at: http://newsroom.fb.com/company-info/.

61. As of August 7, 2014, Google Finance.

62. "Our Mission," Facebook, available at: http://newsroom.fb.com/company-info/.

63. Steven Pearlstein, "Review: 'The Second Machine Age,' by Erik Brynjolfsson and Andrew McAfee," *Washington Post*, January 17, 2014, available at: http://www.washingtonpost.com/opinions/review-the-second-machine-age-by-erik-brynjolfsson-and-andrew-mcafee/2014/01/17/ace0611a-718c-11e3-8b3f-b1666705ca3b_story.html.

64. Chris Taylor, "Instagram Has 100 Million Users, Says Zuckerberg," *Mashable*, February 19, 2014, available at: http://mashable.com/2012/09/11/instagram-100-million/.

65. Adrian Covert, "Facebook Buys WhatsApp for $19 Billion," *CNN Money*, February 19, 2014, available at: http://money.cnn.com/2014/02/19/technology/social/facebook-whatsapp/.

66. Alec Ross, "19 Billion Reasons for Opportunity in Ukraine," *CNN*, February 27, 2014, available at: http://www.cnn.com/2014/02/27/opinion/ross-ukraine-opportunity/.

67. "Welcome to Apache Hadoop!," *Apache Foundation*, available at: http://hadoop.apache.org/.

68. William Uricchio, "The Greatest Art Form of the Twentieth Century," *Journal of Visual Studies*, 13(1): 104, 2014.

69. Kevin Poulsen, "Software Bug Contributed to Blackout," SecurityFocus, February 2, 2004, available at: http://www.securityfocus.com/news/8016.

70. Chris Bronk, Ken Medlock and Dan Wallach, "Is U.S. Vulnerable to a Cyber Attack?" *Houston Chronicle*, May 3, 2009.

71. Texas's CenterPoint, the power distribution utility for much of the greater Houston region, deployed 2.2 million computerized smart meters in the wake of

Hurricane Ike, a large Category 2 storm that is the third costliest on record. The interconnected meters are touted to provide enhanced capacity for detection of grid damage and thus repair. "Centerpoint Energy Completes Smart Meter Installations," CenterPoint, available at: http://www.centerpointenergy.com/services/electricity/competitiveretailers/smartmeters/a3d58d69ef0fe110VgnVCM1000005a1a0d0aRCRD/.

72. Dale Evans, "The Internet of Things: How the Next Evolution of the Internet Is Changing Everything," Cisco, April 2011, available at: http://www.cisco.com/web/about/ac79/docs/innov/IoT_IBSG_0411FINAL.pdf.

73. Rolfe Winkler and Daisuke Wakabayashi, "Google to Buy Nest Labs for $3.2 Billion," *Wall Street Journal*, January 13, 2014.

74. Liz Gannes, "Google's Nest Buys Dropcam for $555 Million," *re/code*, January 20, 2014, available at: http://recode.net/2014/06/20/googles-nest-buys-dropcam-for-555-million/.

75. Nicholas M. Luscombe, Dov Greenbaum, and Mark Gerstein, "What Is Bioinformatics? A Proposed Definition and Overview of the Field," *Methods of Information in Medicine*, 4: 346, 2001.

76. "The Human Genome Project Completion: Frequently Asked Questions," National Human Genome Research Institute, National Institutes of Health, available at: http://www.genome.gov/11006943.

77. "Size of Wikipedia," *Wikipedia*, available at: http://en.wikipedia.org/wiki/Wikipedia:Size_of_Wikipedia.

78. Ben Shneiderman, "A National Initiative for Technology-Mediated Social Participation," Lecture, Rice University, November 2, 2009.

79. Ben Shneiderman, "Science 2.0," *Science*, 319: 1349, 2008.

CHAPTER 3

1. Ronald Deibert, *Black Code: Inside the Battle for Cyberspace*, Random House: Toronto, 2013.

2. Stephen Manuel Wolfson, "The NSA, AT&T, and the Secrets of Room 641A," *I/S: A Journal of Law and Policy for the Information Age*, 3(3), 2007–2008.

3. Vinton Cerf, "Request for Comments 2468: I Remember IANA," *Internet Engineering Task Force*, Accessed September 10, 2014, available at: http://tools.ietf.org/html/rfc2468.

4. David D. Clark, "The Design Philosophy of the DARPA Internet Protocols," *ACM SIGCOMM Computer Communication Review,* 18(4): 114, 1988.

5. Ibid., 106.

6. Cade Metz, "Remembering Jon Postel—And the Day He Hijacked the Internet," *Wired*, October 15, 2012, available at: http://www.wired.com/2012/10/joe-postel/.

7. Hans Klein, "ICANN Reform: Establishing the Rule of Law," Georgia Institute of Technology Internet & Public Policy Project, available at: http://www.internetgovernance.org/wordpress/wp-content/uploads/ICANN-Reform-Establishing-the-Rule-of-Law.pdf.

8. Rajiv Chandrasekaran, "Internet Reconfiguration Concerns Federal Officials," *Washington Post*, January 31, 1998.

9. ICANN was founded in September 1998, just a month before Postel's death, in Marina del Rey, home to USC's Information Sciences Institute.

10. Internet Corporation for Assigned Names and Numbers, "ICANN Asks Commerce Department to Begin DNS Transition," available at: https://www.icann.org/news/icann-pr-1998-11-06-en.

11. Lawrence Lessig, "Open Code and Open Societies: Values of Internet Governance," *Chicago-Kent Law Review*, 74(3): 1406, 1999.

12. Ibid., 1407–1408.

13. These are noticeable on the Internet as the two-letter suffixes to Web addresses, such as .nz for New Zealand, .ly for Libya, .tv for Tuvalu, and so on. The United States is an interesting exception, with its .us suffix rarely used.

14. Milton L. Mueller, *Ruling the Root: Internet Governance and the Taming of Cyberspace*, MIT Press: Cambridge, MA, 2004, 43.

15. National Telecommunications and Information Administration, "NTIA Announces Intent to Transition Key Internet Domain Name Functions," Last modified March 14, 2014, Accessed December 18, 2014, available at: http://www.ntia.doc.gov/press-release/2014/ntia-announces-intent-transition-key-internet-domain-name-functions.

16. See Jack Quarter, "Recent Trends in the Worker-Ownership Movement in Canada: Four Alternative Models," *Economic and Industrial Democracy*, 11(4), 1990. Susan Albers Mohrman and Edward E. Lawler III, "Participative Managerial Behavior and Organizational Change," *Journal of Organizational Change Management*, 1(1), 1988. Anna Vari, "Approaches towards Conflict Resolution in Decision Processes," *Social Decision Methodology for Technological Projects*, Kluwer: Boston, 1989. Joanne Linnerooth, "The Danube River Basin: Negotiating Settlements to Transboundary Environmental Issues," *Natural Resources Journal*, 30, 1990.

17. Don MacLean, "Herding Schrödinger's Cats: Some Conceptual Tools for Thinking about Internet Governance," International Telecommunications Union, Background Paper for the ITU Workshop on Internet Governance, Geneva, February 26–27, 2004.

18. "Multistakeholder Model," *ICANNWiki*, available at: http://icannwiki.com/index.php/Multistakeholder_Model.

19. Karen Frazier, *Merit's History: The Internet Backbone Project, 1987–1995*, Merit Network, Inc: Ann Arbor, MI, 1995, available at: http://www.livinginternet.com/doc/merit.edu/intro.html.

20. ISOC has grown tremendously over the last decade. In 2005, the organization spent approximately $4.3 million on its activities, while in 2012, the year for which data are available, it expended some $33.8 million. In addition, the assets of the organization have grown to approximately $35 million. Internet Society, "Internet Society 2005 Annual Report," Last modified 2006, available at: http://www.isoc.org/isoc/reports/ar2005/ISOCAR05.pdf; Internet Society, "Internet Society 2012 Annual Report," available at: http://www.isoc.org/isoc/reports/ar2005/ISOCAR05.pdf.

21. International Telecommunications Union, "About ITU," available at: http://www.itu.int/en/about/Pages/default.aspx.

22. Adam Peake, "Internet Governance and the World Summit on the Information Society (WSIS)," Report prepared for the Association for Progressive Communications (APC), 3, available at: www.apc.org/documents/governance.pdf.

23. Milton L. Mueller, *Networks and States: The Global Politics of Internet Governance*, MIT Press: Cambridge, MA, 2010.

24. Mark Raymond, "The Internet as a Global Commons," *CIGI*, October 26, 2012, available at: https://www.cigionline.org/publications/2012/10/internet -global-commons.

25. ICANN introduced an Internationalized Domain Names (IDN) program and fast track process in October 2009. "Internationalized Domain Names," *ICANN*, available at: https://www.icann.org/resources/pages/idn-2012-02-25 -en?routing_type=path.

26. Kenneth Neil Cukier, "Who Controls the Internet?" *Foreign Affairs*, 84(6), November/December 2005. See also J. Abley and K. Lindqvist, "Request for Comments: 4786," *Internet Engineering Task Force*, December 2006, available at: http://tools.ietf.org/pdf/rfc4786.pdf.

27. IP addresses in the widely employed IP version 4 (IPv4) are 32 bits in length, which limits the number of total unique IP addresses to 4.3 billion. IP version 6 (IPv6) employs a 128-bit address scheme, considerably expanding address space. A typical IPv4 address is notionally represented as 128.1.1.1 and the website for this book's press, www.praeger.com, was 207.154.67.75 at the time of drafting.

28. National Telecommunications and Information Administration, "U.S. Principles on the Internet's Domain Name and Addressing System," June 30, 2005, available at: http://www.ntia.doc.gov/files/ntia/publications/usdnsprinciples _06302005.pdf.

29. Hans Klein, "ICANN Reform: Establishing the Rule of Law," Georgia Institute of Technology Internet & Public Policy Project, available at: http://www .internetgovernance.org/wordpress/wp-content/uploads/ICANN-Reform -Establishing-the-Rule-of-Law.pdf.

30. *Tunis Commitment*, World Summit of the Information Society, November 18, 2005.

31. D. Weller and B. Woodcock, "Internet Traffic Exchange: Market Developments and Policy Challenges," OECD Digital Economy Papers, No. 207, OECD Publishing: Paris, 2013.

32. Skype traffic represented eight percent of international long distance in 2009 according to the ITU. ICT "Statistics Newslog—Skype's Share of the International Long-Distance Pie on the Increase," International Telecommunications Union, March 31, 2009, available at: http://www.itu.int/ITU-D/ict/news log/Skypes+Share+Of+The+International+Longdistance+Pie+On+The+Increase .aspx.

33. Adam Peake, *Internet Governance and the World Summit on the Information Society (WSIS)*, Association for Progressive Communications, June 2004, 4.

34. William Drake, "Reframing Internet Governance Discourse: Fifteen Baseline Propositions," in *Internet Governance: Toward a Grand Collaboration*, United Nations Information and Communications Technologies Task Force, 2004.

35. Ibid., 160.

36. Declaration of Mark Klein in Support of Plaintiffs' Motion for Preliminary Injunction, *Electronic Frontier Foundation*, June 8, 2006, available at: https://www .eff.org/files/filenode/att/ser_klein_decl.pdf.

37. Olga Khazan, "Gentlemen Reading Each Other's Mail: A Brief History of Diplomatic Spying," *Atlantic Monthly*, June 17, 2003.

38. This evolved into the Five Eyes intelligence-sharing arrangement between the United States, UK, Australia, Canada, and New Zealand. The NSA's roots can be traced to Herbert O. Yardley's Black Chamber, the Cipher Bureau formed and funded by the U.S. Army and Department of State in 1919 to continue code-breaking activities following World War I. Eventually, the Cipher Bureau was closed in 1929 after Secretary of State Henry Stimson deemed it was immoral to decrypt and monitor the diplomatic communications. Code-breaking capacity was very much back in demand with the outbreak of World War II. Americans broke Japanese cryptographic systems and worked closely with the UK code-breaking establishment at Bletchley Park during the war.

39. James Risen, "Obama's Wiretapping Stand Enrages Many Supporters," *New York Times*, July 2, 2008; Eric Lictblau and James Risen, "Officials Say U.S. Wiretaps Exceeded Law," *New York Times*, April 15, 2009.

40. Olga Khazan, "The Creepy, Long-Standing Practice of Undersea Cable Tapping," *Atlantic Monthly*, July 16, 2013.

41. James Bamford, *The Puzzle Palace*, Houghton-Mifflin: New York, 1982.

42. The last, which is essentially a phone-sized device holding as much computing power as a mobile computer, was produced only a few years ago.

43. Olmstead went on to serve four years in prison but was pardoned by FDR in 1935.

44. *Olmstead v. United States*, 277 U.S. 438 (1928), Accessed June 16, 2008, available at: http://caselaw.lp.findlaw.com/scripts/getcase.pl?court=US&vol=277&invol=438.

45. Loch K. Johnson, *A Season of Inquiry, Congress and Intelligence*, Dorsey Press: Chicago, 1988.

46. Robert Mueller, *Electronic Surveillance Manual: Volume I—Procedures and Forms*, U.S. Department of Justice: Washington, D.C., 1991.

47. Whitfield Diffie and Susan Landau, *Privacy on the Line*, MIT Press: Cambridge, MA, 2007, 132.

48. Ibid., 219.

49. Sabra Chartrand, "Clinton Gets a Wiretapping Bill That Covers New Technologies," *New York Times*, October 9, 1994.

50. Patricia Moloney Figiola, *Digital Surveillance: The Communications Assistance for Law Enforcement Act*, Congressional Research Service: Washington, D.C., 2007.

51. 18 U.S.C., Part II, Chapter 206, § 3127, available at: http://www.law.cornell.edu/uscode/text/18/3127.

52. Mark M. Lowenthal, *Intelligence: From Secrets to Policy*, Sage: Thousand Oaks, CA, 2011, 245.

53. Tom Zeller, "Ideas & Trends; Cloak, Dagger, Echelon," *New York Times*, July 16, 2000.

54. Sandra Upson, "Wiretapping Woes: Trouble Ahead for Those Wanting to Monitor Internet-Based Calls," *IEEE Spectrum*, May 2007.

55. There are parallel Web 2.0 issues at play in the IC: first, the use of Internet-hosted social media as a source for collection and, second, adoption of social media and peer production techniques (wikis and blogs). See Adrienne Werner,

Thesis: The Potential Transformative Impact of Web 2.0 Technology on the Intelligence Community, Naval Postgraduate School: Monterey, CA, 2008.

56. Pam Benson and Kevin Bohn, "Senate OKs Immunity for Telecoms in Intelligence Bill," *CNN*, February 12, 2008, available at: http://www.cnn.com/2008/POLITICS/02/12/fisa.senate/.

CHAPTER 4

1. That a cyber attack was a component of the 2007 Israeli air strike on Syria's nuclear facility has been asserted by former senior U.S. national security official Richard Clarke. Paul J. Stringer, *Cyberwarfare: A Reference Handbook*, ABC-CLIO: Santa Barbara, CA, 2015.

2. "The Slashdot effect, also known as slashdotting, occurs when a popular website links to a smaller site, causing a massive increase in traffic. This overloads the smaller site, causing it to slow down or even temporarily become unavailable." Denial-of-service attacks produce a similar outcome. Wikipedia, en.wikipedia.org/wiki/Slashdot_effect.

3. *World Fact Book*, Central Intelligence Agency: Washington, D.C., 2007.

4. Merike Kaeo, "Cyber Attacks on Estonia," Presentation, NANOG 40 2007, Bellevue, WA, June 3–6, 2007.

5. Peter Finn, "Cyber Assaults on Estonia Typify a New Battle Tactic," *Washington Post*, May 19, 2007.

6. Ian Traynor, "Russia Accused of Unleashing Cyberwar to Disable Estonia," *Guardian*, May 17, 2007.

7. "Luzhkov Accuses Estonian Authorities of Abetting Fascism," *Interfax News Service*, available at: http://www.interfax.ru/e/B/0/0.html?id_issue=11721667.

8. Peter Finn, "Cyber Assaults on Estonia Typify a New Battle Tactic," *Washington Post*, May 19, 2007.

9. Miska Rantanen, "Virtual Harassment, but for Real," *Helsingen Sanomat*, June 5, 2007.

10. "Newly Nasty," *Economist*, May 24, 2007.

11. United States Department of Labor, "Technology and Globalization," *Futurework*, September 06, 1999, available at: http://www.dol.gov/oasam/programs/history/herman/reports/futurework/report/chapter6/main.htm.

12. Frank Spellman, *Handbook of Water and Wastewater Treatment Plant Operations*, CRC Press: Boca Raton, FL, 2013, 53.

13. "Internet Security: Fighting the Worms of Mass Destruction," *Economist*, sec. Special Report, November 27, 2003.

14. The self-replicating virus Robert Tappan Morris released onto the pre-commercialized Internet in 1988 knocked roughly half the network offline in a very short amount of time. In response, the first security incident response team was established by the U. S. government via a contract to Carnegie Mellon University. Brendan Kehoe, *Zen and the Art of the Internet*, Prentice Hall: Upper Saddle River, NJ, 1995.

15. John D. Howard, *An Analysis of Security Incidents on the Internet*, doctoral thesis, Carnegie Mellon University, 1997, 53–54.

16. David Cochrane, "For Whose Eyes Only? Cryptanalysis and Frequency Analysis," Department of Mathematics, U.S. Military Academy, available at: http://www.usma.edu/math/military%20math%20modeling/ps5.pdf.

17. Chris Bronk, "Hacking Is Hardly Cyberwar, for Now," *New York Times*, February 28, 2013, available at: http://www.nytimes.com/roomfordebate/2013/02/28/what-is-an-act-of-cyberwar/hacking-is-hardly-cyberwar-for-now.

18. Howard, *An Analysis of Security Incidents on the Internet*, 54.

19. Martin Libicki, *What Is Information Warfare*, NDU Press: Washington, D.C., 1995.

20. Howard, *An Analysis of Security Incidents on the Internet*, 62.

21. Eric Raymond, *The Hacker's Dictionary*, ver 4.2.2, available at: https://archive.org/stream/jarg422/jarg422.txt.

22. John Serabian, "CIA Official Assesses Information Warfare Threat," *U.S. Information Service*, December 10, 1998.

23. Richard O. Hundley, Robert H. Anderson, Tora K. Bikson, and C. Richard Neu, *The Global Course of the Information Revolution: Recurring Themes and Regional Variations*, RAND: Santa Monica, CA, 2003.

24. These efforts, which pay hackers to locate software bugs, are referred to as "bug bounty" programs. Google, Microsoft, Facebook, Mozilla, Twitter, and Github offer bounties in exchange for bug reports.

25. Zhenmin Li, et al., "Have Things Changed Now? An Empirical Study of Bug Characteristics in Modern Open Source Software," *ASID'06*, October 21, 2006, San Jose, CA, USA.

26. On this, see the account of Marcel Lehal Lazar Guccifer, who was convicted of compromising the email accounts of multiple members of the Bush family and Colin Powell as well as a substantial number of government officials in the United States and his native Romania, among others. Andrew Higgins, "For Guccifer, Hacking Was Easy. Prison Is Hard," *New York Times*, November 10, 2014.

27. This is not at all a knock on the Air Force, but does acknowledge that the service did not engage in significant air-to-air combat in the Afghanistan and Iraq wars, and was largely tasked with reconnaissance, logistics, and close-air support missions that rarely put its members in harm's way. Air Force casualties in the two wars were little more than one percent of the total of both killed and wounded.

28. Michael Wynne, "Cyberspace as a Domain in Which the Air Force Flies and Fights," *C4ISR Integration Conference*, Crystal City, VA, November 2, 2006.

29. Marty Graham, "Welcome to Cyberwar Country, USA," *Wired*, February 11, 2008, available at: http://archive.wired.com/politics/security/news/2008/02/cyber_command?currentPage=all.

30. Kevin Poulsen, "Air Force Launches Recruitment Campaign Touting Cyber Command," *Wired*, February 27, 2008, available at: http://www.wired.com/2008/02/air-force-launc/.

31. Ward Carroll, "Inside the Cyber Command Turf Battle," *DefenseTech*, August 15, 2008, available at: http://defensetech.org/2008/08/15/inside-the-cyber-command-turf-battle/.

32. Pamela Hess, "Pentagon Puts Hold on USAF Cyber Effort," *USA Today*, August 13, 2008.

33. Nate Hale, "Cyber Command on Hold?," *In from the Cold* (blog), August 13, 2008, available at: http://formerspook.blogspot.com/2008/08/cyber-command -on-hold.html.

34. Gregg Keizer, "Cyberattacks Knock Out Georgia's Internet Presence," *Computerworld*, August 11, 2008, available at: http://www.computerworld.com/ article/2532289/cybercrime-hacking/cyberattacks-knock-out-georgia-s-internet -presence.html.

35. Siobhan Gorman, "Georgia States Computers Hit by Cyberattack," *Wall Street Journal*, August 12, 2008.

36. Georgia had been a member of the NATO Partnership for Peace program since 1994, but following the 2003 resignation of Eduard Shevardnadze from the presidency, the new government moved to join NATO and sent a contingent of troops to Iraq as part of the international coalition there. In January 2008, a majority of its voters cast ballots in favor of joining the alliance. Following the conflict, movement on Georgian NATO membership has been effectively frozen.

37. John Arquila and David Ronfeldt, "Cyberwar Is Coming!" *Comparative Strategy*, 12(2), Spring 1993.

38. Ibid., 28, 30.

39. Steve Bankes and Carl Builder, *Seizing the Moment: Harnessing Information Technologies*, RAND: Santa Monica, CA, 1992, iii.

40. Arquila and Ronfeldt, 52–53.

41. David A. Baldwin, ed., *Neorealism and Neoliberalism: The Contemporary Debate*, Columbia University Press: New York, 1993.

42. See Roger Hurwitz, *An Augmented Summary of the Harvard, MIT, and University of Toronto Cyber Norms Workshop*, MIT CSAIL and Munk School of Global Affairs, May 2012.

43. J. P. Singh, "Information Technologies, Meta-power, and Transformation in Global Politics," *International Studies Review*, 15(1), March 2013.

44. Carla Bass, *Building Castles on Sand: Ignoring the Riptide of Information Operations*, Air War College: Montgomery, AL, 1998.

45. Giulio Douhet, *Command of the Air*, Air Force History and Museums Program: Washington, D.C., 1998.

46. Although states erecting national firewall systems such as Iran or China may well try a national cyber defense policy largely avoiding entanglement with industry or state-friendly companies.

47. William Gibson, *Neuromancer*, Ace: New York, 1984.

48. Jeanne Meserve, "Sources: Staged Cyber Attack Reveals Vulnerability in Power Grid," *CNN*, September 26, 2007, available at: http://edition.cnn.com/ 2007/US/09/26/power.at.risk/.

CHAPTER 5

1. Beckstrom was a highly impressive candidate for the position holding an economics degree with honors and distinction and MBA from Stanford. He won a Fulbright scholarship to Switzerland to study finance, built and sold a NASDAQ-listed software company, and wrote a best-selling business book on

the concept of leaderless organizations. Siobhan Gorman, "Cybersecurity Chief Resigns," *Wall Street Journal*, March 7, 2009.

2. Jason Miller, "EXCLUSIVE: Turnover at DHS Cyber Operations Continue," *Federal News Radio*, September 15, 2011, available at: http://www.federalnews radio.com/239/2546098/EXCLUSIVE-Turnover-at-DHS-cyber-operations-continue.

3. Gorman, "Cybersecurity Chief Resigns."

4. Rod Beckstrom, Letter of Resignation, Department of Homeland Security, March 5, 2009.

5. Ibid.

6. Beryl Howell, "Seven Weeks: The Making of the USA Patriot Act," *George Washington Law Review*, 72(6), August 2004.

7. A colleague made the observation in relationship with college football, a sort of all-encompassing passion in the author's home state on football. He argued, "DHS is the Texas Tech of the Intelligence Community." In other words, it is big, well resourced, and ambitious, but it fails to hold the same sort of sway as the other agencies, much as Texas Tech is seen as a lesser competitor on the gridiron than its other in-state peers, the University of Texas and Texas A&M. Unnamed intelligence official, personal communication, September 23, 2011.

8. Barack Obama, *Fiscal Year 2015 Budget of the U.S. Government*, Executive Office of the President of the United States: Washington, D.C., March 4, 2014.

9. *Homeland Security: Agency Plans, Implementation, and Challenges Regarding the National Strategy for Homeland Security*, Government Accountability Office: Washington, D.C., January 2005, 17.

10. William J. Clinton, *Executive Order 13010—Critical Infrastructure Protection*, The White House: Washington, D.C., July 15, 1996.

11. William J. Clinton, *Presidential Decision Directive/NSC-63—Critical Infra-structure Protection*, The White House: Washington, D.C., May 22, 1998.

12. Robert F. Dacey, *Critical Infrastructure Protection: Significant Homeland Security Challenges Need to Be Addressed*, General Accountability Office: Washington, D.C., July 9, 2002.

13. "DHS Releases a Brief Documentary History of the Department, 2001–2008," American Immigration Lawyers Association, November 7, 2011, available at: http://www.aila.org/content/default.aspx?docid=37572.

14. This has since happened, with the establishment of the National Cyber Threat Intelligence Integration Center, which reports to the DNI and is housed at Fort Meade. Stephanie Condon, "Critics: Homeland Security Unprepared for Cyberthreats," *cnet*, December 7, 2008, available at: http://www.cnet.com/news/critics-homeland-security-unprepared-for-cyberthreats/.

15. The CSIS commission report is considered at length in the following chapter.

16. William J. Perry, et al., *United States Government Interagency Domestic Terror-ism Concept of Operations Plan (CONPLAN)*, obtained from Federation of American Scientists, available at: http://fas.org/irp/threat/conplan.pdf.

17. Ibid.

18. CDRUSNORTHCOM CONPLAN 3501-8 Defense Support of Civilian Authorities, U.S. Northern Command, Peterson AFB, CO, May 16, 2008, available at: http://www.northcom.mil/Portals/28/Documents/FOIA/Con%20Plan %203501-08%20DSCA.pdf.

19. *National Response Framework*, Department of Homeland Security: Washington, D.C., January 2008.

20. *Cyber Incident Annex*, Department of Homeland Security: Washington, D.C., 2004, CYB-1.

21. *Catastrophic Disaster Response Staff Officer's Handbook*, U.S. Army Center for Army Lessons Learned: Ft. Leavenworth, KS, 2006.

22. *Cyber Incident Annex*, Department of Homeland Security: Washington, D.C., 2004, CYB-6.

23. There is always a possibility that classified guidance exists, but it would not be available due to restrictions regarding dissemination of such information.

24. Saul Hansell, "It's Obama on the iPhone," *New York Times*, October 2, 2008, available at: http://bits.blogs.nytimes.com/2008/10/02/its-obama-on-the-iphone/?_r=0.

25. Brendan Sasso, "Report: China Hacked Obama, McCain Campaigns in 2008," *The Hill*, June 7, 2013, available at: http://thehill.com/policy/technology/304111-report-china-hacked-obama-mccain-campaigns.

26. Barack Obama, *Cyberspace Policy Review: Assuring a Trusted and Resilient Information and Communications Infrastructure*, The White House: Washington, D.C., 2009, vi.

27. *Cyber Storm III Final Report*, Department of Homeland Security: Washington, D.C., July 2011, 3.

28. *National Cyber Incident Response Plan—Interim Version (NCIRP)*, Department of Homeland Security: Washington, DC, September 2010, 3.

29. Ibid., 2007, 3.

30. A note on force protection. The THREATCON identifier was replaced with the designation Force Protection Condition (FPCON) in June 2001. FPCON levels rise with intelligence and to present a deterrent to terror threat. The responses to elevation of FPCON are often very specific and regard all manner of security practices such as spot checks, inspections, patrols, and other physical security measures.

31. SEI organizational roots are in design and development of a highly resilient software for applications in aerospace and the defense sector.

32. "About Us," CERT, Software Engineering Institute, Carnegie Mellon University, Pittsburgh, PA, available at: http://www.cert.org/about/.

33. "What Is a CSIRT?" European Union Agency for Network and Information Security, Athens, Greece, available at: https://www.enisa.europa.eu/activities/cert/support/guide2/introduction/what-is-csirt.

34. "About Us," US-CERT, Department of Homeland Security: Washington, D.C., available at: https://www.us-cert.gov/about-us.

35. "National Cybersecurity and Communications Integration Center," *US-CERT*, available at: https://www.us-cert.gov/nccic.

36. Ibid.

37. IDS systems are typically of two varieties: network based and host based. Network IDS implementations inspect the traffic of data packets between the organization's network and the outside world, flagging suspicious ones for investigation by a human operator. Host-based IDS implementations employ software installed on a computer to monitor its function and look for the presence of known

malicious software or activity. A typical IDS is largely dependent on its database of signature information to determine if certain forms of data transmission, applications, or operations are a threat to the network or a particular computer. Generally, an IDS is only as useful as its signature set. If a threat is known and a signature for it present within the IDS's signature database, it will be detected. If threat is unknown, then the IDS will likely ignore it. State-of-the-art IDS systems now employ pattern-matching and machine-learning techniques to assess if a particular Internet address, message, or piece of computer code may be similar enough to a known malicious item to warrant an alert and a response. The other area of advance is in development of Intrusion Prevention Systems (IPS), which monitor for a suspicious activity that is of a more invasive nature and then automatically institute a mitigation response to isolate the threat.

38. John Rollins and Anna Henning, *Comprehensive National Cybersecurity Initiative: Legal Authorities and Policy Considerations*, Congressional Research Service: Washington, D.C., March 10, 2009, 6.

39. Steven Bellovin, Scott Bradner, Whitfield Diffie, Susan Landau, and Jennifer Rexford, "Can It Really Work? Problems with Extending EINSTEIN 3 to Critical Infrastructure," *Harvard National Security Journal*, 3, 2011, 36.

40. "$20 Million 'Virtual' Border Fence Scrapped," *Associated Press*, April 23, 2008.

41. "Critical Infrastructure and Key Resource Overview," Information Sharing Environment, available at: http://www.ise.gov/mission-partner/critical-infrastructure -and-key-resources.

42. "Fusion Centers and Information Sharing," Bureau of Justice Assistance: Washington, D.C., available at: http://www.ncirc.gov/documents/public/nysic _low_res.pdf.

43. Michael Flynn and Charles Flynn, "Integrating Intelligence: Ten Points for the Commander," *Military Review*, January–February 2012, 4.

44. "Fusion Confusion," *Chicago Tribune*, October 8, 2012.

45. The language for mission is slightly different, specifying "intersection of the private sector, civilian, law enforcement, intelligence, and defense communities" rather than the language in the vision statement cited above. "National Cybersecurity and Communications Integration Center," *US-CERT*, available at: https://www.us-cert.gov/nccic.

46. The author worked closely with a number of information security leaders in the oil and gas industry as they navigated the process of creating an Oil and Natural Gas ISAC (ONG-ISAC) in 2013. What the ISAC; relevant government agencies, which for oil and natural gas industry include not only DHS but also the Departments of Energy and Transportation; and companies are able to do in this framework remains unclear. See Oil and Natural Gas Information Sharing and Analysis Center, available at: www.ongisac.org.

47. George W. Bush, *Homeland Security Presidential Directive-7—Critical Infrastructure Identification, Prioritization and Protection*, The White House: Washington, D.C., June 17, 2004.

48. *The Role of Information Sharing and Analysis Centers (ISACs) in Private/Public Sector Critical Infrastructure Protection*, National Council of ISACs, January 2009, available at: http://www.isaccouncil.org/images/ISAC_Role_in_CIP.pdf.

49. Gus P. Coldebella and Brian M. White, "Foundational Questions Regarding the Federal Role in Cybersecurity," *Journal of National Security Law and Policy*, 4(1): 233, 236, 2010.

50. Ibid.

CHAPTER 6

1. Nelson Peacock, "Cybersecurity Could Be the Next Bipartisan Breakthrough," *The Hill*, January 22, 2014, available at: http://thehill.com/blogs/congress-blog/technology/196026-cybersecurity-could-be-the-next-bipartisan-breakthrough.

2. Myriam Dunn Cavelty and Manuel Suter, "Public–Private Partnerships Are No Silver Bullet: An Expanded Governance Model for Critical Infrastructure Protection," *International Journal of Critical Infrastructure Protection*, 2(4), 2009.

3. Searching on the terms "cyber" and "it depends" casts a shining light on this problem. Consider the expert opinion of due diligence consultancy Kroll's cybersecurity expert when asked what hackers are after. Obviously chagrined in his choice of words, he states nonetheless, "As much as I hate to give this response, it depends. There are variations among industries, but generally hackers are after almost any type of data or digital business asset that can be used to obtain financial gain or competitive advantage in the marketplace." See "Securing Your Company from Cyber Crime," Kroll, available at: http://www.kroll.com/library/Securing_your_company_from_cyber_crime.pdf.

4. Well-defined comprehensive U.S. law on computer security and criminality extends back to the 1986 Computer Fraud and Abuse Act, although U.S. law and policy on unauthorized disclosure of information extends to well before the development of the digital computer.

5. H.R. 2458, *The Federal Information Security Management Act*, U.S. House of Representatives: Washington, D.C., available at: http://csrc.nist.gov/drivers/documents/FISMA-final.pdf.

6. Wm. Arthur Conklin, "Why FISMA Falls Short: The Need for Security Metrics," *WISP 2008*, Montreal, Canada, December 7–9, 2007.

7. "FedRAMP/FISMA: Frequently Asked Questions," *Microsoft*, available at: http://www.microsoft.com/online/legal/v2/en-us/FISMA_FAQ.htm.

8. Ron Ross, Stuart Katzke, and Patricia Toth, "The New FISMA Standards and Guidelines: Changing the Dynamic of Information Security for the Federal Government," Military Communications Conference: MILCOM 2005, Atlantic City, NJ, October 17–20, 2005.

9. See Ronald Ross and L. A. Johnson, *Guide for Applying the Risk Management Framework to Federal Information Systems: A Security Life Cycle Approach*, National Institute of Standards and Technology: Gaithersburg, MD, February 22, 2010.

10. The question asked of proposed amendments to FISMA in 2013 by Government Computing News was "Will Congress continue to grade agency performance based on paperwork compliance, or will it measure actual security?" What actual security constitutes is another question; available at: http://gcn.com/blogs/cybereye/2013/06/security-best-practices-at-root-fisma-amendments.aspx.

11. Robert Silvers, "Rethinking FISMA and Federal Information Security Policy," *New York University Law Review*, 81: 1844–1874, November 2006.

12. Jaikumar Vijayan, "Government Cybersecurity Report Card Coming," *Info-World*, April 12, 2007, available at: http://www.infoworld.com/article/2662880/security/government-cybersecurity-report-card-coming.html.

13. William Jackson, "FISMA Grades: What Do They Mean?" *Government Computing News*, April 23, 2007, available at: http://gcn.com/articles/2007/04/23/fisma-grades-what-do-they-mean.aspx.

14. Yoran is now president of security giant RSA, having joined the company when it acquired his firm, NetWitness, in 2011. Brian Krebs, "Uncle Sam Gets 'D-Plus' on Cyber-Security," *Washington Post*, February 16, 2005.

15. Jerry Davis, *Memorandum: Suspension of Certification and Accreditation Activity*, National Aeronautics and Space Administration: Washington, D.C., May 18, 2010.

16. The Office of Management and Budget does produce a mandated report on FISMA. See "Annual Report to Congress: Federal Information Security Management Act," Office of Management and Budget, February 27, 2015.

17. Joana Lyn Grama, *Legal Issues in Information Security*, Jones & Bartlett Learning: Burlington, MA, 2015.

18. "Panel Must Narrow Cybersecurity Scope," *FCW*, November 4, 2007, available at: http://fcw.com/Articles/2007/11/04/Panel-must-narrow-cybersecurity-scope.aspx?Page=2.

19. While Microsoft has been much maligned for security vulnerabilities in its software, the company's evolving capacity on security of its products deserves merit. While building its Vista desktop operating system, Microsoft undertook a massive review of software coding practices. Fruit of this effort was the company's Security Development Lifecycle, a process designed to dramatically reduce the number of security-related bugs in its software releases. Steve Lipner and Michael Howard, *The Trustworthy Computing Development Lifecycle*, Microsoft Corporation: Redmond, WA, March 2005.

20. David Perera, "New White House Cybersecurity Strategy Needs New Ideas, Says CSIS Commission," *FierceGovernmentIT*, February 1, 2011, available at: http://www.fiercegovernmentit.com/story/new-white-house-cybersecurity-strategy-needs-new-ideas-says-csis-commission/2011-02-01.

21. James Langevin, Michael McCaul, Scott Charney, Harry Raduege, and James Lewis, *Securing Cyberspace for the 44th Presidency: A Report of the CSIS Commission on Cybersecurity for the 44th Presidency*, Center for Strategic and International Studies: Washington, D.C., December 2008, 50.

22. Ibid.

23. Evan Thomas, "Campaign 2008 Secrets: McCain Gambles on Palin," *Newsweek*, November 5, 2008.

24. Jeff Zeleny, "Lose the BlackBerry? Yes He Can, Maybe," *New York Times*, November 15, 2008.

25. Michael Isikoff, "Chinese Hacked Obama, McCain Campaigns, Took Internal Documents, Officials Say," *NBC News*, June 6, 2013, available at: http://investigations.nbcnews.com/_news/2013/06/06/18807056-chinese-hacked-obama-mccain-campaigns-took-internal-documents-officials-say.

26. "Chinese Hacked Obama and McCain Campaigns, Officials Say," *MSNBC*, June 6, 2013, available at: http://www.msnbc.com/msnbc/chinese-hacked -obama-and-mccain-campaigns.

27. Christopher Lee and Zachary Goldfarb, "Stolen VA Laptop and Hard Drive Recovered," *Washington Post*, June 30, 2006.

28. Ellen Nakashima and Brian Krebs, "Contractor Blamed in DHS Data Breaches," *Washington Post*, September 24, 2007.

29. Kim Zetter, "Hackers Targeted U.S. Government Satellites," *Wired*, October 27, 2011, available at: http://www.wired.com/2011/10/hackers-attack-satellites/.

30. Bobbie Johnson, "Obama Orders Review of Cyber Security," *Guardian*, February 10, 2009.

31. Barack Obama, "Remarks by the President on Securing Our Nation's Cyber Infrastructure," The White House: Washington, D.C., May 29, 2009, available at: http://www.whitehouse.gov/the_press_office/Remarks-by-the-President-on -Securing-Our-Nations-Cyber-Infrastructure/.

32. Ibid.

33. Barack Obama, *Cyberspace Policy Review: Assuring a Trusted and Resilient Information and Communications Infrastructure*, The White House: Washington, D.C., 2009, C-12.

34. Obama, "Remarks by the President."

35. Eric Greenwald, "History Repeats Itself: The 60-Day Cyberspace Policy Review in Context," *Journal of National Security Law and Policy*, 4(41) 2010, 60.

36. The caucus stood at 63 members plus the chairs in 2014, with significant representation from both parties. Congressional Cybersecurity Caucus, available at: http://cybercaucus.langevin.house.gov/members.

37. Declan McCullagh, "Bill Would Give President Emergency Control of the Internet," *cnet*, August 28, 2009, available at: http://www.cnet.com/news/bill -would-give-president-emergency-control-of-internet/.

38. One bill, the Reduce Iranian Cyber-Suppression Act, was an international sanction prohibiting U.S. federal agencies from purchasing goods or services from computing and telecommunications firms doing business in Iran. The bill was a response to the heavy Internet censorship imposed in the wake of Iran's 2009 presidential election and ensuing protests. *S. 1475*, 111th Congress, U.S. Senate: Washington, D.C., available at: https://www.congress.gov/bill/111th-congress/ senate-bill/1475/text?q=%7B%22search%22%3A%5B%22%5C%22cyber%5C%22 %22%5D%7D.

39. Chris Bronk, "The Wrong Way to Stop Online Piracy," *Houston Chronicle*, November 25, 2011, available at: http://www.chron.com/opinion/outlook/ article/The-wrong-way-to-stop-online-piracy-2292842.php.

40. ACM US Public Policy Council, *Analysis of SOPA's Impact on DNS and DNSSEC*, Association for Computing Machinery, January 18, 2012.

41. The author signed one such petition, collected by the Center for Democracy and Technology (CDT). See "Organizations and Individuals Opposing SOPA," Center for Democracy and Technology, available at: https://www.cdt.org/ report/list-organizations-and-individuals-opposing-sopa.

42. The blackout effected only the English-language version of Wikipedia and did not entirely block access to Wikipedia content via mobile devices or access

from mirrored or cached repositories of it elsewhere on the Web. "Protests against SOPA and PIPA,"*Wikipedia,* available at: http://en.wikipedia.org/wiki/Protests _against_SOPA_and_PIPA.

43. The proposed law increased penalties for theft of trade secrets. "Summary of SOPA and PIPA," *MasurLaw,* January 20, 2012, available at: http://www .masurlaw.com/resources/summary-of-sopa-and-pipa/.

44. Paul Rosenzweig, "Cybersecurity Act of 2012: Revised Cyber Bill Still Has Problems," *The Heritage Foundation,* July 23, 2012, available at: http://www .heritage.org/research/reports/2012/07/cybersecurity-act-of-2012-revised-cyber -bill-still-has-problems.

45. Ramsey Cox and Jennifer Martinez, "Cybersecurity Act Fails Senate Vote," *The Hill,* August 2, 2012, available at: http://thehill.com/policy/technology/ 241851-cybersecurity-act-fails-to-advance-in-senate.

46. Andrew Couts, "Senate Kills Cybersecurity Act of 2012," *Digital Trends,* August 2, 2012, available at: http://www.digitaltrends.com/web/senate-votes -against-cybersecurity-act-of-2012/.

47. As with prior cyber bills, CISPA was also controversial. Alexandra Petri, "Should You Be Panicking about CISPA?," *Washington Post,* April 17, 2013.

48. Barack Obama, *Presidential Memorandum—Establishment of the Cyber Threat Intelligence Integration Center,* The White House: Washington, D.C., February 25, 2015.

49. National Security Telecommunications Advisory Committee (NSTAC), available at: http://www.ncs.gov/nstac/nstac.html.

50. This is meant to describe the combination of infrastructure process control or data processing systems with Internet Protocol (IP) communications. Examples are Smart Grid electricity distribution and Electronic Medical Record (EMR) systems.

CHAPTER 7

1. One U.S. diplomat recalled a 2006 meeting between International Atomic Energy Agency chief Mohamed ElBaradei and U.S. Undersecretary of State for Arms Control Robert Joseph in which Joseph stated, "We cannot have a single centrifuge spinning in Iran. Iran is a direct threat to the national security of the United States and our allies, and we will not tolerate it. We want you to give us an understanding that you will not say anything publicly that will undermine us." Seymour Hersh, "The Iran Plans," *New Yorker,* April 17, 2006, available at: http:// www.newyorker.com/magazine/2006/04/17/the-iran-plans.

2. Eben Kaplan, "How Libya Got Off the List," *Council on Foreign Relations,* October 16, 2007, available at: http://www.cfr.org/libya/libya-got-off-list/p10855.

3. Western intervention in Libya in the wake of the Arab Spring was unhindered by any concern of a WMD program, something not the case in Syria.

4. The term is borrowed from a 2000 radio interview of Madeline Albright. Christopher Marquis, "U.S. Declares 'Rogue Nations' Are Now 'States of Concern,' " *New York Times,* June 20, 2000.

5. Recounted by a former INR director. Randy Fort, *Emerging Cybersecurity Threats* (conference), Baker Institute for Public Policy, Houston, TX, September 18, 2012.

6. Warren Strobel, John Walcott, and Nancy Youssef, "Cheney Urging Strikes on Iran," *McClatchyDC*, August 9, 2007, available at: http://www.mcclatchydc.com/2007/08/09/18834/cheney-urging-strikes-on-iran.html.

7. *National Intelligence Estimate–Iran: Nuclear Intentions and Capabilities*, National Intelligence Council: Washington, D.C., November 2007, available at: http://www.dni.gov/files/documents/Newsroom/Reports%20and%20Pubs/20071203_release.pdf.

8. Greg Bruno and Sharon Otterman, "National Intelligence Estimates," *Council on Foreign Relations*, May 14, 2008, available at: http://www.cfr.org/iraq/national-intelligence-estimates/p7758.

9. It was also hugely unpopular with those critical of not engaging in military action on Iran. James Philips, "The Iran National Intelligence Estimate: A Comprehensive Guide to What Is Wrong with the NIE," *The Heritage Foundation*, January 11, 2008, available at: http://www.heritage.org/research/reports/2008/01/the-iran-national-intelligence-estimate-a-comprehensive-guide-to-what-is-wrong-with-the-nie.

10. Dan Plafcan, "Intelligence, Diplomacy, and the Management of Credibility," Science, Technology, and Public Policy Program, Gerald R. Ford School of Public Policy, University of Michigan, October 7, 2008, available at: http://stpp.fordschool.umich.edu/news-events/?p=452.

11. Thomas Fingar, *Reducing Uncertainty: Intelligence Analysis and National Security*, Stanford Security Studies: Palo Alto, CA, 2011.

12. *National Intelligence Estimate*.

13. David Sanger and William Broad, "U.S. and Allies Warn Iran over Nuclear 'Deception,'" *New York Times*, September 25, 2009.

14. W.32 refers to the systems the worm could compromise, in this case Microsoft Windows 32-bit operating system machines. Stuxnet was the term produced by "Microsoft from a combination of file names (.stub and MrxNet.sys) found in the code." Kim Zetter, "How Digital Detectives Deciphered Stuxnet, the Most Menacing Malware in History," *Ars Technica*, July 11, 2011, available at: http://arstechnica.com/tech-policy/2011/07/how-digital-detectives-deciphered-stuxnet-the-most-menacing-malware-in-history/.

15. Nicholas Falliere, Liam O Murchu, and Eric Chien, *W.32 Stuxnet Dossier Ver 1.4*, Symantec, February 2011.

16. Device driver software connects the physical hardware of a system to functionality directed by the operating system or binary input-output system.

17. Falliere, et al., *W.32 Stuxnet Dossier Ver 1.4*.

18. Switching in telephony has gradually evolved from manual switching to electro-mechanical systems that gradually incorporated greater portions of computing power as those technologies became available. For an example of pre-computing electro-mechanical switching, consult the following on AT&T's 1951 step-by-step telephone switch. Step-by-Step Switch, AT&T, available at: http://techchannel.att.com/play-video.cfm/2011/7/22/AT&T-Archives-The-Step-by-Step-Switch.

19. See the following comments on the private sector's role in cybersecurity: Amitai Etzioni, "Cybersecurity in the Private Sector," *Issues in Science and Technology*, November 2013, available at: http://issues.org/28-1/etzioni-2/.

20. Symantec's W32.Stuxnet Dossier was revised several times from September 2010 to February 2011. Falliere, et al., *W.32 Stuxnet Dossier Ver 1.4*.

21. VirusBlokAda, "Microsoft Windows Shortcut 'LNK/PIF' Files Automatic File Execution Vulnerability," *Security Focus*, August 11, 2010, available at: http://www.securityfocus.com/bid/41732.

22. A black market for the buying and selling of zero-day exploits exists and prices for them vary widely; however, highly efficacious ones that may be aimed at a massive user base fetch the highest prices. By one estimate, the three exploits contained in Stuxnet might have held a combined cost of nearly $1 million on the zero-day black market. Lilian Ablon, Martin Libicki, and Andrea Golay, *Markets for Cybercrime Tools and Stolen Data*, RAND: Santa Monica, CA, 2014.

23. Galrahn, "Six Hundred Kilobytes of War 2.0," *Information Dissemination*, September 30, 2010, available at: http://www.informationdissemination.net/2010/09/six-hundred-kilobytes-of-war-20.html.

24. Ralph Langer, *To Kill a Centrifuge: A Technical Analysis of What Stuxnet's Creators Tried to Achieve*, The Langer Group, November 2013, available at: http://www.langner.com/en/wp-content/uploads/2013/11/To-kill-a-centrifuge.pdf.

25. William Broad, John Markoff, and David Sanger, "Israeli Test on Worm Called Crucial in Iran Nuclear Delay," *New York Times*, January 15, 2011.

26. Langer, *To Kill a Centrifuge*.

27. Ibid., 8.

28. Pay for working in Iran on securing critical systems was reputedly as much as $20,000 a week. Rumors on this fee circulated in the SCADA security community servicing the energy industry, much of which is undertaken in Houston, TX. Wm. Arthur Conklin, personal communication with the author, September 2011.

29. David Sanger, "Obama Order Sped Up Wave of Cyberattacks against Iran," *New York Times*, June 1, 2012.

30. David Sanger, *Confront and Conceal: Obama's Secret Wars and Surprising Use of American Power*, Crown: New York, 2012.

31. Tobias Buck, "Israel's Army of Tech Startups," *Financial Times*, November 30, 2011.

32. Dan Raviv, "U.S. Pushing Israel to Stop Assassinating Iranian Nuclear Scientists," *CBS News*, March 1, 2014.

33. Langer, *To Kill a Centrifuge*.

34. Tony Smith, "Hacker Jailed for Revenge Sewage Attacks," *The Register*, October 31, 2001, available at: http://www.theregister.co.uk/2001/10/31/hacker_jailed_for_revenge_sewage/.

35. Sanger, "Obama Order Sped Up Wave of Cyberattacks against Iran."

36. The Cryptography and Systems Security Lab at Budapest University for Technology and Economics discovered Duqu in September 2011. Boldizsár Bencsáth, Gábor Pék, Levente Buttyán, and Márk Félegyházi, *Duqu: A Stuxnet-Like Malware Found in the Wild*, Laboratory of Cryptography and Systems Security, Budapest University of Technology and Economics, October 14, 2011, available at: http://www.crysys.hu/publications/files/bencsathPBF11duqu.pdf.

37. Steven Cherry, "Sons of Stuxnet," *IEEE Spectrum*, December 14, 2011, available at: http://spectrum.ieee.org/podcast/telecom/security/sons-of-stuxnet.

38. *W.32.Duqu, The Precursor to the Next Stuxnet* (White Paper), Symantec, November 23, 2011, available at: http://www.symantec.com/content/en/us/enterprise/media/security_response/whitepapers/w32_duqu_the_precursor_to_the_next_stuxnet.pdf.

39. David Kushner, "The Real Story of Stuxnet," *IEEE Spectrum*, February 26, 2011, available at: http://spectrum.ieee.org/telecom/security/the-real-story-of-stuxnet.

40. "Iran 'Finds Fix' for Sophisticated Flame Malware," BBC, May 29, 2012, available at: http://www.bbc.com/news/technology-18253331.

41. The ITU could have shared Flame's code with multiple security firms, the international Computer Emergency Response Team (CERT) community, or academic research institutions that study malware code and produce formal reports and proceedings on their analysis, but chose instead to use Kaspersky. Ellen Nakashima, "Iran Acknowledges That Flame Virus Has Infected Computers Nationwide," *Washington Post*, May 29, 2012, http://www.washingtonpost.com/world/national-security/iran-acknowledges-that-flame-virus-has-infected-computers-nationwide/2012/05/29/gJQAzlEF0U_story.html.

42. "Kaspersky Lab and ITU Research Reveals New Advanced Cyber Threat," *Kaspersky*, May 28, 2012, available at: http://www.kaspersky.com/about/news/virus/2012/Kaspersky_Lab_and_ITU_Research_Reveals_New_Advanced_Cyber_Threat.

43. Alexander Gostev, "The Flame: Questions and Answers," *Securelist*, May 28, 2012, available at: http://www.securelist.com/en/blog/208193522/The_Flame_Questions_and_Answers.

44. Noah Shachtman, "Russia's Top Cyber Sleuth Foils US Spies, Helps Kremlin Pals," *Wired*, July 23, 2012, available at: http://www.wired.com/2012/07/ff_kaspersky/.

45. Harvey Morris, "Israel Gets the Blame for Flame Virus," *New York Times*, May 29, 2012, available at: http://rendezvous.blogs.nytimes.com/2012/05/29/israel-gets-the-blame-for-flame/.

46. Anyone who has developed software knows that working hours usually translate to whenever the coders feel like working, and often over very long stretches of time. This seems to be a stretch; see http://bits.blogs.nytimes.com/2012/05/31/daily-report-researchers-find-clues-in-flame-virus/.

47. Brian Krebs, "Flame Malware Prompts Microsoft Patch," *Krebs on Security*, June 4, 2012, available at: http://krebsonsecurity.com/2012/06/flame-malware-prompts-microsoft-patch/.

48. Jim Finkle, "UPDATE 3-UN Agency Plans Major Warning on Flame Virus Risk," *Reuters*, May 29, 2012, available at: http://www.reuters.com/article/2012/05/29/cyberwar-flame-idUSL1E8GT7X120120529.

49. Pete Gutman, "The Commercial Malware Industry," *DEFCON 15*, Las Vegas, NV, August 3–5, 2007, available at: https://www.defcon.org/images/defcon-15/dc15-presentations/dc-15-gutmann.pdf.

50. Akamai, which produces software for dynamically responding to denial-of-service attacks, is one source for data on the topic. "Top 10 Countries Where

Cyber Attacks Originate," *Government Technology*, available at: http://www
.govtech.com/security/204318661.html.

51. Brian Manzanec, "The Art of (Cyber) War," *Journal of International Security
Affairs*, 16, 2009.

52. Aaron Brantly, "Cyber Actions by State Actors: Motivation and Utility,"
International Journal of Intelligence and Counterintelligence, 27(3), 2014.

53. The number of computers, an upward revision from 30,000, noted in early
press reports comes from an unnamed oil and gas executive.

54. Nicole Perlroth, "Hackers Lay Claim to Saudi Aramco Cyberattack," *New
York Times*, August 23, 2012, available at: http://bits.blogs.nytimes.com/2012/
08/23/hackers-lay-claim-to-saudi-aramco-cyberattack/.

55. Nicole Perlroth, "In Cyberattack on Saudi Firm, U.S. Sees Iran Firing Back,"
New York Times, October 23, 2012.

56. Robert Tuttle, "Virus Shuts RasGas Office Computers, LNG Output Unaffected," *Bloomberg*, August 30, 2012, available at: http://www. bloomberg.com/
news/2012-08-30/ virus-shuts-rasgas-office-computers- lng-output-unaffected-1
-.html.

57. John Roberts, "Cyber Threats to Energy Security, as Experienced by Saudi
Arabia," *Platts*, November 27, 2012, available at: http://blogs.platts.com/2012/
11/27/virus_threats/.

58. Ibid.

59. "Untitled," *Pastebin*, August 15, 2012, available at: http://pastebin.com/
HqAgaQRj.

60. Gregg Kelzer, "Shamoon Malware Cripples Windows PCs to Cover
Tracks," *ComputerWorld*, August 17, 2012, available at: http://www.computer
world.com/article/2505971/cybercrime-hacking/shamoon-malware-cripples
-windows-pcs-to-cover-tracks.html.

61. Perlroth, "In Cyberattack on Saudi Firm."

62. Michael A. Riley and Eric Engleman, "Code in Aramco Cyber Attack
Indicates Lone Perpetrator," *Bloomberg*, October 25, 2012, available at: http://www
.bloomberg.com/news/2012-10-25/code-in-aramco-cyber-attack-indicates-lone
-perpetrator.html.

63. Chris Bronk and Cody Monk, *Cybersecurity and the Energy Industry* (invited
presentation), Council on Foreign Relations, New York, January 23, 2013.

64. Gregory Hale and Richard Sale, "Cyber War Opens New Front," *Offshore
Engineer*, January 1, 2013, available at: http://www.oedigital.com/component/
k2/item/1366-cyber-war-opens-new-front.

65. The author was extensively involved in discussions with information security officials in a number of companies on how to form an ISAC for their industry
in 2012 and 2013. A contract was awarded by the American Petroleum Institute to
Booz Allen Hamilton to begin constructing the ONG-ISAC in 2013.

66. Matthew J. Schwartz, "Banks Hit Downtime Milestone in DDoS Attacks,"
Dark Reading, April 4, 2014, available at: http://www.darkreading.com/attacks
-and-breaches/banks-hit-downtime-milestone-in-ddos-attacks/d/d-id/1109390?.

67. How Lieberman came to the conclusion is unclear. Ellen Nakashima,
"Iran Blamed for Cyberattacks on U.S. Banks and Companies,"*Washington Post*,
September 21, 2012.

68. Don Melvin and Jonathan Fahey, "SWIFT Cuts Off Iran as Sanctions Vice Tightens," *World Post*, March 15, 2012, available at: http://www.huffingtonpost.com/2012/03/15/swift-iran-sanctions_n_1347361.html.

69. Christopher Haress, "Iran's Rouhani Faces Music as Sanctions Bite Harder, Is There a SWIFT Solution in the Works?" *International Business Times*, October 8, 2013, available at: http://www.ibtimes.com/irans-rouhani-faces-music-sanctions-bite-harder-there-swift-solution-works-1417768.

70. Ellen Mesmer, "New Federal Rule Requires Banks to Fight DDoS Attacks," *Network World*, April 4, 2014, available at: http://www.networkworld.com/article/2175847/network-security/new-federal-rule-requires-banks-to-fight-ddos-attacks.html.

71. Patti Domm, "False Rumor of Explosion at White House Causes Stocks to Briefly Plunge; AP Confirms Its Twitter Feed Was Hacked," *CNBC*, April 23, 2013, available at: http://www.cnbc.com/id/100646197#.

72. "Stocks Rebound after Fake Tweet Spooks Investors," *CNN*, April 23, 2013, available at: http://money.cnn.com/2013/04/23/investing/stocks-markets/.

73. Serene Assir, "Syrian Electronic Army Battles for Public Opinion through Cyber Attacks," *AFP*, available at: http://www.huffingtonpost.com/2013/06/09/syrian-electronic-army-battles-public-opinion_n_3412843.html.

74. A perpetrator or perpetrators employing the pseudonym Mister Rero claimed responsibility for hacking Aramco's Twitter account. Waqas, "National Oil Company of Saudi Arabia, Saudi Aramco's Twitter Account Hacked," *Hack-Read*, March 7, 2013, available at: http://www.hackread.com/national-oil-company-of-saudi-arabia-saudi-aramcos-twitter-account-hacked/.

75. "Syria: Thousands Suffering Neurotoxic Symptoms Treated in Hospitals Supported by MSF," *Medecins San Frontieres*, August 24, 2013, available at: http://www.doctorswithoutborders.org/news-stories/press-release/syria-thousands-suffering-neurotoxic-symptoms-treated-hospitals-supported.

76. Steven J. Vaughan-Nichols, "How the Syrian Electronic Army Took Out the New York Times and Twitter Sites," *ZDNet*, August 28, 2013, available at: http://www.zdnet.com/article/how-the-syrian-electronic-army-took-out-the-new-york-times-and-twitter-sites/.

77. Tom Gjelten, "Firms Brace for Possible Retaliatory Cyberattacks from Syria," *NPR*, August 30, 2013, available at: http://www.npr.org/templates/transcript/transcript.php?storyId=217296301.

78. John B. Sheldon, "Geopolitics and Cyber Power: Why Geography Still Matters," *American Foreign Policy Interests: The Journal of the National Committee on American Foreign Policy*, 36(5), 2014.

79. Judson Dressler, Dan Wallach, and Chris Bronk, "Unvalidated Input: Reconsidering Cyberspace as a Warfighting Domain," forthcoming.

CHAPTER 8

1. Joseph Nye, *Soft Power: The Means to Success in World Politics*, PublicAffairs: New York, 2005.

2. While Rice was immediately involved in a broad variety of bilateral and multilateral diplomatic initiatives once confirmed, she did not make a significant policy speech on managerial issues for the Department of State until 2006.

3. Christopher M. Jones, "The Other Side of Powell's Record," *American Diplomacy*, March 2006, available at: http://www.unc.edu/depts/diplomat/item/2006/0103/jone/jonesc_powell.html.

4. Condoleezza Rice, "Transformational Diplomacy: Shaping US Diplomatic Posture in the 21st Century" (speech given at Georgetown School of Foreign Service, January 18, 2006), available at: http://www.cfr.org/us-strategy-and-politics/transformational-diplomacy-shaping-us-diplomatic-posture-21st-century/p9637.

5. George Argyros, Marc Grossman, and Felix Rohatyn, *The Embassy of the Future*, The CSIS Press: Washington, D.C., 2007, 44.

6. U.S. Advisory Commission on Public Diplomacy, "The New Diplomacy: Utilizing Innovative Communication Concepts That Recognize Resource Constraints," June 2003, available at: http://www.state.gov/documents/organization/22956.pdf.

7. *Changing Minds, Winning Peace: A New Strategic Direction for U.S. Public Diplomacy in the Arab and Muslim World*, Report of the Advisory Group on Public Diplomacy for the Arab and Muslim World, Edward P. Djerejian, chairman, prepared for the U.S. House of Representatives Committee on Appropriations, October 1, 2003.

8. Public diplomacy's definition is somewhat dynamic, varied, and evolving. The current State Department public language on the term says, "The mission of American public diplomacy is to support the achievement of U.S. foreign policy goals and objectives, advance national interests, and enhance national security by informing and influencing foreign publics and by expanding and strengthening the relationship between the people and Government of the United States and citizens of the rest of the world." U.S. Department of State, see http://www.state.gov/r/.

9. Fred Kaplan, "Karen Hughes, Stay Home!: What on Earth Is She Doing in the Middle East?," *Slate*, September 29, 2005, available at: http://www.slate.com/articles/news_and_politics/war_stories/2005/09/karen_hughes_stay_home.html.

10. Under Secretary of State for Public Diplomacy and Public Affairs Karen Hughes, "Remarks at the Council on Foreign Relations," New York City, May 10, 2006, available at: http://merln.ndu.edu/archivepdf/nss/state/66098.pdf.

11. Kenon Nakamura and Susan Epstein, *CRS Report for Congress—Diplomacy in the 21st Century: Transformational Diplomacy*, Congressional Research Service: Washington, D.C., August 23, 2007, CRS-13.

12. State's public diplomacy efforts included a project with the Berkman Center at Harvard Law School that would eventually produce a topical and contextual map of blogging activity in Iran and the Farsi language. See John Kelly and Bruce Etling, "Mapping Iran's Online Public: Politics and Culture in the Persian Blogosphere," Harvard University Berkman Center for Internet and Society, April 5, 2008.

13. Andrew Beath, Fotini Christia, and Ruben Enikpolov, "Winning Hearts and Minds through Development? Evidence from a Field Experiment in Afghanistan," The World Bank, July 2012.

14. Timothy L. Thomas, "Al Qaeda and the Internet: The Danger of 'Cyber-planning,' " *Parameters*, 33(1): 112–123, Spring 2003.

15. Steve Moore, "TSA: Fail," *gmancasefile* (blog), January 24, 2012, available at: http://gmancasefile.blogspot.com/2012/01/tsa-fail.html.

16. Tim O'Reilly, "What Is Web 2.0: Design Patterns and Business Models for the Next Generation of Software," *O'Reilly*, September 30, 2005, available at: http://www.oreilly.com/pub/a/web2/archive/what-is-web-20.html.

17. Facebook was once a Harvard-only network and then extended to other elite institutions of higher education before being opened to the general public.

18. Google has owned YouTube since 2006.

19. According to Alexa, a Web metrics firm, Google was #1, Facebook #2, You-Tube #3, and Twitter #9 in global Web traffic in 2012, the year of the Arab Spring revolutions. Blogspot, a blog hosting service, also owned by Google, stood at #8. See Alexa, "Top Sites," Accessed January 30, 2012, available at: http://www.alexa.com/topsites. Also of interest are some of the volume statistics. Twitter claims to transmit an average of 250 million tweets per day and more than 60 hours of video are uploaded to YouTube each minute. See "YouTube, Statistics," YouTube, available at: http://www.youtube.com/t/press_statistics.

20. Specified in William J. Clinton, *Executive Order 13011: Federal Information Technology*, The White House: Washington, D.C., July 16, 1996.

21. Jesse Lichtenstein, "Digital Diplomacy," *New York Times*, July 10, 2010.

22. See Evgeny Morozov, *The Net Delusion: The Dark Side of Internet Freedom*, Public Affairs: New York, 2011.

23. Robert Gates, remarks as delivered as secretary of defense, Kansas State University, November 26, 2007.

24. "Leading through Civilian Power," *The First Quadrennial Diplomacy and Development Review* (QDDR), 2010, 16, available at: http://www.state.gov/s/dmr/qddr/.

25. Ibid., 16–17.

26. Nart Villeneuve, "GhostNet," *Malware Explorer* (blog), March 28, 2009, available at: http://www.nartv.org/2009/03/28/ghostnet/.

27. John Markoff, "Vast Spy System Loots Computers in 103 Countries," *New York Times*, March 28, 2009.

28. David Drummond, "A New Approach to China," Google official blog, January 12, 2010, available at: http://googleblog.blogspot.com/2010/01/new-approach-to-china.html.

29. Ibid.

30. Cecilia Kang, "Secretary Clinton Dines with High-Tech Titans to Talk Diplomacy," *Washington Post*, available at: http://voices.washingtonpost.com/posttech/2010/01/sec_clinton_dines_high-tech_ti.html.

31. Hillary Clinton, "Remarks on Internet Freedom," Department of State: Washington, D.C., January 21, 2010, available at: http://www.state.gov/secretary/rm/2010/01/135519.htm.

32. The Haiti text message donation campaign for the American Red Cross's efforts raised more than $1 million. See http://philanthropy.com/article/Social-Media-Aids-Efforts-t/63566/ and Cecilia Kang, "Haiti Relief via Text Message, Ushering Mobile Donations," *Washington Post*, January 19, 2010, available at:

http://voices.washingtonpost.com/posttech/2010/01/a_record_22_million_has
.html?hpid=topnews.

33. Republished by *Wired:* Bruce Sterling, "Meanwhile, Somewhere at the Chinese Soft Power Retaliation Board," January 24, 2010, available at: http://www.wired.com/2010/01/meanwhile-somewhere-at-the-chinese-soft-power-retaliation-board/.

34. "Chinese Media Lashes Out at Clinton's Internet Demands," *BBC,* January 22, 2010, available at: http://news.bbc.co.uk/2/mobile/asia-pacific/8474466.stm.

35. "Piratage de Google: Clinton menace la Chine à demi-mot," *Le Monde,* January 21, 2010, available at: http://www.lemonde.fr/technologies/article/2010/01/21/piratage-de-google-clinton-menace-la-chine-a-demi-mot_1295010_651865.html#SiKpy1mZjT8F8tLi.99.

36. Elizabeth Dickerson, "Internet Freedom," *Foreign Policy,* January 21, 2010.

37. With early experiments in postcolonial democracy completely sidelined by revolutions and coup d'etats across the Arab world, by 2011 nations from the Maghreb to the Arabian Peninsula fell into three categories: monarchy, dictatorship, and Israel.

38. Largely undertaken by religious organizations.

39. Transcript and online video of Secretary of State Hillary Rodham Clinton at "Town Hall with Tunisian Youth," Palais du Baron d'Erlanger, Tunis, Tunisia, February 25, 2012, available at: http://www.state.gov/secretary/rm/2012/02/184656.htm.

40. Alexis Madrigal, "The Inside Story of How Facebook Responded to Tunisian Hacks," *Atlantic,* January 24, 2011.

41. It appears that Egypt was able to use the Border Gateway Protocol to largely shut down external Internet connectivity. The Myanmar government also shut down outside Internet connectivity during its Saffron Revolution of 2007. James Cowie, "Egypt Leaves the Internet," *Renesys* (blog), January 27, 2011, available at: http://www.renesys.com/blog/2011/01/egypt-leaves-the-internet.shtml.

42. Edward P. Djerejian, personal communication, February 15, 2011.

43. U.S. Embassy Bamako, Mali, Twitter post, March 12, 2012, see https://twitter.com/#!/USEmbassyMali.

44. Fergus Hanson, "Revolution @State: The Spread of Ediplomacy," *Lowy Institute for International Policy,* March 2012, available at: http://lowyinstitute.richmedia-server.com/docs/Hanson_Revolution-at-State.pdf.

45. Ronald Deibert, "International Plug 'n Play: Citizen Activism, the Internet, and Global Public Policy," *International Studies Perspectives,* 1(3), December 2000.

46. That said, foreign policy celebrity is hardly new, but the rapid rise to prominence of new digital media has created a window for new forms of that celebrity.

CHAPTER 9

1. Jessica Yellin, "Obama, Xi Work through Range of Issues in 2-Day Summit," *CNN,* June 10, 2013, February 27, 2015, available at: http://www.cnn.com/2013/06/09/politics/obama-xi-summit.

2. See the annual reports of the U.S.-China Economic and Security Review Commission, available at: http://www.uscc.gov/. The commission, founded in 2000, has not been without criticism from China. In 2012, the Chinese foreign ministry remarked that the commission "has not let go of its Cold War mentality" and that it produces statements "that are harmful to China-U.S. relations." Jim Wolf, "U.S.-China Economic and Security Review Commission Urges Congress to Probe China's Cyber Attacks," *Huffington Post*, available at: http://www.huffingtonpost.com/2012/11/14/us-china-economic-and-security-review -commission_n_2127521.html.

3. The cases of Chi Mak, who was convicted of exporting defense technology information belonging to his employer, L-3 Communications, and Peter Lee, an engineer with TRW, provide exemplars for traditional Chinese espionage activities. See Yudjijit Battacharjee, "How the F.B.I. Cracked a Chinese Spy Ring," *New Yorker*, May 12, 2014; Jeff Gerth and James Risen, "Reports Show Scientist Gave U.S. Radar Secrets to Chinese," *New York Times*, May 10, 1999. The recruitment of U.S. college exchange student Glenn Duffie Shriver and his ultimate conviction exposed Chinese efforts to employ U.S. citizens moving into the ranks of its Intelligence Community; Adam Taylor, "A Cheesy FBI Video Hopes to Stop U.S. Students from Becoming Chinese Spies," *Washington Post*, April 15, 2014, available at: http://www.washingtonpost.com/blogs/worldviews/wp/2014/ 04/15/a-cheesy-fbi-video-hopes-to-stop-u-s-students-from-becoming-chinese -spies/.

4. Bryan Krekel, Patton Adams, and George Bakos, "Occupying the Information High Ground: Chinese Capabilities for Computer Network Operations and Cyber Espionage," *U.S.-China Economic and Security Review Commission*, 2012, Accessed February 27, 2015, available at: http://www2.gwu.edu/~nsarchiv/ NSAEBB/NSAEBB424/docs/Cyber-066.pdf.

5. Daniel Emery, "Governments, IOC and UN Hit by Massive Cyber-Attack," *British Broadcasting Corporation*, August 3, 2011, available at: http://www.bbc .com/news/technology-14387559.

6. Jim Finkle, "State Actor behind Slew of Cyber Attacks," *Reuters*, August 03, 2011, available at: http://www.reuters.com/article/2011/08/03/us-cyberattacks -idUSTRE7720HU20110803.

7. Dmitri Alperovitch, "Revealed: Operation Shady RAT," *McAfee*, 2011, available at: http://www.mcafee.com/us/resources/white-papers/wp-operation -shady-rat.pdf.

8. McAfee Foundstone Professional Services and McAfee Labs, "Global Energy Cyberattacks: 'Night Dragon,' " *McAfee*, 2011, 11, available at: http:// www.mcafee.com/us/resources/white-papers/wp-global-energy-cyberattacks -night-dragon.pdf.

9. Conversation with U.S. intelligence official, April 19, 2011.

10. Two-factor authentication combines something the user knows, such as their ID and password, as well as something they hold, such as a token, or something they are, such as a biometric attribute, for instance, a fingerprint. Robert McMillan, "RSA Warns SecurID Customers after Company Is Hacked," *PCWorld*, March 17, 2011, available at: http://www.pcworld.com/article/222522/article .html.

11. Marketing materials from EMC provide a suggestion of this wide adoption. See "RSA Customer Profiles: RSA SecureID," available at: http://www.emc.com/ collateral/customer-profiles/h11660-rsa-securid-cp.pdf.

12. Matthew J. Schwartz, "RSA SecurID Breach Cost $66 Million," *Information-Week Dark Reading*, July 28, 2011, available at: http://www.darkreading.com/ attacks-and-breaches/rsa-securid-breach-cost-$66-million/d/d-id/1099232?.

13. Email was the fledgling Internet, then-ARPANET's first "killer" application, developed in 1971 by Ray Tomlinson and several collaborators working with ideas presented in the ARPANET Network Working Group's RFC196. Ray Tomlinson, "The First Network Email," *OpenMap*, available at: http://openmap.bbn .com/~tomlinso/ray/firstemailframe.html; Richard Watson, "RFC 196 – A Mail Box Protocol," *Network Working Group*, July 20, 1971, available at: https://tools .ietf.org/html/rfc196.

14. Email has grown enormously important in the contemporary workplace. Pew surveyed American workers and found in 2014 that 61 percent of those surveyed believed "email is 'very important' for doing their job" and that almost half of those surveyed worked outside of the office more than once a month. While email provides great connectivity, its Achilles' heel is in how its tremendous interoperability may be used to deliver messages containing malware payloads or Web links that can compromise system integrity. Kristen Purcell and Lee Rainie, "Technology's Impact on Workers," *Pew Research Center*, December 30, 2014, available at: http://www.pewinternet.org/2014/12/30/technologys-impact-on-workers/.

15. RSAFraudAction Research Labs, "Anatomy of an Attack," *RSA: Speaking of Security* (blog), April 1, 2011, available at: https://blogs.rsa.com/anatomy-of-an -attack/.

16. Michael Riley and Ashlee Vance, "Inside the Chinese Boom in Corporate Espionage," *Bloomberg*, March 15, 2012, available at: http://www.bloomberg .com/bw/articles/2012-03-14/inside-the-chinese-boom-in-corporate-espionage.

17. Matt Egan, "Hack the Hackers? Companies Itching to Go on Cyber Offense," *Fox Business*, December 7, 2012, available at: http://www.foxbusiness .com/technology/2012/12/07/hack-hackers-companies-itching-to-go-on-cyber -offense/.

18. Ulrich Clauß, "Hack Back—When a Cyber Attack Victim Turns 'Digital Vigilante,' " *Worldcrunch*, July 21, 2012, available at: http://www.worldcrunch .com/hack-back-when-cyber-attack-victim-turns-digital-vigilante/tech-science/ hack-back-when-a-cyber-attack-victim-turns-digital-vigilante-/c4s5887/.

19. Ibid.

20. Jordan Robertson, "Is Hacking in Self-Defense Legal? It Depends, Says Army Cyber Lawyer," *Bloomberg*, July 23, 2012, available at: http://go.bloomberg .com/tech-blog/2012-07-23-is-hacking-in-self-defense-legal-it-depends-says -army-cyber-lawyer/.

21. Conversation with cybersecurity consulting principal, September 14, 2012.

22. *APT 1: Exposing One of China's Cyber Espionage Units*, Mandiant: Washington, D.C., February 18, 2013.

23. In considering Mandiant, a contractor to multiple government agencies, a question arises as to how much the *APT 1* report was informed by classified sources or methods. Although Mandiant extensively noted the report with information

found from the Internet, it is worth wondering how much of that information covered initial discoveries facilitated by classified activity. *APT 1*, February 18, 2013.

24. Dan Wallach, conversation, February 19, 2013.

25. Protesting the conduct of the United States in Vietnam, Ellsberg felt compelled to release the documents to educate the American public as to undisclosed actions undertaken in the escalation of the war. Copying the documents by Xerox machine took far more time than required to make digital copies today.

26. "Public Attitudes toward the War in Iraq: 2003–2008," *Pew Research Center*, March 19, 2008, available at: http://www.pewresearch.org/2008/03/19/public-attitudes-toward-the-war-in-iraq-20032008/.

27. Chris Cillizza, "Obama Lays Out Ethics Rules," *Washington Post*, November 11, 2008.

28. Susan Schmidt and James V. Grimaldi, "The Fast Rise and Steep Fall of Jack Abramoff," *Washington Post*, December 29, 2005.

29. Jimmy Wales, "Opening Plenary (Transcript)" (presentation), Wikimania: Cambridge, MA, August 4, 2006, available at: http://wikimania2006.wikimedia.org/wiki/Opening_Plenary_%28transcript%29.

30. Large open projects enlisting the efforts of volunteers have often been in some way run by powerful but generally respected figures in the project community. Linus Torvalds, who oversaw creation of the Linux open source computer operating system, is one, and Richard Stallman, founder of the Free Software Foundation, which advocates for the creation of nonproprietary computer software, is another of these figures. Wales, who has traveled widely on Wikipedia business and even endorsed a watch brand avoided taking Wikipedia toward profit-seeking status and possibly great personal wealth. Amy Chozick, "Jimmy Wales Is Not an Internet Billionaire," *New York Times*, June 27, 2013.

31. Julian Assange, "About WikiLeaks," WikiLeaks, May 7, 2011, available at: https://wikileaks.org/About.html.

32. Patrick J. Lyons, "Of Orwell, Wikipedia and Guantánamo Bay," *New York Times*, December 14, 2007.

33. William Glaberson, "Red Cross Monitors Barred from Guantánamo," *New York Times*, November 16, 2007.

34. Jonathan D. Glater, "Judge Reverses His Order Disabling Web Site," *New York Times*, March 1, 2008.

35. Ida A. Brudnick, *The Congressional Research Service and the American Legislative Process*, Congressional Research Service: Washington, D.C., April 12, 2011.

36. Stephanie Strom, "Pentagon Sees a Threat from Online Muckrakers," *New York Times*, March 17, 2010.

37. "WikiLeaks Posts Video of 'US Military Killings' in Iraq," *BBC*, April 6, 2010, available at: http://news.bbc.co.uk/2/hi/americas/8603938.stm.

38. Before Manning's arrest, only one diplomatic cable had been released, documenting a U.S. Embassy Reykjavik meeting with officials from Iceland's government. Many more would follow. Kevin Poulsen and Kim Zetter, "U.S. Intelligence Analyst Arrested in Wikileaks Video Probe," *Wired*, June 6, 2010, available at: http://www.wired.com/2010/06/leak/.

39. "A Note to Readers: Piecing Together the Reports, and Deciding What to Publish," *New York Times*, July 25, 2010.

40. James Fallows, "On the AfPak / Wikileaks Documents," *Atlantic*, July 26, 2010, available at: http://www.theatlantic.com/politics/archive/2010/07/on-the-afpak-wikileaks-documents/60379/.

41. Scott Shane and Andrew W. Lehren, "Leaked Cables Offer Raw Look at U.S. Diplomacy," *New York Times*, sec. World, November 28, 2010.

42. Edward P. Djereijian and Christopher Bronk, *Foreign Policy*, "How Disastrous Is WikiLeaks for the State Department?" December 1, 2010, available at: http://foreignpolicy.com/2010/12/01/how-disastrous-is-wikileaks-for-the-state-department/.

43. Christopher Beam, "The WikiLeaks Cables as Literature," *Slate*, December 1, 2010, available at: http://www.slate.com/articles/news_and_politics/politics/2010/12/dispatches.single.html.

44. Christian Stöcker, "Leak at WikiLeaks: A Dispatch Disaster in Six Acts," *Spiegel Online*, September 1, 2011, available at: http://www.spiegel.de/international/world/leak-at-wikileaks-a-dispatch-disaster-in-six-acts-a-783778.html.

45. Jennifer K. Elsea, *Criminal Prohibitions on the Publication of Classified Defense Information*, Washington, D.C.: Congressional Research Service, September 9, 2013.

46. Kerry was described generally as willing to engage in dialog on hard issues, but perhaps lacking a "golden touch." J. Dana Stuster, "America's Next Top Diplomat," *Foreign Policy*, December 21, 2012, available at: http://foreign policy.com/2012/12/21/americas-next-top-diplomat/.

47. Zack Whittaker, "Wikileaks: How the Diplomatic Cables Sparked the 2011 Arab Revolutions," *ZDNet*, June 22, 2011, available at: http://www.zdnet.com/article/wikileaks-how-the-diplomatic-cables-sparked-the-2011-arab-revolutions/.

48. Ian Black, "WikiLeaks Cables: Tunisia Blocks Site Reporting 'Hatred' of First Lady," *Guardian*, December 7, 2010, available at: http://www.theguardian.com/world/2010/dec/07/wikileaks-tunisia-first-lady.

49. Naval Postgraduate School faculty member, conversation, November 6, 2013.

50. Keith Alexander omitted the Middle Passage, a point raised by Roger Hurwitz in oral remarks, 56th Annual Convention of the International Studies Association, February 19, 2015. For Alexander's remarks, see Emil Protalinski, "NSA: Cybercrime Is 'the Greatest Transfer of Wealth in History,' " *ZDNet*, July 10, 2012, available at: http://www.zdnet.com/article/nsa-cybercrime-is-the-greatest-transfer-of-wealth-in-history/.

51. United States Department of Justice, "U.S. Charges Five Chinese Military Hackers for Cyber Espionage against U.S. Corporations and a Labor Organization for Commercial Advantage," May 19, 2014, available at: http://www.justice.gov/opa/pr/us-charges-five-chinese-military-hackers-cyber-espionage-against-us-corporations-and-labor.

52. Ellen Nakashima, "Indictment of PLA Hackers Is Part of Broad U.S. Strategy to Curb Chinese Cyberspying," *Washington Post*, May 22, 2014.

53. Joe Lieberman, "Questions for the Record Submitted to Under Secretary Robert Kennedy," Senate Committee on Homeland Security and Government

Affairs, March 10, 2011, available at: http://www.fas.org/irp/congress/2011_hr/infoshare-qfr.pdf.

54. Charlie Savage, "Manning Is Acquitted of Aiding the Enemy," *New York Times*, July 30, 2013.

55. "Julian Assange's Backers Lose £200,000 Bail Money," *Telegraph*, September 4, 2012, available at: http://www.telegraph.co.uk/news/worldnews/wikileaks/9519767/Julian-Assanges-backers-lose-200000-bail-money.html.

56. Jonathan Marcus, "Ukraine Crisis: Transcript of Leaked Nuland-Pyatt Call," *BBC*, February 7, 2014, available at: http://www.bbc.com/news/world-europe-26079957.

57. Jack Moore, "Concerns over Quality Continue to Plague OPM's Background Investigations," *Federal News Radio*, May 14, 2014, available at: http://federalnewsradio.com/congress/2014/05/concerns-over-quality-continue-to-plague-opms-background-investigations/.

58. Adam Mazmanian, "OPM Merges Security Investigation Databases," *FCW*, May 29, 2014, available at: http://fcw.com/Articles/2014/05/29/security-check-databases-merged.aspx?Page=1.

59. Mary Louis Hoffman, "OPM to Consolidate Staff, Contractor Security Clearance Records," *ExecutiveGov*, May 30, 2014, available at: http://www.executivegov.com/2014/05/opm-to-consolidate-staff-contractor-security-clearance-records/.

60. The author meekly asked his mother to type his entries for him onto the form in 2001, when seeking federal employment.

61. "e-QIP Application," *Office of Personnel Management*, available at: https://www.opm.gov/investigations/e-qip-application/.

62. David Perera, "Office of Personnel Management Didn't Encrypt Feds' Data Hacked by Chinese," *Politico*, June 4, 2015, available at: http://www.politico.com/story/2015/06/personal-data-of-4-million-federal-employees-hacked-118655.html.

63. David Auerbach, "The OPM Breach Is a Catastrophe," *Slate*, June 16, 2015, available at: http://www.slate.com/articles/technology/future_tense/2015/06/opm_hack_it_s_a_catastrophe_here_s_how_the_government_can_stop_the_next.html.

64. Perera, "Office of Personnel Management."

65. "CyTech Services Confirms Assistance to OPM Breach Response," *PRWEB*, June 15, 2015, available at: http://www.prweb.com/releases/2015/06/prweb12787823.htm.

66. Robert Hackett, "A Product Demo May Have Revealed What Could Be the Biggest Ever Government Data Breach," *Fortune*, June 12, 2015, available at: http://fortune.com/2015/06/12/cytech-product-demo-opm-breach/.

67. Corporate information security official, conversation, November 12, 2013.

68. "About Us," *KeyPoint Government Solutions*, available at: http://www.keypoint.us.com/AboutUs/History.

69. Evan Perez and Shimon Prokupecz, "First on CNN: U.S. Data Hack May Be 4 Times Larger Than the Government Originally Said," *CNN*, June 23, 2015, available at: http://www.cnn.com/2015/06/22/politics/opm-hack-18-milliion/.

70. Erin Kelly, "OPM Hack Q&A: What We Know and What We Don't," *USA Today*, June 27, 2015, available at: http://www.usatoday.com/story/news/politics/2015/06/27/opm-hack-questions-and-answers/29333211/.

71. A data breach also occurred at USIS, another OPM contractor. "48,000 Federal Employees Potentially Affected by Second Background Check Hack," *Nextgov*, December 18, 2014, available at: http://www.nextgov.com/cybersecurity/2014/12/opm-alerts-feds-second-background-check-breach/101622/.

72. Michael Esser, *Final Audit Report: Federal Information Security Management Act Audit FY2014*, Office of Personnel Management: Washington, D.C., November 12, 2014, i.

73. Sean Gallager, "Why the 'Biggest Government Hack Ever' Got Past the Feds," *Ars Technica*, June 8, 2015, available at: http://arstechnica.com/security/2015/06/why-the-biggest-government-hack-ever-got-past-opm-dhs-and-nsa/.

74. Sean Lyngaas, "Rogers Mum on OPM Attribution, but Says Hack Shows Value of Data," June 24, 2015, available at: http://fcw.com/articles/2015/06/24/rogers-opm-attribution.aspx.

75. Brian Krebs, "Catching Up on the OPM Breach," *Krebs on Security*, June 15, 2015, available at: http://krebsonsecurity.com/2015/06/catching-up-on-the-opm-breach/.

76. Ellen Nakashima, "Chinese Breach Data of 4 Million Federal Workers," *Washington Post*, June 4, 2015, available at: https://www.washingtonpost.com/world/national-security/chinese-hackers-breach-federal-governments-personnel-office/2015/06/04/889c0e52-0af7-11e5-95fd-d580f1c5d44e_story.html.

77. Tom Risen, "Obama Considers Sanctions after Cyberattacks," *US News*, June 15, 2015, http://www.usnews.com/news/articles/2015/06/15/obama-considers-sanctions-after-opm-breach.

78. Ellen Nakashima, "U.S. Decides against Publicly Blaming China for Data Hack," *Washington Post*, July 21, 2015, available at: https://www.washingtonpost.com/world/national-security/us-avoids-blaming-china-in-data-theft-seen-as-fair-game-in-espionage/2015/07/21/03779096-2eee-11e5-8353-1215475949f4_story.html.

79. Katherine Archuleta, "OPM: Data Breach," Testimony, Committee on Oversight and Government Reform, U.S. House of Representatives, June 16, 2015, available at: http://oversight.house.gov/wp-content/uploads/2015/06/Archuleta-OPM-Statement-6-16-Data-Breach.pdf.

80. Tal Kopan and David Perera, "Oversight Chairman: Fire Leaders of Hacked Agency," *Politico*, June 16, 2015, available at: http://www.politico.com/story/2015/06/katherine-archuleta-opm-computer-hack-house-119067.html.

CHAPTER 10

1. Glenn Greenwald, "NSA Collecting Phone Records of Millions of Verizon Customers Daily," *Guardian*, June 5, 2013.

2. Aaron Blake, "Edward Snowden Reveals Himself as NSA Leaker," *Washington Post*, June 9, 2013.

3. Lana Lam, "Snowden Leaves Hong Kong 'on His Own Accord', Arrives in Moscow with WikiLeaks Help," *South China Morning Post*, August 29, 2013, available at: http://www.scmp.com/news/hong-kong/article/1267261/snowden-leaves-hong-kong-his-own-accord-arrives-moscow-wikileaks-help.

4. How Snowden boarded an international flight with a canceled passport and without a valid visa for entry into Russia, a requisite for all American travelers to the country, is one of the many unanswered questions of the Snowden Affair; see http://articles.latimes.com/2013/jun/30/world/la-fg-wn-putin-edward-snowden -20130630.

5. Allegedly, documents covering the domestic surveillance undertaken via U.S. telecommunications firms and the PRISM operation targeting U.S. Internet and software firms were among the last copied before Edward Snowden departed for Hong Kong. Edward Jay Epstein, "Was Snowden's Heist a Foreign Espionage Operation?" *Wall Street Journal*, May 9, 2014.

6. Laura Poitras, *Citizenfour*, Film, Praxis Films, Participant Media, HBO Films, October 10, 2014.

7. Glenn Greenwald, "NSA Collecting Phone Records of Millions of Verizon Customers Daily," *Guardian*, June 5, 2013.

8. Glenn Greenwald and Ewen MacAskill, "NSA Prism Program Taps in to User Data of Apple, Google and Others," *Guardian*, June 7, 2013.

9. Satirical newspaper *The Onion* produced a fake news story on the topic well before Snowden's breach. "CIA's Facebook Program Dramatically Cut Agency's Costs," *Onion*, available at: http://www.theonion.com/video/cias-facebook -program-dramatically-cut-agencys-cos,19753/.

10. Larry Page and David Drummond, "What the . . .?," *Official Google Blog*, June 7, 2013, available at: http://googleblog.blogspot.com/2013/06/what.html.

11. "A Petition for Greater Transparency," *Transparency Report*, Google, September 9, 2013, available at: http://googlepublicpolicy.blogspot.com/2013/ 09/a-petition-for-greater-transparency.html.

12. Mark Rumold and David Sobel, "Government Says Secret Court Opinion on Law Underlying PRISM Program Needs to Stay Secret,"*Electronic Frontier Foundation*, June 7, 2013, available at: https://www.eff.org/deeplinks/2013/06/ government-says-secret-court-opinion-law-underlying-prism-program-needs -stay.

13. See U.S. Senator Ron Wyden's letter to General Keith Alexander, October 10, 2012, available at: http://www.wyden.senate.gov/download/?id=f752080a-d541 -4a2f-be83-bece34731d3c&download=1.

14. Spencer Ackerman and Dan Roberts, "NSA Surveillance: Lawmakers Urge Disclosure as Obama 'Welcomes' Debate," *Guardian*, June 9, 2013.

15. Bill Keller, "Disillusioned Nation: From Dick Cheney to Edward Snowden," *New York Times*, June 10, 2013, available at: http://keller.blogs.nytimes .com/2013/06/10/disillusioned-nation/?_r=0.

16. Spencer Ackerman, "NSA Chief Claims 'Focused' Surveillance Disrupted More Than 50 Terror Plots," *Guardian*, June 19, 2013.

17. The *Washington Post*'s Barton Gelman also published from Snowden material, apparently receiving some documentation from Snowden before failing to employ a sufficient level of cryptographic security to satisfy the leaker's concerns for maintaining confidentiality of communications. Mackenzie Weinger, "Barton Gellman, Glenn Greenwald Feud over NSA Leaker," *Politico*, June 10, 2013, available at: http://www.politico.com/story/2013/06/edward-snow den-nsa-leaker-glenn-greenwald-barton-gellman-92505.html.

18. Ewen MacAskill, Nick Davies, Nick Hopkins, Julian Borger, and James Ball, "GCHQ Intercepted Foreign Politicians' Communications at G20 Summits," *Guardian*, June 17, 2013.

19. The G20 slides offered corroborative evidence of soured U.S. and UK relations with Turkey, extending back as far perhaps as the Erdogan government's decision to forbid use of Turkish territory for the U.S.-led invasion of Iraq in 2003.

20. "Embassy Espionage: The NSA's Secret Spy Hub in Berlin," *Der Spiegel*, October 27, 2013, available at: http://www.spiegel.de/international/germany/cover-story-how-nsa-spied-on-merkel-cell-phone-from-berlin-embassy-a-930205-2.html.

21. Frank Zeller, "Germany Drops Probe into Alleged US Tapping of Merkel Cellphone," *AFP*, June 12, 2015, available at: http://news.yahoo.com/germany-drops-probe-alleged-us-tapping-merkel-cellphone-090650693.html.

22. George Packer, "The Quiet German: The Astonishing Rise of Angela Merkel, the Most Powerful Woman in the World," *New Yorker*, December 1, 2014.

23. Colum Lynch, "Brazil President Condemns NSA Spying," *Washington Post*, September 24, 2013.

24. James Risen and Laura Poitras, "Spying by N.S.A. Ally Entangled U.S. Law Firm," *New York Times*, February 15, 2014.

25. Adam Liptak, "Justices Turn Back Challenge to Broader U.S. Eavesdropping," *New York Times*, February 26, 2013.

26. Colin Freeze and Stephanie Nolen, "Charges That Canada Spied on Brazil Unveil CSEC's Inner Workings," *Globe and Mail*, October 7, 2013.

27. *NETmundial Multistakeholder Agreement*, NETmundial Global Multistakeholder Meeting on the Future of Internet Governance, Sao Paulo, Brazil, April 23–24, 2014, available at: http://netmundial.br/wp-content/uploads/2014/04/NETmundial-Multistakeholder-Document.pdf.

28. Moshe Y. Vardi, "The End of the American Network: Can the Internet Be Liberated from Government Meddling?," *Communications of the ACM*, 56(11): 5, 2013.

29. Lawrence E. Strickling, "Remarks by Assistant Secretary Strickling at the State of the Net Conference 1/27/2015," presentation, State of the Net Conference, Washington, D.C., January 27, 2015, available at: http://www.ntia.doc.gov/speechtestimony/2015/remarks-assistant-secretary-strickling-state-net-conference-1272015.

30. Maeli Astruc, "Will ICANN Be the Next International Organisation in Geneva?," *Intellectual Property Watch*, March 2, 2014, available at: http://www.ip-watch.org/2014/03/02/internet-governance-will-icann-be-the-next-international-organisation-in-geneva/.

31. Rory Carroll, "Hillary Clinton: People Felt Betrayed by NSA Surveillance," *Guardian*, February 24, 2015.

32. The agency's roots can be traced to Herbert O. Yardley's Black Chamber, the Cipher Bureau formed and funded by the U.S. Army and Department of State in 1919 to continue code-breaking activities following World War I. Eventually, the Cipher Bureau was closed in 1929 after Secretary of State Henry Stimson deemed it was immoral to decrypt and monitor the diplomatic communications. Code-breaking capacity was very much back in demand with the outbreak of World

War II. Americans broke Japanese cryptographic systems and worked closely with the UK code-breaking establishment at Bletchley Park during the war. David Kahn, *The Codebreakers: The Story of Secret Writing*, Scribner: New York, 1996.

33. Whitfield Diffie and Susan Landau, *Privacy on the Line: The Politics of Wiretapping and Encryption*, MIT Press: Cambridge, MA, 2007.

34. Charles Mann, "Homeland Insecurity," *Atlantic Monthly*, September 2002, 5.

35. Nicole Perlroth, Jeff Larson, and Scott Shane, "N.S.A. Able to Foil Basic Safeguards of Privacy on Web," *New York Times*, September 5, 2013.

36. National Institute of Standards and Technology, "Supplemental ITL Bulletin for September 2013," *Information Technology Laboratory Bulletins*, September 2013, available at: http://csrc.nist.gov/publications/nistbul/itlbul2013_09 _supplemental.pdf.

37. Bruce Schneider, "NSA Surveillance: A Guide to Staying Secure," *Guardian*, September 6, 2013.

38. "Inside TAO: Documents Reveal Top NSA Hacking Unit," *Der Spiegel*, December 29, 2013, available at: http://www.spiegel.de/international/world/ the-nsa-uses-powerful-toolbox-in-effort-to-spy-on-global-networks-a-940969. html.

39. Ibid.

40. Barton Gellman, Ashkan Soltani, and Andrea Peterson, "How We Know the NSA Had Access to Internal Google and Yahoo Cloud Data,"*Washington Post*, November 4, 2013.

41. Adrian Covert, "Gmail at 10: How Google Dominated E-mail," *CNNMoney*, April 1, 2014, available at: http://money.cnn.com/2014/04/01/technology/ gmail/.

42. Sean Gallagher, "Googlers Say 'F*** You' to NSA, Company Encrypts Internal Network," *Ars Technica*, November 6, 2013, available at: http://arstechnica .com/information-technology/2013/11/googlers-say-f-you-to-nsa-company -encrypts-internal-network/.

43. CATO Institute, "The 2014 Cato Institute Surveillance Conference," presentation, The 2014 Cato Institute Surveillance Conference, Washington, D.C., December 12, 2014, available at: http://www.cato.org/events/2014-cato-institute -surveillance-conference.

44. Mark J. Cox, *Google Plus* (blog), April 9, 2014, available at: https://plus .google.com/ MarkJCox/posts/TmCbp3BhJma.

45. Michael A. Riley, "NSA Said to Have Used Heartbleed Bug, Exposing Consumers," *Bloomberg*, April 11, 2014, available at: http://www.bloomberg.com/ news/articles/2014-04-11/nsa-said-to-have-used-heartbleed-bug-exposing -consumers.

46. Epstein, "Was Snowden's Heist a Foreign Espionage Operation?"

47. "Snowden, NSA, and Counterintelligence," *The XX Committee* (blog), September 4, 2013, available at: http://20committee.com/2013/09/04/snowden -nsa-and-counterintelligence/.

48. Joshua Foust, "Has Wikileaks Been Infiltrated by Russian Spies?" *War Is Boring* (blog), August 29, 2013, available at: https://medium.com/war-is-boring/ has-wikileaks-been-infiltrated-by-russian-spies-b876a8bc035a.

49. James Ball, "Israel Shamir and Julian Assange's Cult of Machismo," *Guardian*, November 8, 2011, available at: http://www.theguardian.com/commentis free/cifamerica/2011/nov/08/israel-shamir-julian-assange-cult-machismo and http://www.thelocal.de/20110210/33025.

50. Barton Gellman, "Code Name 'Verax': Snowden, in Exchanges with Post Reporter, Made Clear He Knew Risks," *Washington Post*, June 9, 2013, available at: http://www.washingtonpost.com/world/national-security/code-name -verax-snowden-in-exchanges-with-post-reporter-made-clear-he-knew-risks/ 2013/06/09/c9a25b54-d14c-11e2-9f1a-1a7cdee20287_story.html.

51. "Defense Contractor Charged in Hawaii with Communicating Classified Information to Person Not Entitled to Receive Such Information," U.S Attorney's Office, District of Hawaii, March 18, 2013, available at: http://www.fbi.gov/ honolulu/press-releases/2013/defense-contractor-charged-in-hawaii-with -communicating-classified-information-to-person-not-entitled-to-receive-such -information.

52. "Oahu Defense Contractor Sentenced on Espionage Charges," *Hawaii Reporter*, September 18, 2014, available at: http://www.hawaiireporter.com/ oahu-defense-contractor-sentenced-on-espionage-charges.

53. Public acts of dissent in the Intelligence Community represent a perilous path. While much has been made of the CIA's employment of torture in terrorist detention, only one government employee, John Kiriakou, was sentenced to two years in federal prison for leaking information on waterboarding to the press. "CIA Whistleblower John Kiriakou Given More Than Two Years in Prison," *Guardian*, January 25, 2013.

54. The report made several intelligence policy prescriptions, which were revisited in the recent DNI; Richard Clarke, Michael Morrell, Geoffrey Stone, Cass Sunstein, and Peter Swire, *Liberty and Security in a Changing World: Report and Recommendations of the President's Review Group on Intelligence and Communication Technologies*, The White House: Washington, D.C., December 12, 2013, available at: http://www.whitehouse.gov/sites/default/files/docs/2013-12-12_rg_final _report.pdf.

55. Office of the Director of National Intelligence, "Signals Intelligence Reform 2015 Anniversary Report," *IC on the Record* (blog), January 17, 2015, available at: http://icontherecord.tumblr.com/ppd-28/2015/overview.

56. "[T]he term 'United States person' means any United States citizen or alien admitted for permanent residence in the United States, and any corporation, partnership, or other organization organized under the laws of the United States," 22 U.S.C. Sec 6010.

57. "PPD-28 Section 4 Procedures," National Security Agency: Fort Meade, MD, January 12, 2015, available at: https://www.nsa.gov/public_info/_files/ nsacss_policies/PPD-28.pdf.

58. The U.S. government's actions came after large Internet firms such as Google and Facebook published their own transparency reports detailing the number of requests from the U.S. and other governments requesting specific data from their firms. Telecommunications firms have since followed suit.

59. Committee on Responding to Section 5(d) of Presidential Policy Directive 28: The Feasibility of Software to Provide Alternatives to Bulk Signals Intelligence

Collection, Computer Science and Telecommunications Board; Division on Engineering and Physical Sciences, National Research Council, *The Bulk Collection of Signals Intelligence: Technical Options*, National Research Council: Washington, D.C., 2015, available at: http://www.nap.edu/catalog/19414/bulk-collection-of-signals-intelligence-technical-options.

60. "The End of the Snowden Operation," *The XX Committee* (blog), January 18, 2014, available at: http://20committee.com/2014/01/18/the-end-of-the-snowden-operation/.

61. Christopher Bronk, "Webtapping: Securing the Internet to Save Us from Transnational Terror?" *First Monday*, 13(11), 2008, available at: http://ojs-prod-lib.cc.uic.edu/ojs/index.php/fm/article/view/2192/2052.

CHAPTER 11

1. Willie Sutton and Edward Linn, *Where the Money Was: The Memoirs of a Bank Robber*, Viking Press: New York, 2004, 160.

2. Deborah Lamm Weisel, *Bank Robbery*, U.S. Department of Justice, Office of Community Policing Services, March 2007, available at: http://www.cops.usdoj.gov/Publications/e03071267.pdf.

3. Stacey Cowley, "FBI Director: Cybercrime Will Eclipse Terrorism," *CNN*, March 2, 2012, available at: http://money.cnn.com/2012/03/02/technology/fbi_cybersecurity/.

4. Mark Krebs, "Sources: Target Investigating Data Breach," *Krebs on Security*, December 13, 2013, available at: http://krebsonsecurity.com/2013/12/sources-target-investigating-data-breach/.

5. Nicholas Ballasay, "Target Breach: CUNA/CBA Member Costs Top $200M," *Credit Union Times*, February 18, 2014, available at: http://www.cutimes.com/2014/02/18/target-breach-cuna-cba-member-costs-top-200m.

6. Google Finance, available at: https://www.google.com/finance.

7. Anne D'Innocenzo, "Data-Breach Costs Take Toll on Target Profit," *Yahoo! News*, February 26, 2014, available at: http://news.yahoo.com/data-breach-costs-toll-target-profit-123047290—finance.html.

8. "Target Reports Fourth Quarter and Full-Year 2013 Earnings," *Target*, February 26, 2014, available at: http://investors.target.com/phoenix.zhtml?c=65828&p=irol-newsArticle&ID=1903678&highlight=.

9. A number of factors contributed to Steinhafel's eventual sacking beyond the data breach. Paul Ziobro and Serena Ng, "Retailer Target Lost Its Way under Ousted CEO Gregg Steinhafel," *Wall Street Journal*, June 23, 2014.

10. Dale Jorgenson, "Information Technology and the U.S. Economy," *The American Economic Review*, 91(1), 2001.

11. Hélène Baudchon, "The Aftermath of the 'New Economy' Bust: A Case Study of Five OECD Countries, No 2002–08," *Observatoire Français des conjectures Economiques*, December 2002.

12. George Stigler, "The Economics of Information," *The Journal of Political Economy*, 69(3), 1961.

13. Google Finance, available at: https://investor.google.com/financial/tables.html.

14. William. S. Comanor and Thomas A. Wilson, "Advertising, Market Structure and Performance," *The Review of Economics and Statistics*, 49: 423–440, 1967; Phillip Nelson, "The Economic Consequences of Advertising," *Journal of Business*, 48: 213–241, 1975; and Kyle Bagwell, "The Economic Analysis of Advertising," Columbia University, Department of Economics Discussion Paper Series, August 2005.

15. "For Students Doing Reports," *Recording Industry Association of America*, available at: http://www.riaa.com/faq.php.

16. Josh Rogin, "NSA Chief: Cybercrime Constitutes the 'Greatest Transfer of Wealth in History,' " *Foreign Policy*, July 9, 2012, available at: http://thecable .foreignpolicy.com/posts/2012/07/09/nsa_chief_cybercrime_constitutes_the _greatest_transfer_of_wealth_in_history.

17. James Lewis and Stewart Baker, *The Economic Impact of Cybercrime and Cyber Espionage*, Center for Strategic and International Studies, July 2013, available at: http://csis.org/files/publication/60396rpt_cybercrime-cost_0713_ph4_0.pdf.

18. *United States Attorneys' Annual Statistical Report*, Department of Justice: Washington, D.C., 2012.

19. *18 U.S. Code Sec. 1030, Fraud and Related Activity in Connection to Computers*, Legal Information Institute, Cornell University, available at: https://www.law .cornell.edu/uscode/text/18/1030.

20. Orin Kerr, "Vagueness Challenges to the Computer Fraud and Abuse Act," *Minnesota Law Review*, 94: 1587, 2010.

21. *U.S. v. Drew*, 259 F.R.D. 449, Central District of California.

22. Kristen Archick, *CRS Report for Congress—Cybercrime: The Council of Europe Convention*, Congressional Research Service: Washington, D.C., April 26, 2002.

23. Shannon Hopkins, "Cybercrime Convention: A Positive Beginning to a Long Road Ahead," *Journal of High Technology Law, 2(1), 2003*.

24. FBI's staff includes "34,787 permanent positions (13,082 Special Agents (SAs), 3,026 Intelligence Analysts (IAs), and 18,679 professional staff (PS)) and 36,442 full time equivalents (FTE)," *FY 2014 Budget and Request to Congress*, Federal Bureau of Investigation: Washington, D.C., April 2013, available at: http://www .justice.gov/sites/default/files/jmd/legacy/2013/11/17/fbi-justification.pdf.

25. "Cybercriminals: Wanted BJORN DANIEL SUNDIN by the FBI 20k Reward," *CyberWarZone*, February 2, 2012, available at: http://www.cyberwar zone.com/cyberwarfare/cybercriminals-wanted-bjorn-daniel-sundin-fbi-20k -reward#sthash.

26. "FBI Includes Latvian-Born Russian Citizen on Its List of Most Wanted Cyber Criminals," *LETA*, November 6, 2011, available at: http://www.leta.lv/ eng/home/important/5943B5CE-DC91-4FC9-8443-899F0D2D4E93/.

27. James Verini, "The Great Cyberheist," *New York Times*, November 10, 2010.

28. David Jones and Jim Finkle, "U.S. Indicts Hackers in Biggest Cyber Fraud Case in History," *Reuters*, July 25, 2013, available at: http://www.reuters.com/ article/2013/07/25/us-usa-hackers-creditcards-idUSBRE96O0RI20130725.

29. Joseph Menn, *Fatal System Error: The Hunt for the New Crime Lords Who Are Bringing Down the Internet*, PublicAffairs: New York, 2010.

30. "FBI Cyber Action Teams: Traveling the World to Catch Cyber Criminals," Federal Bureau of Investigation news stories, March 6, 2006, available at: http:// www.fbi.gov/news/stories/2006/march/cats030606.

31. "Turk, Moroccan Nabbed in Huge Worm Case," *CNN Money,* August 26, 2005, available at: http://money.cnn.com/2005/08/26/technology/worm_arrest/.

32. David S. Wall, *Cybercrime: The Transformation of Crime in the Information Age,* Polity: London, 2007.

CHAPTER 12

1. Thomas Fingar, "Sources of Instability in the Middle East," *The Global Energy Market: Comprehensive Strategies to Meet Geopolitical and Financial Risks,* Baker Institute for Public Policy, Rice University, May 21, 2008.

2. Lev Grossman, "You—Yes, You—Are TIME's Person of the Year," *Time,* December 26, 2006.

3. Jody Williams, *My Name Is Jody Williams: A Vermont Girl's Winding Path to the Nobel Peace Prize,* University of California Press: Berkeley, CA, 2013.

4. Max Weber, *Politics as Vocation (Politik als Beruf),* Munich University, January 1919.

5. Alexander Vacca and Mark Davidson, "The Regularity of Irregular Warfare," *Parameters,* Spring 2011.

6. Jon Street, " 'Islamic State Hacking Division' Likely Used Google to Create U.S. Military 'Hit List': Analysis," *The Blaze,* March 23, 2015, available at: http://www.theblaze.com/stories/2015/03/23/islamic-state-hacking-division-likely-used-google-to-create-u-s-military-hit-list-analysis/.

7. Orson Scott Card, *Ender's Game,* Tor: New York, 1991, 207–208.

8. In December 2014, the German *Bundesamt für Sicherheit in der Informationstechnik* (BSI—Federal Office for Information Security) released a report chronicling the destruction of a steel mill's blast furnace by cyber means. Robert M. Lee, Michael J. Assante, and Tim Conway, *German Steel Mill Cyber Attack,* SANS Industrial Control Systems, December 30, 2014.

9. Debate continues regarding the possibility that Iranian forces were able to subvert the flight control system of a U.S. RQ-170 UAV and bring it down in Iran. See Adam Rawnsley, "Iran's Alleged Drone Hack: Tough, but Possible," *Wired,* December 11, 2011, available at: http://www.wired.com/2011/12/iran-drone-hack-gps/; David Axe, "Nah, Iran Probably Didn't Hack CIA's Stealth Drone," *Wired,* April 24, 2012, available at: http://www.wired.com/2012/04/iran-drone-hack/. For the Russian version, see "How Iran Hacked Super-Secret CIA Stealth Drone," *RT,* December 15, 2011, available at: http://rt.com/usa/iran-drone-hack-stealth-943/.

10. James Der Derian, "The Simulation Syndrome: From War Games to Game Wars," *Social Text,* Spring 1990.

11. "The Great Disrupter's New Targets," *Economist,* September 20, 2014.

12. "Made in China?" *Economist,* March 14, 2015.

13. Edward Hallett Carr, *The Twenty Years' Crisis, 1919–1939: An Introduction to the Study of International Relations,* Harper Perennial: New York, 1964.

14. Arkady Bukh, "The Real Cybercrime Geography," *TechCrunch,* January 4, 2015, available at: http://techcrunch.com/2015/01/04/after-sony-whats-the-real-cybercrime-geography/.

15. Roger Hurwitz, "The Play of States: Norms and Security in Cyberspace," *American Foreign Policy Interests*, 36(5), 2014.

16. P. K. Manadhata and J. M. Wing, "An Attack Surface Metric," *IEEE Transactions on Software Engineering*, 37(3), 2010.

17. Heartbleed is an error in the OpenSSL software libraries that service encrypted server-to-browser sessions that allowed unrestricted data queries of servers. Shellshock is a bug in the Unix operating system (the Bash Shell) that permitted unauthorized users to gain access to systems.

18. *Security Implications of Microsoft Windows Vista*, Symantec: Cupertino, CA, 2007, available at: http://www.symantec.com/avcenter/reference/Security _Implications_of_Windows_Vista.pdf.

19. Jordan Robertson and Michael A. Riley, "JPMorgan Goes to War," *Bloomberg*, February 19, 2015, available at: http://www.bloomberg.com/news/articles/ 2015-02-19/jpmorgan-hires-cyberwarriors-to-repel-data-thieves-foreign-powers.

20. Daniel Terdiman, "Stuxnet Delivered to Iranian Nuclear Plant on Thumb Drive," *cnet*, April 12, 2012, available at: http://www.cnet.com/news/stuxnet -delivered-to-iranian-nuclear-plant-on-thumb-drive/.

21. Ashton Carter, *The DoD Cyber Strategy*, Department of Defense: Washington, D.C., April 2015, 5.

22. Ibid., 26.

23. While no mention of DEVGRU is to be found on a DoD Web server, a Google News search yields 961 articles about the naval special operations unit known to have been a key part of U.S. counterterror and counterinsurgency missions since its inception. Samantha Heig, "Who's Who in the Osama Bin Laden Raid," *New Yorker*, August 2, 2011, available at: http://www.newyorker.com/news/ news-desk/whos-who-in-the-osama-bin-laden-raid.

24. Master Chief Dave, *Strategic Multilayer Analysis, 5th Annual Conference*, Natcher Hall, National Institutes of Health, November 30, 2011.

25. Ibid.

Bibliography

BOOKS

Argyros, George, Marc Grossman, and Felix Rohatyn, *The Embassy of the Future*, The CSIS Press: Washington, DC, 2007.

Aspray, William, ed., *Computing before Computers*, Iowa State University Press: Ames, 1990.

Baldwin, David A., ed., *Neorealism and Neoliberalism: The Contemporary Debate*, Columbia University Press: New York, 1993.

Bamford, James, *The Puzzle Palace*, Houghton-Mifflin: New York, 1982.

Bass, Carla, *Building Castles on Sand: Ignoring the Riptide of Information Operations*, Air War College: Montgomery, AL, 1998.

Brynjolfsson, Erik and Brian Kahin, *Understanding the Digital Economy*, MIT Press: Cambridge, MA, 2000.

Brynjolfsson, Erik and Andrew McAfee, *Race against the Machine: How the Digital Revolution Is Accelerating Innovation, Driving Productivity, and Irreversibly Transforming Employment and the Economy*, Digital Frontier Press: Cambridge, MA, 2012.

Card, Orson Scott, *Ender's Game*, Tor: New York, 1991.

Carr, Edward Hallett, *The Twenty Years' Crisis, 1919–1939: An Introduction to the Study of International Relations*, Harper Perennial: New York, 1964.

Castells, Manuel, *The Rise of the Network Society, The Information Age: Economy, Society and Culture Vol. I*, Oxford University Press: Cambridge, MA, 1996.

Ceruzzi, Paul, *A History of Modern Computing*, MIT Press: Cambridge, MA, 2003.

Deibert, Ronald, *Black Code: Inside the Battle for Cyberspace*, Random House: Toronto, 2013.

Diffie, Whitfield and Susan Landau, *Privacy on the Line: The Politics of Wiretapping and Encryption*, MIT Press: Cambridge, MA, 2007.

Douhet, Giulio, *Command of the Air*, Air Force History and Museums Program: Washington, DC, 1998.

Fingar, Thomas, *Reducing Uncertainty: Intelligence Analysis and National Security*, Stanford Security Studies: Palo Alto, CA, 2011.

Gibson, William, *Neuromancer*, Ace: New York, 1984.

Gleick, James, *The Information: A History, a Theory, a Flood*, Pantheon: New York, 2011.

Grama, Joana Lyn, *Legal Issues in Information Security*, Jones & Bartlett Learning: Burlington, MA, 2015.

Hundley, Richard O., Robert H. Anderson, Tora K. Bikson, and C. Richard Neu, *The Global Course of the Information Revolution: Recurring Themes and Regional Variations*, RAND: Santa Monica, CA, 2003.

Johnson, Loch K., *A Season of Inquiry, Congress and Intelligence*, Dorsey Press: Chicago, IL, 1988.

Kahn, David, *The Codebreakers: The Story of Secret Writing*, Scribner: New York, 1996.

Kehoe, Brendan, *Zen and the Art of the Internet*, Prentice Hall: Upper Saddle River, NJ, 1995.

Kshetri, Nir, *Cybercrime and Cybersecurity in the Global South*, Palgrave: London, 2013.

Libicki, Martin, *What Is Information Warfare*, NDU Press: Washington, DC, 1995.

Libicki, Martin, *Conquest in Cyberspace: National Security and Information Warfare*, Cambridge University Press: Cambridge, 2007.

Lipner, Steve and Michael Howard, *The Trustworthy Computing Development Lifecycle*, Microsoft Corporation: Redmond, WA, March 2005.

Lowenstein, Roger, *Origins of the Crash: The Great Bubble and Its Undoing*, Penguin: New York, 2004.

Lowenthal, Mark M. *Intelligence: From Secrets to Policy*, Sage: Thousand Oaks, CA, 2011.

Menn, Joseph, *Fatal System Error: The Hunt for the New Crime Lords Who Are Bringing Down the Internet*, PublicAffairs: New York, 2010.

Morozov, Evgeny, *The Net Delusion: The Dark Side of Internet Freedom*, Public Affairs: New York, 2011.

Mueller, Milton L., *Ruling the Root: Internet Governance and the Taming of Cyberspace*, MIT Press: Cambridge, MA, 2004.

Mueller, Milton L., *Networks and States: The Global Politics of Internet Governance*, MIT Press: Cambridge, MA, 2010.

Nickles, David, *Under the Wire: How the Telegraph Changed Diplomacy*, Harvard University Press: Cambridge, MA, 2003.

Nye, Joseph, *Soft Power: The Means to Success in World Politics*, PublicAffairs: New York, 2005.

Sanger, David, *Confront and Conceal: Obama's Secret Wars and Surprising Use of American Power*, Crown: New York, 2012.

Singer, Peter W. and Allan Friedman, *Cybersecurity and Cyberwar: What Everyone Needs to Know*, Oxford University Press: Cambridge, MA, 2014.

Spellman, Frank, *Handbook of Water and Wastewater Treatment Plant Operations*, CRC Press: Boca Raton, FL, 2013.

Stringer, Paul J., *Cyberwarfare, a Reference Handbook*, ABC-CLIO: Santa Barbara, CA, 2015.

Sutton, Willie and Edward Linn, *Where the Money Was: The Memoirs of a Bank Robber*, Viking Press: New York, 2004.

Varian, Hal, Joseph Farrell, and Carl Shapiro, *The Economics of Information Technology*, Cambridge University Press: Cambridge, UK, 2004.

Wall, David S., *Cybercrime: The Transformation of Crime in the Information Age*, Polity: London, 2007.

Weber, Max, *Politics as Vocation (Politik als Beruf)*, Munich University: Munich, 1919.

Wiener, Norbert, *Cybernetics: Or Control and Communication in the Animal and the Machine*, Hermann & Cie: Paris & MIT Press: Cambridge, MA, 1948.

Yergin, Daniel and Joseph Stanislaw, *The Commanding Heights: The Battle for the World Economy*, Free Press: New York, 1998.

Zetter, Kim, *Countdown to Zero Day: Stuxnet and the Launch of the World's First Digital Weapon*, Crown: New York, 2014.

REPORTS AND OFFICIAL DOCUMENTS

Abley, J. and K. Lindqvist, "Request for Comments: 4786," *Internet Engineering Task Force*, December 2006, available at: http://tools.ietf.org/pdf/rfc4786.pdf.

Ablon, Lilian, Martin Libicki, and Andrea Golay, *Markets for Cybercrime Tools and Stolen Data*, RAND: Santa Monica, CA, 2014.

ACM U.S. Public Policy Council, *Analysis of SOPA's Impact on DNS and DNSSEC*, Association for Computing Machinery, January 18, 2012.

Air Traffic Control: FAA Needs a More Comprehensive Approach to Address Cybersecurity as Agency Transitions to Next Gen, GAO-15-370, Government Accountability Office: Washington, DC, April 14, 2015.

Alperovitch, Dmitri, "Revealed: Operation Shady RAT," McAfee, 2011, available at: http://www.mcafee.com/us/resources/white-papers/wp-operation -shady-rat.pdf.

Annual Report to Congress: Federal Information Security Management Act, Office of Management and Budget: Washington, DC, February 27, 2015.

APT 1: Exposing One of China's Cyber Espionage Units, Mandiant: Washington, DC, February 18, 2013.

Archick, Kristen, *CRS Report for Congress—Cybercrime: The Council of Europe Convention*, Congressional Research Service: Washington, DC, April 26, 2002.

Bankes, Steve and Carl Builder, *Seizing the Moment: Harnessing Information Technologies*, RAND: Santa Monica, CA, 1992.

Baudchon, Hélène, "The Aftermath of the 'New Economy' Bust: A Case Study of Five OECD Countries, No 2002–08," *Observatoire Français des conjectures Economiques*, OECD Publishing: Paris, December 2002.

Beath, Andrew, Fotini Christia, and Ruben Enikpolov, *Winning Hearts and Minds through Development? Evidence from a Field Experiment in Afghanistan*, The World Bank: Washington DC, July 2012.

Bencsáth, Boldizsár, Gábor Pék, Levente Buttyán, and Márk Félegyházi, *Duqu: A Stuxnet-Like Malware Found in the Wild*, Laboratory of Cryptography and Systems Security, Budapest University of Technology and Economics,

October 14, 2011, available at: http://www.crysys.hu/publications/files/
bencsathPBF11duqu.pdf.

Bhushan, Abhay, Ken Pogran, Ray Tomlinson, and Jim White, *RFC 561—Standard-izing Network Mail Headers*, September 5, 1973.

Brudnick, Ida A., *The Congressional Research Service and the American Legislative Process*, Congressional Research Service: Washington, DC, April 12, 2011.

Bruno, Greg and Sharon Otterman, "National Intelligence Estimates," *Council on Foreign Relations*, May 14, 2008, available at: http://www.cfr.org/iraq/national-intelligence-estimates/p7758.

Bush, George W., *Homeland Security Presidential Directive-7—Critical Infrastructure Identification, Prioritization and Protection*, The White House: Washington, DC, June 17, 2004.

Carter, Ashton, *The DoD Cyber Strategy*, Department of Defense: Washington, DC, April 2015.

Catastrophic Disaster Response Staff Officer's Handbook, U.S. Army Center for Army Lessons Learned: Ft. Leavenworth, KS, 2006.

CDRUSNORTHCOM CONPLAN 3501-8 Defense Support of Civilian Authorities, U.S. Northern Command, Peterson AFB, CO, May 16, 2008, available at: http://www.northcom.mil/Portals/28/Documents/FOIA/Con%20Plan%203501-08%20DSCA.pdf.

Cerf, Vinton, Internet Engineering Task Force, "Request for Comments 2468: I Remember IANA," Accessed September 10, 2014, available at: http://tools.ietf.org/html/rfc2468.

Cerf, Vinton and Robert Kahn, "A Protocol for Packet Network Intercommunication," *IEEE Transactions on Communications*, May 1974.

Changing Minds, Winning Peace: A New Strategic Direction for U.S. Public Diplomacy in the Arab and Muslim World, Report of the Advisory Group on Public Diplomacy for the Arab and Muslim World, Edward P. Djerejian, chairman, prepared for the U.S. House of Representatives Committee on Appropriations, October 1, 2003.

Clarke, Richard, Michael Morrell, Geoffrey Stone, Cass Sunstein, and Peter Swire, *Liberty and Security in a Changing World: Report and Recommendations of The President's Review Group on Intelligence and Communication Technologies*, The White House: Washington, DC, December 12, 2013, available at: http://www.whitehouse.gov/sites/default/files/docs/2013-12-12_rg_final_report.pdf.

Clinton, Hillary R., "Leading through Civilian Power," *The First Quadrennial Diplomacy and Development Review* (QDDR), 2010, available at: http://www.state.gov/s/dmr/qddr/.

Clinton, William J., *Executive Order 13010: Critical Infrastructure Protection*, The White House: Washington, DC, July 15, 1996.

Clinton, William J., *Executive Order 13011: Federal Information Technology*, The White House: Washington, DC, July 16, 1996.

Clinton, William J., *Presidential Decision Directive/NSC-63—Critical Infrastructure Protection*, The White House: Washington, DC, May 22, 1998.

Cochrane, David, "For Whose Eyes Only? Cryptanalysis and Frequency Analysis," Department of Mathematics, U.S. Military Academy, available at: http://www.usma.edu/math/military%20math%20modeling/ps5.pdf.

Committee on Responding to Section 5(d) of Presidential Policy Directive 28: The Feasibility of Software to Provide Alternatives to Bulk Signals Intelligence Collection, Computer Science and Telecommunications Board; Division on Engineering and Physical Sciences, National Research Council, *The Bulk Collection of Signals Intelligence: Technical Options,* National Research Council: Washington, DC, 2015, available at: http://www.nap.edu/catalog/19414/bulk-collection-of-signals-intelligence-technical-options.

"Critical Infrastructure and Key Resource Overview," *Information Sharing Environment,* Office of the Director of National Intelligence: Washington, DC, available at: http://www.ise.gov/mission-partner/critical-infrastructure-and-key-resources.

Cyber Incident Annex, Department of Homeland Security: Washington, DC, 2004.

Cyber Storm III Final Report, Department of Homeland Security: Washington, DC, July 2011.

Dacey, Robert F., *Critical Infrastructure Protection: Significant Homeland Security Challenges Need to Be Addressed,* General Accountability Office: Washington, DC, July 9, 2002.

Davis, Jerry, *Memorandum: Suspension of Certification and Accreditation Activity,* National Aeronautics and Space Administration: Washington, DC, May 18, 2010.

18 U.S.C., Part II, Chapter 206, § 3127, available at: http://www.law.cornell.edu/uscode/text/18/3127.

Elsea, Jennifer K., *Criminal Prohibitions on the Publication of Classified Defense Information,* Congressional Research Service: Washington, DC, September 9, 2013.

Esser, Michael, *Final Audit Report: Federal Information Security Management Act Audit FY2014,* Office of Personnel Management: Washington, DC, November 12, 2014.

Evans, Dale, "The Internet of Things How the Next Evolution of the Internet Is Changing Everything," Cisco, April 2011, available at: http://www.cisco.com/web/about/ac79/docs/innov/IoT_IBSG_0411FINAL.pdf.

Falliere, Nicholas, Liam O Murchu, and Eric Chien, *W.32 Stuxnet Dossier Ver 1.4,* Symantec: Mountain View, CA, February 2011.

Figliola, Patricia Moloney, *Digital Surveillance: The Communications Assistance for Law Enforcement Act,* Congressional Research Service: Washington, DC, 2007.

Frankston, Robert, *The Computer Utility as a Marketplace for Computer Services,* Master's Thesis, MIT, 1974, available at: http://www.frankston.com/public/?name=TR128.

Frazier, Karen, *Merit's History: The Internet Backbone Project, 1987–1995,* Merit Network, Inc., 1995, available at: http://www.livinginternet.com/doc/merit.edu/intro.html.

"Fusion Centers and Information Sharing," Bureau of Justice Assistance: Washington, DC, available at: http://www.ncirc.gov/documents/public/nysic_low_res.pdf.

FY 2014 Budget and Request to Congress, Federal Bureau of Investigation: Washington, DC, April 2013, available at: http://www.justice.gov/sites/default/files/jmd/legacy/2013/11/17/fbi-justification.pdf.

Hanson, Fergus, "Revolution @State: The Spread of Ediplomacy," *Lowy Institute for International Policy*, March 2012, http://lowyinstitute.richmedia-server.com/docs/Hanson_Revolution-at-State.pdf.

Homeland Security: Agency Plans, Implementation, and Challenges Regarding the National Strategy for Homeland Security, Government Accountability Office: Washington, DC, January 2005.

Howard, John D., *An Analysis of Security Incidents on the Internet*, Doctoral Thesis, Carnegie Mellon University: Pittsburgh, PA, 1997.

Hurwitz, Roger, *An Augmented Summary of the Harvard, MIT, and University of Toronto Cyber Norms Workshop*, MIT CSAIL and Munk School of Global Affairs: Cambridge, MA, May 2012.

Internet Society, "Internet Society 2005 Annual Report." Last modified 2006, available at: http://www.isoc.org/isoc/reports/ar2005/ISOCAR05.pdf

Internet Society, "Internet Society 2012 Annual Report," available at: http://www.isoc.org/isoc/reports/ar2005/ISOCAR05.pdf.

Jones, Christopher M., "The Other Side of Powell's Record," *American Diplomacy*, March 2006, available at: http://www.unc.edu/depts/diplomat/item/2006/0103/jone/jonesc_powell.html.

Kaplan, Eben, "How Libya Got Off the List," *Council on Foreign Relations*, October 16, 2007, available at: http://www.cfr.org/libya/libya-got-off-list/p10855.

"Kaspersky Lab and ITU Research Reveals New Advanced Cyber Threat," *Kaspersky*, May 28, 2012, available at: http://www.kaspersky.com/about/news/virus/2012/Kaspersky_Lab_and_ITU_Research_Reveals_New_Advanced_Cyber_Threat.

Kelly, John and Bruce Etling, *Mapping Iran's Online Public: Politics and Culture in the Persian Blogosphere*, Harvard University Berkman Center for Internet and Society: Cambridge, MA, April 5, 2008.

Klein, Hans, "ICANN Reform: Establishing the Rule of Law," Georgia Institute of Technology Internet & Public Policy Project, available at: http://www.internetgovernance.org/wordpress/wp-content/uploads/ICANN-Reform-Establishing-the-Rule-of-Law.pdf.

Krekel, Bryan, Patton Adams, and George Bakos, "Occupying the Information High Ground: Chinese Capabilities for Computer Network Operations and Cyber Espionage." *U.S.-China Economic and Security Review Commission*, 2012, available at: http://www2.gwu.edu/~nsarchiv/NSAEBB/NSAEBB424/docs/Cyber-066.pdf (accessed February 27, 2015).

Langer, Ralph, *To Kill a Centrifuge: A Technical Analysis of What Stuxnet's Creators Tried to Achieve*, The Langer Group, November 2013, available at: http://www.langner.com/en/wp-content/uploads/2013/11/To-kill-a-centrifuge.pdf.

Langevin, James, Michael McCaul, Scott Charney, Harry Raduege, and James Lewis, *Securing Cyberspace for the 44th Presidency: A Report of the CSIS Commission on Cybersecurity for the 44th Presidency*, Center for Strategic and International Studies: Washington, DC, December 2008.

Lee, Robert M., Michael J. Assante, and Tim Conway, *German Steel Mill Cyber Attack*, SANS Industrial Control Systems: Washington, DC, December 30, 2014.

Leed, Maren, "Offensive Cyber Capabilities at the Operational Level," *Center for Strategic International Studies*, 2013.

Lerner, Barry et al., *Brief History of the Internet*, Internet Society, available at: http://www.internetsociety.org/internet/what-internet/history-internet/brief-history-internet.

Lewis, James and Stewart Baker, *The Economic Impact of Cybercrime and Cyber Espionage*, Center for Strategic and International Studies, July 2013, available at: http://csis.org/files/publication/60396rpt_cybercrime-cost_0713_ph4_0.pdf.

MacLean, Don, "Herding Schrödinger's Cats: Some Conceptual Tools for Thinking about Internet Governance," International Telecommunications Union, Background Paper for the ITU Workshop on Internet Governance, Geneva, February 26–27, 2004.

Marquis-Boire, Morgan et al., *Planet Blue Coat: Mapping Global Censorship and Surveillance Tools*, Citizen Lab: Toronto, January 15, 2013.

McAfee Foundstone Professional Services and McAfee Labs, "Global Energy Cyberattacks: Night Dragon," McAfee, 2011, available at: http://www.mcafee.com/us/resources/white-papers/wp-global-energy-cyberattacks-night-dragon.pdf.

Mueller, Robert, *Electronic Surveillance Manual: Volume I—Procedures and Forms*, U.S. Department of Justice: Washington, DC, 1991.

Nakamura, Kenon and Susan Epstein, *CRS Report for Congress—Diplomacy in the 21st Century: Transformational Diplomacy*, Congressional Research Service: Washington, DC, August 23, 2007.

National Institute of Standards and Technology, "Supplemental ITL Bulletin for September 2013," *Information Technology Laboratory Bulletins*, September 2013, available at: http://csrc.nist.gov/publications/nistbul/itlbul2013_09_supplemental.pdf.

National Intelligence Estimate–Iran: Nuclear Intentions and Capabilities, National Intelligence Council: Washington, DC, November 2007, available at: http://www.dni.gov/files/documents/Newsroom/Reports%20and%20Pubs/20071203_release.pdf.

National Response Framework, Department of Homeland Security: Washington, DC, January 2008.

National Telecommunications and Information Administration, "U.S. Principles on the Internet's Domain Name and Addressing System," June 30, 2005, available at: http://www.ntia.doc.gov/files/ntia/publications/usdnsprinciples_06302005.pdf.

NETmundial Multistakeholder Agreement, NETmundial Global Multistakeholder Meeting on the Future of Internet Governance, Sao Paulo, Brazil, April 23–24, 2014, available at: http://netmundial.br/wp-content/uploads/2014/04/NETmundial-Multistakeholder-Document.pdf.

Neuman, Peter G. et al., *A Provably Secure Operating System*, Stanford Research Institute: Menlo Park, CA, June 1975.

Obama, Barack, *Cyberspace Policy Review: Assuring a Trusted and Resilient Information and Communications Infrastructure*, The White House: Washington, DC, 2009.

Obama, Barack, *Fiscal Year 2015 Budget of the U.S. Government*, Executive Office of the President of the United States: Washington, DC, March 4, 2014.

Obama, Barack, "A New Tool against Cyber Threats," *Medium*, April 1, 2015, available at: https://medium.com/@PresidentObama/a-new-tool-against -cyber-threats-1a30c188bc4.

Obama, Barack, *Presidential Memorandum—Establishment of the Cyber Threat Intelli-gence Integration Center*, The White House: Washington, DC, February 25, 2015.

Obama, Barack, "Remarks by the President on Security our Nation's Cyberinfras-tructure," The White House: Washington, DC, May 29, 2009, available at: http://www.whitehouse.gov/the_press_office/Remarks-by-the-President-on -Securing-Our-Nations-Cyber-Infrastructure/.

Peake, Adam, "Internet Governance and the World Summit on the Information Society (WSIS)," Prepared for the Association for Progressive Communications (APC), 3, available at: www.apc.org/documents/governance.pdf.

Perry, William J. et al., *United States Government Interagency Domestic Terrorism Concept of Operations Plan (CONPLAN)*, obtained from Federation of American Scientists, available at: http://fas.org/irp/threat/conplan.pdf.

Philips, James, "The Iran National Intelligence Estimate: A Comprehensive Guide to What Is Wrong with the NIE," *The Heritage Foundation*, January 11, 2008, available at: http://www.heritage.org/research/reports/2008/01/the-iran -national-intelligence-estimate-a-comprehensive-guide-to-what-is-wrong-with -the-nie.

Plafcan, Dan, "Intelligence, Diplomacy, and the Management of Credibility," Science, Technology, and Public Policy Program, Gerald R. Ford School of Pub-lic Policy, University of Michigan, October 7, 2008, available at: http://stpp .fordschool.umich.edu/news-events/?p=452.

"PPD-28 Section 4 Procedures," National Security Agency: Fort Meade, MD, January 12, 2015, available at: https://www.nsa.gov/public_info/_files/nsacss _policies/PPD-28.pdf.

"Public Attitudes toward the War in Iraq: 2003–2008," Pew Research Center, March 19, 2008, available at: http://www.pewresearch.org/2008/03/19/ public-attitudes-toward-the-war-in-iraq-20032008/.

Purcell, Kristen and Lee Rainie, "Technology's Impact on Workers," Pew Research Center, December 30, 2014, available at: http://www.pewinternet.org/2014/ 12/30/technologys-impact-on-workers/.

Raymond, Mark, "The Internet as a Global Commons," CIGI, October 26, 2012, available at: https://www.cigionline.org/publications/2012/10/internet -global-commons.

The Role of Information Sharing and Analysis Centers (ISACs) in Private/Public Sector Critical Infrastructure Protection, National Council of ISACs, January 2009, available at: http://www.isaccouncil.org/images/ISAC_Role_in _CIP.pdf.

Rollins, John and Anna Henning, *Comprehensive National Cybersecurity Inititiative: Legal Authorities and Policy Considerations*, Congressional Research Service: Washington, DC, March 10, 2009.

Rosenzweig, Paul, "Cybersecurity Act of 2012: Revised Cyber Bill Still Has Problems," The Heritage Foundation, July 23, 2012, available at: http://www .heritage.org/research/reports/2012/07/cybersecurity-act-of-2012-revised -cyber-bill-still-has-problems.

Ross, Ronald and Arnold Johnson, *Guide for Applying the Risk Management Framework to Federal Information Systems: A Security Life Cycle Approach*, National Institute of Standards and Technology: Gaithersburg, MD, February 22, 2010.

Security Implications of Microsoft Windows Vista, Symantec: Cupertino, CA, 2007, available at: http://www.symantec.com/avcenter/reference/Security_Implications_of_Windows_Vista.pdf.

"The 2014 Cato Institute Surveillance Conference," presentation, The 2014 Cato Institute Surveillance Conference, Washington, DC, December 12, 2014, available at: http://www.cato.org/events/2014-cato-institute-surveillance-conference.

United States Attorneys' Annual Statistical Report, Department of Justice: Washington, DC, 2012.

United States Department of Labor, "Technology and Globalization," Futurework, September 6, 1999, available at: http://www.dol.gov/oasam/programs/history/herman/reports/futurework/report/chapter6/main.htm.

U.S. Advisory Commission on Public Diplomacy, "The New Diplomacy: Utilizing Innovative Communication Concepts That Recognize Resource Constraints," June 2003, available at: http://www.state.gov/documents/organization/22956.pdf.

Vardi, Moshe Y., "The End of the American Network: Can the Internet Be Liberated from Government Meddling?," *Communications of the ACM*, 56(11), 2013, 5.

W.32.Duqu, The Precursor to the Next Stuxnet (White Paper), Symantec, November 23, 2011, available at: http://www.symantec.com/content/en/us/enterprise/media/security_response/whitepapers/w32_duqu_the_precursor_to_the_next_stuxnet.pdf.

Ware, Willis H., *Security and Privacy in Computer Systems*, RAND: Santa Monica, CA, April 1967.

Watson, Richard, "RFC 196—A Mail Box Protocol," Network Working Group, July 20, 1971, available at: https://tools.ietf.org/html/rfc196.

Weisel, Deborah Lamm, *Bank Robbery*, U.S. Department of Justice, Office of Community Policing Services, March 2007, available at: http://www.cops.usdoj.gov/Publications/e03071267.pdf.

Weller, Dennis and Bill Woodcock, "Internet Traffic Exchange: Market Developments and Policy Challenges," OECD Digital Economy Papers, No. 207, OECD Publishing, Paris, 2013.

Werner, Adrienne, *Thesis: The Potential Transformative Impact of Web 2.0 Technology on the Intelligence Community*, Naval Postgraduate School: Monterey, CA, 2008.

BOOK CHAPTERS AND JOURNAL ARTICLES

Arquilla, John and David Ronfeldt, "Cyberwar Is Coming!" *Comparative Strategy*, 12(2), Spring 1993.

Bagwell, Kyle, "The Economic Analysis of Advertising," Columbia University, Department of Economics Discussion Paper Series, August 2005.

Bellovin, Steven, Scott Bradner, Whitfield Diffie, Susan Landau, and Jennifer Rexford, "Can It Really Work? Problems with Extending EINSTEIN 3 to Critical Infrastructure," *Harvard National Security Journal*, 3, 2011, 36.

Brantly, Aaron, "Cyber Actions by State Actors: Motivation and Utility," *International Journal of Intelligence and Counterintelligence*, 27(3), 2014, 465–484.

Bronk, Christopher, "Webtapping: Securing the Internet to Save Us from Transnational Terror?" *First Monday*, 13(11), 2008, available at: http://ojs-prod-lib.cc.uic .edu/ojs/index.php/fm/article/view/2192/2052.

Brynjolfsson, Erik, "The Productivity Paradox of Information Technology," *Communications of the ACM*, 36(12), 1993, 66–77.

Burks, Arthur W., Herman H. Goldstine, and John von Neumann, "Preliminary Discussions of the Logical Design of an Electronic Computing Instrument," in A. H. Taub, ed., *Collected Works of John von Neuman*, MacMillan: New York, 1947.

Carr, Nicholas, "IT Doesn't Matter," *Harvard Business Review*, May 2003.

Cavelty, Myriam Dunn and Manuel Suter, "Public–Private Partnerships Are No Silver Bullet: An Expanded Governance Model for Critical Infrastructure Protection," *International Journal of Critical Infrastructure Protection*, 2(4), 2009, 179–187.

Clark, David D., "The Design Philosophy of the DARPA Internet Protocols," *ACM SIGCOMM Computer Communication Review*, 18(4), 1988, 1–10.

Coldebella, Gus P. and Brian M. White, "Foundational Questions Regarding the Federal Role in Cybersecurity," *Journal of National Security Law and Policy*, 4(1), 2010, 236.

Comanor, William S. and Thomas. A. Wilson, "Advertising, Market Structure and Performance," *The Review of Economics and Statistics*, 49, 1967, 423–440.

Conklin, Wm. Arthur, "Why FISMA Falls Short: The Need for Security Metrics," *WISP 2008*, Montreal, Canada, December 7–9, 2007.

Cukier, Kenneth Neil, "Who Controls the Internet?" *Foreign Affairs*, 84(6), November/ December 2005, 7–13.

Deibert, Ronald, "International Plug 'n Play: Citizen Activism, the Internet, and Global Public Policy," *International Studies Perspectives*, 1(3), December 2000, 255–272.

Der Derian, James, "The Simulation Syndrome: From War Games to Game Wars," *Social Text*, Spring 1990.

Drake, William, "Reframing Internet Governance Discourse: Fifteen Baseline Propositions," *Internet Governance: Toward a Grand Collaboration*, 2004.

Dressler, Judson, Dan Wallach, and Chris Bronk, "Unvalidated Input: Reconsidering Cyberspace as a Warfighting Domain," forthcoming.

Etzioni, Amitai, "Cybersecurity in the Private Sector," *Issues in Science and Technology*, November 2013, available at: http://issues.org/28-1/etzioni-2/.

Flynn, Michael and Charles Flynn, "Integrating Intelligence: Ten Points for the Commander," *Military Review*, January–February 2012, 4.

Gerovitch, Slava, "InterNyet: Why the Soviet Union Did Not Build a Nationwide Computer Network," *History and Technology*, 24(4), December 2008, 335–350.

Gostev, Alexander, "The Flame: Questions and Answers," *Securelist*, May 28, 2012, available at: http://www.securelist.com/en/blog/208193522/The_Flame _Questions_and_Answers.

Greenwald, Eric, "History Repeats Itself: The 60-Day Cyberspace Policy Review in Context," *Journal of National Security Law and Policy*, 4, 2010, 41.

Gutman, Pete, "The Commercial Malware Industry," *DEFCON 15*, Las Vegas, NV, August 3–5, 2007, available at: https://www.defcon.org/images/defcon-15/dc15-presentations/dc-15-gutmann.pdf.

Haigh, Thomas, "Los Alamos Bets on ENIAC: Nuclear Monte Carlo Simulations, 1947–1948," *IEEE Annals of the History of Computing*, July–September 2014.

Hopkins, Shannon, "Cybercrime Convention: A Positive Beginning to a Long Road Ahead," *Journal of High Technology Law*, 2(1), 2003, 101.

Howell, Beryl, "Seven Weeks: The Making of the USA Patriot Act," *George Washington Law Review*, 72(6), August 2004, 1145.

Hurwitz, Roger, "The Play of States: Norms and Security in Cyberspace," *American Foreign Policy Interests*, 36(5), 2014.

Jorgenson, Dale, "Information Technology and the U.S. Economy," *The American Economic Review*, 91(1), 2001, 1–32.

Kerr, Orin, "Vagueness Challenges to the Computer Fraud and Abuse Act," *Minnesota Law Review*, 94, 2010, 1587.

Li, Zhenmin et al., "Have Things Changed Now? An Empirical Study of Bug Characteristics in Modern Open Source Software," *ASID'06*, October 21, 2006, San Jose, California, USA.

Licklider, J.C.R. and Welden Clark, "On-Line Man-Computer Communication," *AIEE-IRE '62* (Spring) Proceedings of the May 1–3, 1962, spring joint computer conference, 113–128.

Lin, Herbert, "Laying an Intellectual Foundation for Cyberdeterrence: Some Initial Steps," in *The Secure Information Society*, Jörg Krüger, Bertram Nickolay, and Sandro Gaycken, eds., Springer: New York, 2013, 17–53.

Linnerooth, Joanne, "The Danube River Basin: Negotiating Settlements to Transboundary Environmental Issues," *Natural Resources Journal*, 30, 1990, 629.

Luscombe, Nicholas. M., Dov Greenbaum, and Mark Gerstein, "What Is Bioinformatics? A Proposed Definition and Overview of the Field," *Methods of Information in Medicine*, 4, 2001, 346.

Manadhata, Pratyusa K. and Jeanette M. Wing, "An Attack Surface Metric," *IEEE Transactions on Software Engineering*, 37(3), 2010, 371–386.

Manzanec, Brian, "The Art of (Cyber) War," *Journal of International Security Affairs*, 16, 2009, 84.

Mohrman, Susan Albers and Edward E. Lawler III, "Participative Managerial Behavior and Organizational Change," *Journal of Organizational Change Management*, 1(1), 1988, 45–59.

Moore, Gordon, "Cramming More Components onto Integrated Circuits," *Electronics*, 38(8), April 19, 1965.

Mueller, Milton, "ICANN and Internet Regulation," *Communications of the ACM*, 42(6), June 1999, 497–520.

Nelson, Philip, "The Economic Consequences of Advertising," *Journal of Business*, 48, 1975, 213–241.

Nye, Joseph, "Nuclear Lessons for Cyber Security," *Strategic Studies Quarterly*, Winter 2011, 19.

Quarter, Jack, "Recent Trends in the Worker-Ownership Movement in Canada: Four Alternative Models," *Economic and Industrial Democracy*, 11(4), 1990, 529–552.

Ross, Ron, Stuart Katzke, and Patricia Toth, "The New FISMA Standards and Guidelines: Changing the Dynamic of Information Security for the Federal Government," *Military Communications Conference: MILCOM 2005*, October 17–20, 2005, Atlantic City, NJ.

Saltzer, Jerome and Michael Schroeder, "The Protection of Information in Computer Systems," *Communications of the ACM*, 17(7), July 1974.

Sheldon, John B., "Geopolitics and Cyber Power: Why Geography Still Matters," *American Foreign Policy Interests: The Journal of the National Committee on American Foreign Policy*, 36(5), 2014.

Shneiderman, Ben, "Science 2.0," *Science*, 319, 2008, 1349–1350.

Silvers, Robert, "Rethinking FISMA and Federal Information Security Policy," *New York University Law Review*, 81, November 2006, 1844–1874.

Singh, J. P., "Information Technologies, Meta-power, and Transformation in Global Politics," *International Studies Review*, 15(1), March 2013.

Stigler, George, "The Economics of Information," *The Journal of Political Economy*, 69(3), 1961, 213–225.

Thomas, Timothy L., "Al Qaeda and the Internet: The Danger of 'Cyberplanning'," *Parameters*, 33(1), Spring 2003, 112–123.

Turing, Alan, "Intelligent Machinery, a Heretical Theory," in K. Furukawa, D. Michie, and S. Muggleton eds., *Machine Intelligence 15*, Oxford University Press: Oxford, UK, 1999.

Uricchio, William, "The Greatest Art Form of the Twentieth Century," *Journal of Visual Studies*, 13(1), 2014.

Vacca, Alexander and Mark Davidson, "The Regularity of Irregular Warfare," *Parameters*, Spring 2011.

Vari, Anna, "Approaches towards Conflict Resolution in Decision Processes," *Social Decision Methodology for Technological Projects*, 1989.

Wolfson, Stephen Manuel, "The NSA, AT&T, and the Secrets of Room 641A," *I/S: A Journal of Law and Policy for the Information Age*, 3(3), 2007–2008, 411.

NEWS ARTICLES

Ackerman, Spencer, "NSA Chief Claims 'Focused' Surveillance Disrupted More Than 50 Terror Plots," *Guardian*, June 19, 2013.

Ackerman, Spencer and Dan Roberts, "NSA Surveillance: Lawmakers Urge Disclosure as Obama 'Welcomes' Debate," *Guardian*, June 9, 2013.

Assir, Serene, "Syrian Electronic Army Battles for Public Opinion through Cyber Attacks," *AFP*, available at: http://www.huffingtonpost.com/2013/06/09/syrian-electronic-army-battles-public-opinion_n_3412843.html.

Astruc, Maeli, "Will ICANN Be the Next International Organisation in Geneva?," *Intellectual Property Watch*, March 2, 2014, available at: http://www.ip-watch.org/2014/03/02/internet-governance-will-icann-be-the-next-international-organisation-in-geneva/.

Auerbach, David, "The OPM Breach Is a Catastrophe," *Slate*, June 16, 2015, available at: http://www.slate.com/articles/technology/future_tense/2015/06/opm_hack_it_s_a_catastrophe_here_s_how_the_government_can_stop_the_next.html.

Axe, David, "Nah, Iran Probably Didn't Hack CIA's Stealth Drone," *Wired*, April 24, 2012, available at: http://www.wired.com/2012/04/iran-drone-hack/.

Ball, James, "Israel Shamir and Julian Assange's Cult of Machismo," *Guardian*, November 8, 2011, available at: http://www.theguardian.com/commentisfree/cifamerica/2011/nov/08/israel-shamir-julian-assange-cult-machismo and http://www.thelocal.de/20110210/33025.

Ballasay, Nicholas, "Target Breach: CUNA/CBA Member Costs Top $200M," *Credit Union Times*, February 18, 2014, available at: http://www.cutimes.com/2014/02/18/target-breach-cuna-cba-member-costs-top-200m.

Battacharjee, Yudjijit, "How the F.B.I. Cracked a Chinese Spy Ring," *New Yorker*, May 12, 2014.

Beam, Christopher, "The WikiLeaks Cables as Literature," *Slate*, December 1, 2010, available at: http://www.slate.com/articles/news_and_politics/politics/2010/12/dispatches.single.html.

Bennett, Dashiell, "8 Dot-Coms That Spent Millions on Super Bowl Ads and No Longer Exist," *Business Insider*, February 2, 2011.

Benson, Pam and Kevin Bohn, "Senate OKs Immunity for Telecoms in Intelligence Bill," *CNN*, February 12, 2008, available at: http://www.cnn.com/2008/POLITICS/02/12/fisa.senate/.

Black, Ian, "WikiLeaks Cables: Tunisia Blocks Site Reporting 'Hatred' of First Lady," *Guardian*, December 7, 2010, http://www.theguardian.com/world/2010/dec/07/wikileaks-tunisia-first-lady.

Blake, Aaron, "Edward Snowden Reveals Himself as NSA Leaker," *Washington Post*, June 9, 2013.

Broad, William, John Markoff, and David Sanger, "Israeli Test on Worm Called Crucial in Iran Nuclear Delay," *New York Times*, January 15, 2011.

Bronk, Chris, "Hacking Is Hardly Cyberwar, for Now," *New York Times*, February 28, 2013, available at: http://www.nytimes.com/roomfordebate/2013/02/28/what-is-an-act-of-cyberwar/hacking-is-hardly-cyberwar-for-now.

Bronk, Chris, "The Wrong Way to Stop Online Piracy," *Houston Chronicle*, November 25, 2011, available at: http://www.chron.com/opinion/outlook/article/The-wrong-way-to-stop-online-piracy-2292842.php.

Bronk, Chris, Ken Medlock, and Dan Wallach, "Is U.S. Vulnerable to a Cyber Attack?" *Houston Chronicle*, May 3, 2009.

Buck, Tobias, "Israel's Army of Tech Startups," *Financial Times*, November 30, 2011.

Carroll, Rory, "Hillary Clinton: People Felt Betrayed by NSA Surveillance," *Guardian*, February 24, 2015.

Carroll, Ward, "Inside the Cyber Command Turf Battle," *DefenseTech*, August 15, 2008, available at: http://defensetech.org/2008/08/15/inside-the-cyber-command-turf-battle/.

Chandrasekaran, Rajiv, "Internet Reconfiguration Concerns Federal Officials," *Washington Post*, January 31, 1998.

Chartrand, Sabra, "Clinton Gets a Wiretapping Bill That Covers New Technologies," *New York Times*, October 9, 1994.
Cherry, Steven, "Sons of Stuxnet," *IEEE Spectrum*, December 14, 2011, available at:
http://spectrum.ieee.org/podcast/telecom/security/sons-of-stuxnet.
"Chinese Hacked Obama and McCain Campaigns, Officials Say," *MSNBC*, June 6,
2013, available at: http://www.msnbc.com/msnbc/chinese-hacked-obama-
and-mccain-campaigns.
"Chinese Media Lashes Out at Clinton's Internet Demands," *BBC*, January 22,
2010, available at: http://news.bbc.co.uk/2/mobile/asia-pacific/8474466.stm.
Chozick, Amy, "Jimmy Wales Is Not an Internet Billionaire," *New York Times*,
June 27, 2013.
Cillizza, Chris, "Obama Lays Out Ethics Rules," *Washington Post*, November
11, 2008.
Clauss, Ulrich, "Hack Back—When a Cyber Attack Victim Turns 'Digital Vigilante'," *Worldcrunch*, July 21, 2012, available at: http://www.worldcrunch
.com/hack-back-when-cyber-attack-victim-turns-digital-vigilante/tech-science/
hack-back-when-a-cyber-attack-victim-turns-digital-vigilante-/c4s5887/.
Condon, Stephanie, "Critics: Homeland Security Unprepared for Cyberthreats,"
cnet, December 7, 2008, available at: http://www.cnet.com/news/critics
-homeland-security-unprepared-for-cyberthreats/.
Couts, Andrew, "Senate Kills Cybersecurity Act of 2012," *Digital Trends*, August 2,
2012, http://www.digitaltrends.com/web/senate-votes-against-cybersecurity
-act-of-2012/.
Covert, Adrian, "Facebook Buys WhatsApp for $19 billion," *CNN Money*, Febru-
ary 19, 2014, available at: http://money.cnn.com/2014/02/19/technology/
social/facebook-whatsapp/.
Covert, Adrian, "Gmail at 10: How Google Dominated E-mail," *CNN Money*, April1,
2004, available at: http://money.cnn.com/2014/04/01/technology/gmail/.
Cowley, Stacey, "FBI Director: Cybercrime Will Eclipse Terrorism," *CNN*, March 2,
2012, available at: http://money.cnn.com/2012/03/02/technology/fbi
_cybersecurity/.
Cox, Ramsey and Jennifer Martinez, "Cybersecurity Act Fails Senate Vote," *Hill*,
August 2, 2012, available at: http://thehill.com/policy/technology/241851
-cybersecurity-act-fails-to-advance-in-senate.
Dickerson, Elizabeth, "Internet Freedom," *Foreign Policy*, January 21, 2010.
D'Innocenzo, Anne, "Data-Breach Costs Take Toll on Target profit," *Yahoo! News*,
February 26, 2014, available at: http://news.yahoo.com/data-breach-costs-toll
-target-profit-123047290—finance.html.
Djereijian, Edward P. and Christopher Bronk, *Foreign Policy*, "How Disastrous Is
WikiLeaks for the State Department?" December 1, 2010, available at: http://
foreignpolicy.com/2010/12/01/how-disastrous-is-wikileaks-for-the-state
-department/.
Domm, Patti, "False Rumor of Explosion at White House Causes Stocks to Briefly
Plunge; AP Confirms Its Twitter Feed Was Hacked," *CNBC*, April 23, 2013,
available at: http://www.cnbc.com/id/100646197#.
Egan, Matt, "Hack the Hackers? Companies Itching to Go on Cyber Offense," *Fox
Business*, December 7, 2012, available at: http://www.foxbusiness.com/

technology/2012/12/07/hack-hackers-companies-itching-to-go-on-cyber
-offense/.

"Embassy Espionage: The NSA's Secret Spy Hub in Berlin," *Der Spiegel*, October 27, 2013, available at: http://www.spiegel.de/international/germany/
cover-story-how-nsa-spied-on-merkel-cell-phone-from-berlin-embassy-a
-930205-2.html.

Epstein, Edward Jay, "Was Snowden's Heist a Foreign Espionage Operation?,"
Wall Street Journal, May 9, 2014.

Fallows, James, "On the AfPak/Wikileaks Documents," *Atlantic*, July 26, 2010,
available at: http://www.theatlantic.com/politics/archive/2010/07/on-the
-afpak-wikileaks-documents/60379/.

Finkle, Jim, " 'State Actor' Behind Slew of Cyber Attacks," *Reuters*, August 3, 2011,
available at: http://www.reuters.com/article/2011/08/03/us-cyberattacks
-idUSTRE7720HU20110803.

Finn, Peter, "Cyber Assaults on Estonia Typify a New Battle Tactic," *Washington
Post*, May 19, 2007.

Foust, Joshua, "Has Wikileaks Been Infiltrated by Russian Spies?" *War Is Boring*
(blog), August 29, 2013, available at: https://medium.com/war-is-boring/
has-wikileaks-been-infiltrated-by-russian-spies-b876a8bc035a.

Freeze, Colin and Stephanie Nolen, "Charges That Canada Spied on Brazil Unveil
CSEC's Inner Workings," *Globe and Mail*, October 7, 2013.

"Fusion Confusion," *Chicago Tribune*, October 8, 2012.

Gallagher, Sean, "Googlers Say 'F*** You' to NSA, Company Encrypts Internal
Network," *Ars Technica*, November 6, 2013, available at: http://arstechnica
.com/information-technology/2013/11/googlers-say-f-you-to-nsa-company
-encrypts-internal-network/.

Gallager, Sean, "Why the 'Biggest Government Hack Ever' Got Past the Feds," *Ars
Technica*, June 8, 2015, available at: http://arstechnica.com/security/2015/06/
why-the-biggest-government-hack-ever-got-past-opm-dhs-and-nsa/.

Gannes, Liz, "Google's Nest Buys Dropcam for $555 Million," *re/code*, January 20,
2014, available at: http://recode.net/2014/06/20/googles-nest-buys-dropcam
-for-555-million/.

Gellman, Barton, Ashkan Soltani, and Andrea Peterson, "How We Know the NSA
Had Access to Internal Google and Yahoo Cloud Data," *Washington Post*,
November 4, 2013.

Gerth, Jeff and James Risen, "Reports Show Scientist Gave U.S. Radar Secrets to
Chinese," *New York Times*, May 10, 1999.

Glaberson, William, "Red Cross Monitors Barred from Guantánamo," *New York
Times*, November 16, 2007.

Glater, Jonathan D., "Judge Reverses His Order Disabling Web Site," *New York
Times*, March 1, 2008.

Gorman, Siobhan, "Cybersecurity Chief Resigns," *Wall Street Journal*, March 7, 2009.

Gorman, Siobhan, "Georgia States Computers Hit by Cyberattack," *Wall Street
Journal*, August 12, 2008.

Graham, Marty, "Welcome to Cyberwar Country, USA," *Wired*, February 11, 2008,
available at: http://archive.wired.com/politics/security/news/2008/02/
cyber_command?currentPage=all.

"The Great Disrupter's New Targets," *Economist*, September 20, 2014.

Greenwald, Glenn, "NSA Collecting Phone Records of Millions of Verizon Customers Daily," *Guardian*, June 5, 2013.

Greenwald, Glenn and Ewen MacAskill, "NSA Prism Program Taps in to User Data of Apple, Google and Others," *Guardian*, June 7, 2013.

Grimaldi, James V., "The Fast Rise and Steep Fall of Jack Abramoff," *Washington Post*, December 29, 2005.

Grossman, Lev, "You—Yes, You—Are TIME's Person of the Year," *Time*, December 26, 2006.

Hackett, Robert, "A Product Demo May Have Revealed What Could Be the Biggest Ever Government Data Breach," *Fortune*, June 12, 2015, available at: http://fortune.com/2015/06/12/cytech-product-demo-opm-breach/.

Hale, Gregory and Richard Sale, "Cyber War Opens New Front," *Offshore Engineer*, January 1, 2013, available at: http://www.oedigital.com/component/k2/item/1366-cyber-war-opens-new-front.

Hansell, Saul, "It's Obama on the iPhone," *New York Times*, October 2, 2008, available at: http://bits.blogs.nytimes.com/2008/10/02/its-obama-on-the-iphone/?_r=0.

Haress, Christopher, "Iran's Rouhani Faces Music as Sanctions Bite Harder, Is There a SWIFT Solution in the Works?" *International Business Times*, October 8, 2013, available at: http://www.ibtimes.com/irans-rouhani-faces-music-sanctions-bite-harder-there-swift-solution-works-1417768.

Heig, Samantha, "Who's Who in the Osama Bin Laden Raid," *New Yorker*, August 2, 2011, available at: http://www.newyorker.com/news/news-desk/whos-who-in-the-osama-bin-laden-raid.

Hersh, Seymour, "The Iran Plans," *New Yorker*, April 17, 2006, available at: http://www.newyorker.com/magazine/2006/04/17/the-iran-plans.

Higgins, Andrew, "For Guccifer, Hacking Was Easy. Prison Is Hard," *New York Times*, November 10, 2014.

Hoffman, Mary Louis, OPM to Consolidate Staff, Contractor Security Clearance Records, ExecutiveGov, May 30, 2014, available at: http://www.executivegov.com/2014/05/opm-to-consolidate-staff-contractor-security-clearance-records/.

"How Iran Hacked Super-Secret CIA Stealth Drone," *RT*, December 15, 2011, available at: http://rt.com/usa/iran-drone-hack-stealth-943/.

"Inside TAO: Documents Reveal Top NSA Hacking Unit," *Der Spiegel*, December 29, 2013, available at: http://www.spiegel.de/international/world/the-nsa-uses-powerful-toolbox-in-effort-to-spy-on-global-networks-a-940969.html.

"Iran 'Finds Fix' for Sophisticated Flame Malware," *BBC*, May 29, 2012, available at: http://www.bbc.com/news/technology-18253331.

Isikoff, Michael, "Chinese Hacked Obama, McCain Campaigns, Took Internal Documents, Officials Say," *NBC News*, June 6, 2013, available at: http://investigations.nbcnews.com/_news/2013/06/06/18807056-chinese-hacked-obama-mccain-campaigns-took-internal-documents-officials-say.

Johnson, Bobbie, "Obama Orders Review of Cyber Security," *Guardian*, February 10, 2009.

Jones, David and Jim Finkle, "U.S. Indicts Hackers in Biggest Cyber Fraud Case in History," *Reuters*, July 25, 2013, available at: http://www.reuters.com/article/2013/07/25/us-usa-hackers-creditcards-idUSBRE96O0RI20130725.

"Julian Assange's Backers Lose £200,000 Bail Money," *Telegraph*, September 4, 2012, available at: http://www.telegraph.co.uk/news/worldnews/wikileaks/9519767/Julian-Assanges-backers-lose-200000-bail-money.html.

Kang, Cecilia, "Haiti Relief via Text Message, Ushering Mobile Donations," *Washington Post*, January 19, 2010, available at: http://voices.washingtonpost.com/posttech/2010/01/a_record_22_million_has.html?hpid=topnews.

Kang, Cecilia, "Secretary Clinton Dines with High-Tech Titans to Talk Diplomacy," *Washington Post*, available at: http://voices.washingtonpost.com/posttech/2010/01/sec_clinton_dines_high-tech_ti.html.

Kaplan, Fred, "Karen Hughes, Stay Home!: What on Earth Is She Doing in the Middle East?," *Slate*, September 29, 2005, available at: http://www.slate.com/articles/news_and_politics/war_stories/2005/09/karen_hughes_stay_home.html.

Keizer, Gregg, "Cyberattacks Knock Out Georgia's Internet Presence," *Computerworld*, August 11, 2008, available at: http://www.computerworld.com/article/2532289/cybercrime-hacking/cyberattacks-knock-out-georgia-s-internet-presence.html.

Keller, Bill, "Disillusioned Nation: From Dick Cheney to Edward Snowden," *New York Times*, June 10, 2013, available at: http://keller.blogs.nytimes.com/2013/06/10/disillusioned-nation/?_r=0.

Kelly, Erin, "OPM Hack Q&A: What We Know and What We Don't," *USA Today*, June 27, 2015, available at: http://www.usatoday.com/story/news/politics/2015/06/27/opm-hack-questions-and-answers/29333211/.

Kelzer, Gregg, "Shamoon Malware Cripples Windows PCs to Cover Tracks," *Computer World*, August 17, 2012, available at: http://www.computerworld.com/article/2505971/cybercrime-hacking/shamoon-malware-cripples-windows-pcs-to-cover-tracks.html.

Khazan, Olga, "The Creepy, Long-Standing Practice of Undersea Cable Tapping," *Atlantic Monthly*, July 16, 2013.

Khazan, Olga, "Gentlemen Reading Each Others' Mail: A Brief History of Diplomatic Spying," *Atlantic Monthly*, June 17, 2003.

Kopan, Tal and David Perera, "Oversight Chairman: Fire Leaders of Hacked Agency," *Politico*, June 16, 2015, available at: http://www.politico.com/story/2015/06/katherine-archuleta-opm-computer-hack-house-119067.html.

Krebs, Brian, "Catching Up on the OPM Breach," *Krebs on Security*, June 15, 2015, available at: http://krebsonsecurity.com/2015/06/catching-up-on-the-opm-breach/.

Krebs, Brian, "Flame Malware Prompts Microsoft Patch," *Krebs on Security*, June 4, 2012, http://krebsonsecurity.com/2012/06/flame-malware-prompts-microsoft-patch/.

Krebs, Brian, "Uncle Sam Gets 'D-Plus' on Cyber-Security," *Washington Post*, February 16, 2005.

Kushner, David, "The Real Story of Stuxnet," *IEEE Spectrum*, February 26, 2011, available at: http://spectrum.ieee.org/telecom/security/the-real-story-of-stuxnet.

Lam, Lana, "Snowden Leaves Hong Kong 'on His Own Accord', Arrives in Moscow with WikiLeaks Help," *South China Morning Post*, August 29, 2013, available at: http://www.scmp.com/news/hong-kong/article/1267261/snowden-leaves-hong-kong-his-own-accord-arrives-moscow-wikileaks-help.

Lichtenstein, Jesse, "Digital Diplomacy," *New York Times*, July 10, 2010.

Lictblau, Eric and James Risen, "Officials Say U.S. Wiretaps Exceeded Law," *New York Times*, April 15, 2009.

Liptak, Adam, "Justices Turn Back Challenge to Broader U.S. Eavesdropping," *New York Times*, February 26, 2013.

Lunden, Ingrid, "Internet Ad Spend to Reach $121B in 2014, 23% of $537B Total Ad Spend, Ad Tech Boosts Display," *TechCrunch*, April 7, 2014, available at: http://techcrunch.com/2014/04/07/internet-ad-spend-to-reach-121b-in-2014 -23-of-537b-total-ad-spend-ad-tech-gives-display-a-boost-over-search/.

"Luzhkov Accuses Estonian Authorities of Abetting Fascism," *Interfax News Service*, available at: http://www.interfax.ru/e/B/0/0.html?id_issue=11721667.

Lynch, Colum, "Brazil President Condemns NSA Spying," *Washington Post*, September 24, 2013.

Lyngaas, Sean, "Rogers Mum on OPM Attribution, But Says Hack Shows Value of Data," *FCW*, June 24, 2015, available at: http://fcw.com/articles/2015/06/24/rogers-opm-attribution.aspx.

Lyons, Patrick J., "Of Orwell, Wikipedia and Guantánamo Bay," *New York Times*, December 14, 2007.

MacAskill, Ewen, Nick Davies, Nick Hopkins, Julian Borger, and James Ball, "GCHQ Intercepted Foreign Politicians' Communications at G20 Summits," *Guardian*, June 17, 2013.

"Made in China?" *Economist*, March 14, 2015.

Madrigal, Alexis, "The Inside Story of How Facebook Responded to Tunisian Hacks," *Atlantic*, January 24, 2011.

Mankad, Shawn and George Michailidis, "Discovering the Ecosystem of an Electronic Financial Market with a Dynamic Machine-Learning Method," *Algorithmic Finance*, 2(2), 2013, 151–165.

Mann, Charles, "Homeland Insecurity," *Atlantic Monthly*, September 2002.

Marcus, Jonathan, "Ukraine Crisis: Transcript of Leaked Nuland-Pyatt Call," *BBC*, February 7, 2014, available at: http://www.bbc.com/news/world-europe -26079957.

Markoff, John, "Computer Wins on 'Jeopardy!': Trivial, It's Not," *New York Times*, February 16, 2011.

Marquis, Christopher, "U.S. Declares 'Rogue Nations' Are Now 'States of Concern'," *New York Times*, June 20, 2000.

Mazmanian, Adam, "OPM Merges Security Investigation Databases," *FCW*, May 29, 2014, available at: http://fcw.com/Articles/2014/05/29/security -check-databases-merged.aspx?Page=1.

McCullagh, Declan, "Bill Would Give President Emergency Control of the Internet," *CNET*, August 28, 2009, available at: http://www.cnet.com/news/bill -would-give-president-emergency-control-of-internet/.

McMillan, Robert, "RSA Warns SecurID Customers after Company Is Hacked," *PCWorld*, March 17, 2011, available at: http://www.pcworld.com/article/222522/article.html.

Melvin, Don and Jonathan Fahey, "SWIFT Cuts Off Iran as Sanctions Vice Tightens," *The World Post*, March 15, 2012, available at: http://www.huffingtonpost .com/2012/03/15/swift-iran-sanctions_n_1347361.html.

Meserve, Jeanne, "Sources: Staged Cyber Attack Reveals Vulnerability in Power Grid," *CNN*, September 26, 2007, available at: http://edition.cnn.com/2007/ US/09/26/power.at.risk/.

Mesmer, Ellen, "New Federal Rule Requires Banks to Fight DDoS Attacks," *Network World*, April 4, 2014, available at: http://www.networkworld.com/ article/2175847/network-security/new-federal-rule-requires-banks-to-fight -ddos-attacks.html.

Metz, Cade, "Remembering Jon Postel—And the Day He Hijacked the Internet," *Wired*, October 15, 2012, available at: http://www.wired.com/2012/10/ joe-postel/.

Morris, Harvey, "Israel Gets the Blame for Flame Virus," *New York Times*, May 29, 2012. http://rendezvous.blogs.nytimes.com/2012/05/29/israel-gets-the -blame-for-flame/.

Nakashima, Ellen, "Chinese Breach Data of 4 Million Federal Workers," *Washington Post*, June 4, 2015, available at: https://www.washingtonpost .com/world/national-security/chinese-hackers-breach-federal-governments -personnel-office/2015/06/04/889c0e52-0af7-11e5-95fd-d580f1c5d44e_story .html.

Nakashima, Ellen, "Indictment of PLA Hackers Is Part of Broad U.S. Strategy to Curb Chinese Cyberspying," *Washington Post*, May 22, 2014.

Nakashima, Ellen, "Iran Acknowledges That Flame Virus Has Infected Computers Nationwide," *Washington Post*, May 29, 2012, http://www.washingtonpost .com/world/national-security/iran-acknowledges-that-flame-virus-has -infected-computers-nationwide/2012/05/29/gJQAzlEF0U_story.html

Nakashima, Ellen, "Iran Blamed for Cyberattacks on U.S. Banks and Companies," *Washington Post*, September 21, 2012.

Nakashima, Ellen, "U.S. Decides against Publicly Blaming China for Data Hack," *Washington Post*, July 21, 2015, available at: https://www.washingtonpost .com/world/national-security/us-avoids-blaming-china-in-data-theft-seen -as-fair-game-in-espionage/2015/07/21/03779096-2eee-11e5-8353-12154759 49f4_story.html.

"National Oil Company of Saudi Arabia, Saudi Aramco's Twitter Account Hacked," *HackRead*, March 7, 2013, available at: http://www.hackread.com/ national-oil-company-of-saudi-arabia-saudi-aramcos-twitter-account-hacked/.

"Newly Nasty," *Economist*, May 24, 2007.

"A Note to Readers: Piecing Together the Reports, and Deciding What to Publish," *New York Times*, July 25, 2010.

"Oahu Defense Contractor Sentenced on Espionage Charges," *Hawaii Reporter*, September 18, 2014, available at: http://www.hawaiireporter.com/oahu -defense-contractor-sentenced-on-espionage-charges.

O'Reilly, Tim, "What Is Web 2.0: Design Patterns and Business Models for the Next Generation of Software," *O'Reilly*, September 30, 2005, available at: http:// www.oreilly.com/pub/a/web2/archive/what-is-web-20.html.

Packer, George, "The Quiet German: The Astonishing Rise of Angela Merkel, the Most Powerful Woman in the World," *New Yorker*, December 1, 2014.

"Panel Must Narrow Cybersecurity Scope," *FCW*, November 4, 2007, available at: http://fcw.com/Articles/2007/11/04/Panel-must-narrow-cybersecurity-scope .aspx?Page=2.

Peacock, Nelson, "Cybersecurity Could Be the Next Bipartisan Breakthrough," *Hill*, January 22, 2014, available at: http://thehill.com/blogs/congress-blog/technology/196026-cybersecurity-could-be-the-next-bipartisan-breakthrough.

Pearlstein, Steven, "Review: 'The Second Machine Age,' by Erik Brynjolfsson and Andrew McAfee," *Washington Post*, January 17, 2014, available at: http://www .washingtonpost.com/opinions/review-the-second-machine-age-by-erik -brynjolfsson-and-andrew-mcafee/2014/01/17/ace0611a-718c-11e3-8b3f-b1 666705ca3b_story.html.

Perera, David, "Office of Personnel Management Didn't Encrypt Feds' Data Hacked by Chinese," *Politico*, June 4, 2015, available at: http://www.politico .com/story/2015/06/personal-data-of-4-million-federal-employees-hacked -118655.html.

Perez, Evan and Shimon Prokupecz, "First on CNN: U.S. Data Hack May Be 4 Times Larger than the Government Originally Said," *CNN*, June 23, 2015, available at: http://www.cnn.com/2015/06/22/politics/opm-hack-18 -milliion/.

Perlroth, Nicole, "Hackers Lay Claim to Saudi Aramco Cyberattack," *New York Times*, August 23, 2012, available at: http://bits.blogs.nytimes.com/2012/08/23/hackers-lay-claim-to-saudi-aramco-cyberattack/.

Perlroth, Nicole, "In Cyberattack on Saudi Firm, U.S. Sees Iran Firing Back," *New York Times*, October 23, 2012.

Perlroth, Nicole, Jeff Larson, and Scott Shane, "N.S.A. Able to Foil Basic Safeguards of Privacy on Web," *New York Times*, September 5, 2013.

Peterson, Tim, "Facebook's Mobile Revenue Climbs to $2.5 Billion as Ad Prices Soar," *AdvertisingAge*, January 28, 2015, available at: http://adage.com/article/digital/facebook-s-mobile-revenue-hits-2-5-billion-prices-soar/296869/.

Petri, Alexandra, "Should You Be Panicking about CISPA?," *Washington Post*, April 17, 2013.

"Piratage de Google: Clinton menace la Chine à demi-mot," *Le Monde*, January 21, 2010.

Poulsen, Kevin, "Air Force Launches Recruitment Campaign Touting Cyber Command," *Wired*, February 27, 2008, available at: http://www.wired.com/2008/02/air-force-launc/.

Poulsen, Kevin, "Software Bug Contributed to Blackout," *Security Focus*, February 2, 2004, available at: http://www.securityfocus.com/news/8016.

Poulsen, Kevin and Kim Zetter, "U.S. Intelligence Analyst Arrested in Wikileaks Video Probe," *Wired*, June 6, 2010, available at: http://www.wired.com/2010/06/leak/.

Protalinski, Emil, "NSA: Cybercrime Is 'The Greatest Transfer of Wealth in History'," *ZDNet*, July 10, 2012, available at: http://www.zdnet.com/article/nsa-cybercrime-is-the-greatest-transfer-of-wealth-in-history/.

Rantanen, Miska, "Virtual Harassment, but for Real," *Helsingen Sanomat*, June 5, 2007.

Raviv, Dan, "U.S. Pushing Israel to Stop Assassinating Iranian Nuclear Scientists," *CBS News*, March 1, 2014.

Rawnsley, Adam, "Iran's Alleged Drone Hack: Tough, but Possible," *Wired*, December 11, 2011, available at: http://www.wired.com/2011/12/iran-drone-hack-gps/.

Riley, Michael A., "NSA Said to Have Used Heartbleed Bug, Exposing Consumers," *Bloomberg*, April 11, 2014, available at: http://www.bloomberg.com/news/articles/2014-04-11/nsa-said-to-have-used-heartbleed-bug-exposing-consumers.

Riley, Michael A. and Eric Engleman, "Code in Aramco Cyber Attack Indicates Lone Perpetrator," *Bloomberg*, October 25, 2012, available at: http://www.bloomberg.com/news/2012-10-25/code-in-aramco-cyber-attack-indicates-lone-perpetrator.html.

Riley, Michael and Ashlee Vance, "Inside the Chinese Boom in Corporate Espionage," *Bloomberg*, March 15, 2012, available at: http://www.bloomberg.com/bw/articles/2012-03-14/inside-the-chinese-boom-in-corporate-espionage.

Risen, James, "Obama's Wiretapping Stand Enrages Many Supporters," *New York Times*, July 2, 2008.

Risen, James and Laura Poitras, "Spying by N.S.A. Ally Entangled U.S. Law Firm," *New York Times*, February 15, 2014.

Risen, Tom, "Obama Considers Sanctions after Cyberattacks," *U.S. News*, June 15, 2015, http://www.usnews.com/news/articles/2015/06/15/obama-considers-sanctions-after-opm-breach.

Roberts, John, "Cyber Threats to Energy Security, as Experienced by Saudi Arabia," *Platts*, November 27, 2012, available at: http://blogs.platts.com/2012/11/27/virus_threats/.

Robertson, Jordan, "Is Hacking in Self-Defense Legal? It Depends, Says Army Cyber Lawyer," *Bloomberg*, July 23, 2012, available at: http://go.bloomberg.com/tech-blog/2012-07-23-is-hacking-in-self-defense-legal-it-depends-says-army-cyber-lawyer/.

Rogow, Geoffrey, "Rise of the (Market) Machines," *MarketBeat*, June 19, 2009, http://blogs.wsj.com/marketbeat/2009/06/19/rise-of-the-market-machines/.

Rosencrance, Linda, "Teen Hacker 'Mafiaboy' Sentenced," *Computerworld*, September 13, 2001, available at: http://www.computerworld.com/article/2583318/security0/teen-hacker—mafiaboy—sentenced.html.

Ross, Alec, "19 Billion Reasons for Opportunity in Ukraine," *CNN*, February 27, 2014, available at: http://www.cnn.com/2014/02/27/opinion/ross-ukraine-opportunity/.

Sanger, David, "Obama Order Sped Up Wave of Cyberattacks against Iran," *New York Times*, June 1, 2012.

Sasso, Brendan, "Report: China Hacked Obama, McCain Campaigns in 2008," *Hill*, June 7, 2013, available at: http://thehill.com/policy/technology/304111-report-china-hacked-obama-mccain-campaigns.

Savage, Charlie, "Manning Is Acquitted of Aiding the Enemy," *New York Times*, July 30, 2013.

Schneier, Bruce, "NSA Surveillance: A Guide to Staying Secure," *Guardian*, September 6, 2013.

Schofield, Hugh, "Minitel: The Rise and Fall of the France-Wide Web," *BBC*, June 27, 2012, available at: http://www.bbc.com/news/magazine-186 10692.

Schwartz, Matthew J., "Banks Hit Downtime Milestone in DDoS Attacks," *Dark Reading*, April 4, 2014, available at: http://www.darkreading.com/attacks -and-breaches/banks-hit-downtime-milestone-in-ddos-attacks/d/d-id/ 1109390?.

Schwartz, Matthew J., "RSA SecurID Breach Cost $66 Million," *InformationWeek Dark Reading*, July 28, 2011, available at: http://www.darkreading.com/ attacks-and-breaches/rsa-securid-breach-cost-$66-million/d/d-id/1099232?.

Shachtman, Noah, "Russia's Top Cyber Sleuth Foils U.S. Spies, Helps Kremlin Pals," *Wired*, July 23, 2012, available at: http://www.wired.com/2012/07/ff _kaspersky/.

Shane, Scott and Andrew W. Lehren, "Leaked Cables Offer Raw Look at U.S. Diplomacy," *New York Times*, sec. World, November 28, 2010.

Singel, Ryan, "Analysis: Google's Ad Targeting Turns Algorithms on You," *Wired*, March 11, 2009, available at: http://www.wired.com/2009/03/google-ad -annou/.

Smith, Tony, "Hacker Jailed for Revenge Sewage Attacks," *Register*, October 31, 2001, available at: http://www.theregister.co.uk/2001/10/31/hacker_jailed _for_revenge_sewage/.

Sterling, Bruce, "Meanwhile, Somewhere at the Chinese Soft Power Retaliation Board," January 24, 2010, available at: http://www.wired.com/2010/01/ meanwhile-somewhere-at-the-chinese-soft-power-retaliation-board/.

Stöcker, Christian, "Leak at WikiLeaks: A Dispatch Disaster in Six Acts," *Spiegel Online*, September 01, 2011, available at: http://www.spiegel.de/international/ world/leak-at-wikileaks-a-dispatch-disaster-in-six-acts-a-783778.html.

"Stocks Rebound after Fake Tweet Spooks Investors," *CNN*, April 23, 2013, available at: http://money.cnn.com/2013/04/23/investing/stocks-markets/.

Strobel, Warren, John Walcott, and Nancy Youssef, "Cheney Urging Strikes on Iran," *McClatchyDC*, August 9, 2007, available at: http://www.mcclatchydc .com/2007/08/09/18834/cheney-urging-strikes-on-iran.html.

Strom, Stephanie, "Pentagon Sees a Threat from Online Muckrakers," *New York Times*, March 17, 2010.

Stuster, J. Dana, "America's Next Top Diplomat," *Foreign Policy*, December 21, 2012, available at: http://foreignpolicy.com/2012/12/21/americas-next-top -diplomat/.

Taylor, Adam, "A Cheesy FBI Video Hopes to Stop U.S. Students from Becoming Chinese Spies," *Washington Post*, April 15, 2014, available at: http://www .washingtonpost.com/blogs/worldviews/wp/2014/04/15/a-cheesy-fbi -video-hopes-to-stop-u-s-students-from-becoming-chinese-spies/.

Taylor, Chris, "Instagram Has 100 Million Users, Says Zuckerberg," *Mashable*, February 19, 2014, available at: http://mashable.com/2012/09/11/instagram -100-million/.

Thomas, Evan, "Campaign 2008 Secrets: McCain Gambles on Palin," *Newsweek*, November 5, 2008.

Traynor, Ian, "Russia Accused of Unleashing Cyberwar to Disable Estonia," *Guardian*, May 17, 2007.

"Turk, Moroccan Nabbed in Huge Worm Case," *CNN Money*, August 26, 2005, available at: http://money.cnn.com/2005/08/26/technology/worm_arrest/.

Tuttle, Robert, "Virus Shuts RasGas Office Computers, LNG Output Unaffected," *Bloomberg*, August 30, 2012, available at: http://www. bloomberg.com/news/2012-08-30/virus-shuts-rasgas-office-computers-lng-output-unaffected-1-.html.

"$20 Million 'Virtual' Border Fence Scrapped," *Associated Press*, April 23, 2008.

Upson, Sandra, "Wiretapping Woes: Trouble Ahead for Those Wanting to Monitor Internet-Based Calls," *IEEE Spectrum*, May 2007.

Vaughan-Nichols, Steven J., "How the Syrian Electronic Army Took Out the New York Times and Twitter Sites," *ZDNet*, August 28, 2013, available at: http://www.zdnet.com/article/how-the-syrian-electronic-army-took-out-the-new-york-times-and-twitter-sites/.

Verini, James, "The Great Cyberheist," *New York Times*, November 10, 2010.

Vijayan, Jaikumar, "Government Cybersecurity Report Card Coming," *InfoWorld*, April 12, 2007, available at: http://www.infoworld.com/article/2662880/security/government-cybersecurity-report-card-coming.html.

Weinger, Mackenzie, "Barton Gellman, Glenn Greenwald Feud over NSA Leaker," *Politico*, June 10, 2013, available at: http://www.politico.com/story/2013/06/edward-snowden-nsa-leaker-glenn-greenwald-barton-gellman-92505.html.

Whittaker, Zack, "Wikileaks: How the Diplomatic Cables Sparked the 2011 Arab Revolutions," *ZDNet*, June 22, 2011, available at: http://www.zdnet.com/article/wikileaks-how-the-diplomatic-cables-sparked-the-2011-arab-revolutions/.

"WikiLeaks Posts Video of 'U.S. Military Killings' in Iraq," *BBC*, April 6, 2010, available at: http://news.bbc.co.uk/2/hi/americas/8603938.stm.

Winkler, Rolfe and Daisuke Wakabayashi, "Google to Buy Nest Labs for $3.2 Billion," *Wall Street Journal*, January 13, 2014.

Wolf, Jim, "U.S.-China Economic and Security Review Commission Urges Congress to Probe China's Cyber Attacks," *Huffington Post*, available at: http://www.huffingtonpost.com/2012/11/14/us-china-economic-and-security-review-commission_n_2127521.html.

Yellin, Jessica, "Obama, Xi Work through Range of Issues in 2-Day Summit," *CNN*, June 10, 2013, available at: http://www.cnn.com/2013/06/09/politics/obama-xi-summit.

Zeleny, Jeff, "Lose the BlackBerry? Yes He Can, Maybe," *New York Times*, November 15, 2008.

Zeller, Frank, "Germany Drops Probe into Alleged U.S. Tapping of Merkel Cellphone," *AFP*, June 12, 2015, available at: http://news.yahoo.com/germany-drops-probe-alleged-us-tapping-merkel-cellphone-090650693.html.

Zeller, Tom, "Ideas & Trends; Cloak, Dagger, Echelon," *New York Times*, July 16, 2000.

Zetter, Kim, "Hackers Targeted U.S. Government Satellites," *Wired*, October 27, 2011, available at: http://www.wired.com/2011/10/hackers-attack-satellites/.

Zetter, Kim, "How Digital Detectives Deciphered Stuxnet, the Most Menacing Malware in History," *Ars Technica*, July 11, 2011, available at: http://arstechnica.com/tech-policy/2011/07/how-digital-detectives-deciphered-stuxnet-the-most-menacing-malware-in-history/.

Ziobro, Paul and Serena Ng, "Retailer Target Lost Its Way under Ousted CEO Gregg Steinhafel," *Wall Street Journal*, June 23, 2014.

Index

advanced persistent threat, 110,
111–112, 117
Ahmadinejad, Mahmoud, 84
Al Arabiya, 102
Alexander, Keith, 127, 142
Al Hurrah, 102
Al Jazeera, 102
Alperovitch, Dmitri, 105–106, 109
Al Qaeda, 34, 40, 96, 158
Amazon, 11, 22, 25
American Civil Liberties
Union, 39, 128
America Online (AOL), 70, 94
Anonymous, 89
Apple, 11, 20–21, 59, 127, 151
Arab Spring, 7, 31, 93–97, 115
ARPANET, 4, 17–20, 30, 36
Arquila, John, 50–51
artificial intelligence, 14
Assange, Julian, 114–118, 135
AT&T, 6, 12, 17, 27, 35, 67, 127
attack surface, 154
Aurora (test), 54
Australian Signals Directorate, 129

Baker, Stewart, 142
Beckstrom, Rod, 54–57

Ben Ali, Zine al-Abidine, 6, 33,
101–102, 116
Big Data, 5, 14, 24
Bitcoin, 14
BlackBerry, 73, 127–129
Boden, Vitek, 44
Brandeis, Louis, 37
Brazil, 94, 129, 130, 153
Budapest Convention on Cybercrime,
138, 145

Calce, Michael (a.k.a. *Mafiaboy*), 11
Carnegie Mellon Computer
Emergency Response Team, 60
Carr, Edward Hallett, 2, 11, 153
Center for Strategic and International
Studies, 57, 71–74
Cerf, Vinton, 17–19, 27, 30
certification and accreditation, 70
Chardin, Pierre Teilhard de, 50
Charney, Scott, 71
Chertoff, Michael, 63
China, 7, 9, 35, 72–73, 94, 98–100,
106–117, 123–124, 134–135, 153–154
Church Committee, 37
Cisco Systems, 23, 99
Citizen Lab, 99, 107

Clapper, James, 127
Clarke, Arthur C., 149
Clinton, Bill, 56
Clinton, Hillary, 93, 97–99, 112, 131
Code Red, 88
Cohen, Jared, 97, 104
Commission on Cybersecurity for the
    44th Presidency, 71–74
Communications Assistance for Law
    Enforcement Act (CALEA), 38
Communications Security
    Establishment Canada (CSEC), 130
Computer Fraud and Abuse Act, 144
computer network attack, 41
computer network exploitation, 41
Computer Security Incident Response
    Team, 62
Conficker, 88
Council on Foreign Relations, 95, 104
Counterinsurgency, 48, 96, 98
Craigslist, 76
critical infrastructure, 1, 2, 53, 56–58,
    63, 65
Critical Infrastructure Assurance
    Office, 56
critical infrastructure protection
    (CIP), 56
CrowdStrike, 109
cryptanalysis, 45
Cutting Sword of Justice, 88
cyber attack, 7, 41–49, 52–53, 58, 63–64,
    68–69, 86–88, 92, 110, 142, 154–155
cybercrime, 1, 8, 58, 87, 138–148, 153
cyber geopolitics, 2, 7, 153
Cyber Intelligence Sharing and
    Prevention Act, 77–78
cyber power, 52, 93
Cyber Security Act of 2012, 77
Cybersecurity Act of 2009, 75
cybersecurity report card, 70
Cyberspace Policy Review: Assuring a
    Trusted and Resilient Information and
    Communications Infrastructure, 59, 74
Cyber Storm III (exercise), 59
CyTech, 121

Dalai Lama, 99
Dave, Master Chief, 157

Defense Advanced Research Projects
    Agency, 4, 17, 61
Deibert, Ronald, 99
Difference Engine, 13
Diffie-Hellman key exchange, 131
Director of National Intelligence,
    127–128
distributed denial of service (DDoS), 6,
    42–43, 83, 90
Domain Name System (DNS),
    19, 26–29, 32, 76, 107
Domain Name System Security
    Extensions (DNSSEC), 76
Douhet, Giulio, 52
Duqu, 86

eBay, 11, 25, 33
EINSTEIN, 61–64, 120, 122
Electronic Frontier Foundation, 39, 127
Electronic Numerical Integrator And
    Computer (ENIAC), 4, 13
Electronic Pearl Harbor, 44
Electronic Privacy Information
    Center, 39
Electronic Questionnaires for
    Investigative Processing
    (e-QIP), 119
Ender's Game, 150–151
Estonia, 6, 41–45, 47, 49, 52–53,
    86, 90, 152
European Union, 42, 145
Executive Order 13010, 56

Facebook, 6, 22–23, 39, 88, 93, 96–97,
    101–103, 126, 150, 152
Federal Bureau of Investigation, 1–2,
    37–38, 56–58, 72, 78, 110–111, 120,
    131, 139–147, 155
Federal Information Security
    Management Act, 69–71, 121–122
Fingar, Tom, 81, 149
Five Eyes, 128–129, 153–154
Flame, 86–89, 106
flash crash, 90
Foreign Intelligence Surveillance Act,
    126, 128, 135
Foreign Intelligence Surveillance
    Court, 126–127

Forum of Incident Response and
    Security Teams, 62
France, 18, 88, 91, 154
fusion center, 64–65

Gates, Robert, 81, 98
Gellman, Barton, 135
GhostNet, 99, 106
Gibson, William, 3, 52
Gonzalez, Albert, 146
Google, 6, 11, 21–23, 39, 76, 96, 99–100,
    105, 109, 126, 133, 141, 150, 152,
    154–155, 157
Google Ideas, 104
Government Communications
    Headquarters (GCHQ), 7, 36,
    125, 128, 133
Government Interagency Domestic
    Terrorism Concept of Operations
    Plan (CONPLAN), 57–58
Great Firewall, 9, 63
Greenwald, Glenn, 125, 133–134
guild, 19, 28

hacker, 11, 26, 41, 44, 46–49, 73, 89–91,
    105, 109–110, 114, 116, 121–123, 147,
    153, 155
Hadoop, 22
Hathaway, Melissa, 59, 73
Hayden, Michael, 86, 123
Heartbleed, 133, 154
Homeland Security Presidential
    Directive 7, 65
Hughes, Karen, 95
Hypponen, Mikko, 86

India, 22, 82, 88, 94, 107–108, 126, 153
Information Sharing and Analysis
    Center, 56, 65, 78
initial public offering (IPO), 11, 21
Intel, 15, 106, 142
intellectual property, 99, 142
International Organization for
    Standardization, 19
International Telecommunications
    Union, 19, 30, 32–34, 86–87, 130
Internet Assigned Numbers Authority
    (IANA), 19–20, 27–29, 33–34

Internet Corporation for Assigned
    Names and Numbers (ICANN), 6,
    20, 27–35, 87, 130
Internet Crime Complaint
    Center, 142, 143
Internet Engineering Task Force
    (IETF), 19, 27, 29, 32–33
Internet Freedom, 7, 97–100, 129
Internet Governance Forum
    (IGF), 32, 34
Internet "kill switch," 75–76
Internet Protocol (IP), 3–5, 17–19,
    23–24, 27, 32, 43, 62, 76, 82
Internet Society, 30
The Interview (movie), 1
intrusion detection system, 62–63, 73,
    106, 120
Iran, 7, 80–90, 95, 153, 156
Islamic State, 6, 150
Ivy Bells, 36

Jobs, Steve, 20
Jong Un, Kim, 1

Kahn, Robert, 17, 27
Kaspersky, Eugene, 87
Kaspersky Lab, 86–89
Katz v. United States, 37
KeyPoint, 122
Klein, Mark, 35, 39, 67, 126
Kleinrock, Leonard, 4–5
Krebs, Brian, 141

Langer, Ralph, 83–85
Langevin, James, 71, 75
Lewis, James, 57, 71, 142
liability, 8, 66–67
Libicki, Martin, 4, 46, 50
Licklider, J. C. R., 16

MacAskill, Ewan, 125
machine learning, 14–15
malware, 72, 82–91, 107–111, 121, 147
Mandiant, 110–111, 116
Manning, Chelsea, 7, 93, 112–117,
    144, 154
McAfee, 14, 105–107, 109, 142
McCaul, Michael, 71, 75

McLuhan, Marshall, 22
Menn, Joseph, 147
Metcalfe, Bob, 18
Microsoft, 12, 16, 20, 24, 71, 84, 87, 99,
    147, 150, 155; PowerPoint, 125, 135;
    Windows (OS), 16, 83–84, 86, 88,
    147, 155
Minitel, 18
Mitnick, Kevin, 146
Moore, Gordon and Moore's
    Law, 16, 24
Morozov, Evgeny, 97
Morris Worm, 5, 45, 61, 82, 144, 150
Mozilla, 76
Muller, Robert, 140
multi-stakeholderism, 29

NASDAQ, 11, 90
Natanz, 82–85, 156
National Counterterrorism Center, 77
National Cyber Incident Response
    Plan, 59, 61
National Cyber Risk Alert
    Levels, 59–61
National Information Exchange
    Model, 65
National Institute of Standards and
    Technology (NIST), 57, 61, 119
National Intelligence Council, 81
National Intelligence Estimate, 81–82
National Response Framework, 58
National Science Foundation, 16,
    18–19, 28–31
National Security Agency, 7, 27, 35–39,
    44, 52, 54, 66–67, 78, 85–86, 116–117,
    120, 124–137, 144, 154–155; Echelon,
    38–39; Hawaii Signals Intelligence
    Center, 125; PRISM, 126–127, 135;
    Tailored Access Operations,
    131–132
National Strategy to Secure
    Cyberspace, 72
National Telecommunications and
    Information Administration
    (NTIA), 32
Net Centric Diplomacy, 116–117
NETmundial, 130
Neuromancer, 52

New York Stock Exchange, 15, 90
Night Dragon, 89, 106
NORAD, 15
North Atlantic Treaty Organization,
    42–43, 52–53, 128, 153
Northeast Blackout of 2003, 23
North Korea, 1, 80–81, 88, 105, 123
Northrop Grumman, 105
NSFNET, 19, 30–31
Nye, Joseph, 4, 50, 93

Office of Management and Budget,
    69–72, 122
Office of Personnel Management,
    118–122
Office of the Director of National
    Intelligence, 78, 133
Office of the National
    Counterintelligence Executive, 78
Oil and Natural Gas Information
    Sharing and Analysis Center, 89
Olmstead v. United States, 37
Olympic Games, 85–86
O'Murchu, Liam, 83
Open Systems Interconnect, 19
Operation Shady RAT, 106–107
Organization for Economic
    Co-operation and Development, 33

Patriot Act, 38, 55, 127, 144
Peace of Westphalia, 150
Poitras, Laura, 125–126, 138
Postel, Jon, 19–20, 27–28
Powell, Colin, 94–95
Presidential Decision Directive 63, 56
Presidential Policy Directive 28,
    135–136
President's Review Group on
    Intelligence and Communications
    Technologies, 135
Privacy and Civil Liberties Oversight
    Board, 135
programmable logic controller (PLC),
    83–84
PROTECT Intellectual Property Act, 76

Quadrennial Diplomacy and
    Development Review, 98

Raduege, Harry, 71
RAND Corporation, 15, 50, 112,
Recording Industry Association of
    America, 142
remote access toolkit (RAT), 86, 106
Request for Comment (RFC), 18
Rice, Condoleezza, 94
Rockefeller, Jay, 75
Ronfeldt, David, 50–51
Room 641A, 27, 35–37, 126, 136
Ross, Alec, 97
RSA Security, 108–109, 140
Russia, 6, 9, 34–35, 41–43, 49–53, 86–88,
    91–92, 94–95, 108–109, 117, 124–125,
    128, 134–135, 137–138, 146–147,
    152–156
Russian Business Network
    (RBN), 49, 147
Russo-Georgian War (2008), 49

SABRE, 16
Sanger, David, 85
Saudi Aramco, 7, 64, 88–89, 153
Schindler, John, 134, 136
Schmidt, Eric, 99
Schneier, Bruce, 132
Semi-Automatic Ground Environment
    (SAGE), 15
Sensenbrenner, John, 127
Shamoon, 64, 88–89, 153
Shneiderman, Ben, 25
Siemens Simatic Series 7
    (programmable logic
    controller), 83–84
signals intelligence (SIGINT),
    36, 39–40
Silicon Valley, 5–10, 12, 15, 21, 23, 26,
    76, 96, 102–103, 124, 126–127, 154
SIPRNet, 114, 116
60-Day Cyberspace Policy Review, 73
Skype, 33, 39
Snowden, Edward, 7, 124–125, 127,
    130–137, 153–155
Society for Worldwide Interbank
    Financial Transfers (SWIFT), 90
Soft power, 50, 93, 98
Software Engineering Institute, 60
Sony, 1, 123, 141

Stop Online Piracy Act, 76
Stuxnet, 7, 82–88, 151–152, 155–156
supervisory control and data
    acquisition (SCADA), 83, 85–88, 132
Sutton, Willie, 138
Swartz, Aaron, 144
Symantec, 82–83, 89
Syrian Electronic Army, 90–91

Target, 8, 140–141
top-level domain (TLD), 28, 114
traffic light protocol, 66
Transmission Control Protocol (TCP),
    17–19, 27
Trusted Internet Connection, 62
Tunis Commitment, 32
Turing, Alan, 3, 13–14
Twitter, 18, 21, 39, 90, 93, 96–97, 99–104

Udall, Mark, 127
Unit 61938, 110–111
United Nations, 27, 30–32, 34, 130;
    Working Group on Internet
    Governance, 31
United States v. Drew, 144
University of Southern California's
    Information Sciences Institute, 28
Unix, 17, 46
U.S. Air Force Cyber Command, 48–49
U.S. Cyber Command, 41, 117, 122
U.S. Department of Commerce, 6, 29,
    35, 42, 130
U.S. Department of Defense, 1, 4,
    15–16, 18–19, 28, 41–42, 49,
    58, 81, 98, 114, 116–117, 120,
    124, 132, 142, 155–156
U.S. Department of Energy's Idaho
    National Lab, 18, 53, 84
U.S. Department of Homeland
    Security, 7, 53–56, 60, 62–67, 73–75,
    77, 120–122, 156; National
    Communications System, 57;
    National Cyber Security Division,
    58, 62; National Cybersecurity and
    Communications Integration
    Center, 59, 61–62, 65; National
    Cybersecurity Center, 54–55, 57;
    National Infrastructure Protection

Center, 56–57; National Protection
and Programs Directorate,
54–55; National Security
Telecommunications Advisory
Committee, 78; U.S. Cyber
Emergency Readiness Team,
61–62, 70
U.S. Department of Labor, 43
U.S. Department of State, 66, 81, 95–99,
102–104, 114–116, 125; Bureau of
Intelligence and Research, 81;
Virtual Presence Post, 94
U.S. Intelligence Community, 35

Vernadsky, Vladimir, 50
VirusBlokAda, 82
Voice over Internet Protocol, 39

Wales, Jimmy, 112
war driving, 146–147
weapons of mass destruction, 80
Web 2.0, 96
Weber, Max, 150

Weiner, Norbert, 3
Western Union, 12, 116
WikiLeaks, 7, 93, 98, 113–117, 134–135,
144, 154
Wikipedia, 25, 76, 112–113
Williams, Jody, 149
World Conference on International
Telecommunications (WCIT), 87
World Summit of the Information
Society, 31–34, 100
Wyden, Ron, 127
Wynne, Michael, 48

Xerox PARC, 18
Xi Jinping, 105, 133

Yahoo, 11, 39, 133
YouTube, 18, 25, 39, 93, 96–97, 102

zero-day vulnerability, 70,
83–84, 86
Zotob, 147
Zuckerberg, Mark, 22

About the Author

CHRIS BRONK is an assistant professor of information and logistics technology at the University of Houston's College of Technology. His introduction to computers came in 1982, when his parents overlooked his request for an Atari 2600 game console and instead bought an Apple II. He has held multiple appointments at Rice University, including as a fellow at the James A. Baker III Institute for Public Policy, and retains an appointment in Rice's Computer Science Department and computer security lab. He also holds a fellowship at the University of Toronto's Munk School of Global Affairs.

Chris has published on a number of areas, including the employment of collaboration software in public organizations, technologies for border management and security, virtual currencies, big data analyses of terror events, and policy related to telecommunications and Internet governance. The focus of his work, however, has been on cybersecurity. He has published articles in *Survival, The Electricity Journal; Strategic Studies Quarterly; Latin American Policy; American Intelligence Journal*; and *First Monday*. In addition, he regularly presents to the conferences of the International Studies Association, and has written extensively on the intersection of international relations and cybersecurity. He has presented his work or participated in workshops at institutions of higher learning, including Harvard University, MIT, the Army War College, Texas A&M, Air University, West Point, Southern Methodist University, El Colegio de México, Central European University, the University of Toronto, and the University of Bologna. His work has been supported by the National Science Foundation, the Department of Defense, Deloitte, Microsoft, and AT&T.

In addition to his work in scholarship, Chris expends significant effort in informing policymakers and the public. He is chair of the Digital Governance Committee of the Association for Computing Machinery's U.S. Public Policy Council and from 2009 to 2015 was a senior advisor to the Office of eDiplomacy at the Department of State. He has provided opinion or comment to a number of news outlets, including *The Wall Street Journal; Foreign Policy; NPR; The Guardian; Der Spiegel; CNN; The Houston Chronicle; ABC; Scientific American*; and *The New York Times*.